Implementing Performance Assessment
Promises, Problems, and Challenges

Implementing Performance Assessment
Promises, Problems, and Challenges

Edited by

Michael B. Kane
American Institutes for Research
Washington, DC

Ruth Mitchell
American Association for Higher Education
Washington, DC

LEA LAWRENCE ERLBAUM ASSOCIATES, PUBLISHERS
1996 Mahwah, New Jersey

Lawrence Erlbaum Associates, Inc., Publishers
10 Industrial Avenue
Mahwah, New Jersey 07430

Cover design by Gail Silverman

Library of Congress Cataloging-in-Publication Data

Implementing performance assessment : promises, problems,
and challenges / edited by Michael B. Kane, Ruth Mitchell
       p. cm.
    Edited conference papers.
    Includes bibliographical references and index.
    ISBN 0-8058-2131-7 (c). — ISBN 0-8058-2132-5 (p)
    1. Educational tests and measurements—United States.
2. Academic achievement—United States. 3. Educational
evaluation—United States. 4. Educational
change—United States. I. Kane, Michael B. II. Mitchell,
Ruth.
LB3051.I465 1996
371.2'6—dc20   95-37860
                                             CIP

Printed in the United States of America
10 9 8 7 6 5 4 3 2 1

Contents

Preface

The 10 chapters constituting this collection of essays on performance assessments were commissioned by Pelavin Research Institute (PRI) of the American Insitutes for Research (AIR), under a contract with the Office of Educational Research and Improvement (OERI) of the U.S. Department of Education. In 1991, OERI issued a request for proposals entitled "Studies of Education Reform." Twelve topics were listed under this general heading, each reflecting some aspect of the reform movement that had placed education at the forefront of the national agenda in the late 1980s. PRI was awarded a 3-year contract to study assessment of student performance, which was understood to mean studying the contribution to education reform made by performance-based assessments such as portfolios.

Contractors for all 12 components of the project were required to hold a national conference within the initial year of their project and to commission papers to focus the conference participants on important aspects of the reform topic. PRI, in collaboration with the OERI Study of Curriculum Reform, held a national conference on performance assessment and curriculum reform as a presession to the Annual Student Assessment Conference, organized by the Education Commission of the States, in Boulder, Colorado, in June of 1992.

The assessment component of the presession conference consisted of discussions of the content of the commissioned papers that would later appear as chapters in this collection, as well as demonstrations of performance assessment by practitioners. In addition, a literature review was distributed to participants in advance of the conference. The review has been updated and now serves as the introductory chapter of this book. It discusses contemporary as well as historical events in the performance assessment movement and places the content of the book in a broader context. Although the papers were not read to the audience, their thesis and major points were presented by authors (where possible), and were further developed by two responders. As we hoped, the responses and ensuing discussion in many cases produced positive changes.

The larger and more significant context for these chapters is the increasing commitment across the nation to performance assessment as a reform strategy. California pioneered in this area with statewide open-ended mathematics assessments in the late 1980s; Vermont then chose portfolios for its first statewide assessment. Maryland and Arizona followed (two of our authors, Lois Easton and Paul Koehler, had firsthand experience with the Arizona developments, as administrators in the state education department). Kentucky soon seized the spotlight by committing its statewide education reform to performance assessment, eventually to be accompanied by rewards to schools exhibiting outstanding performances and sanctions for those exhibiting inadequate achievement at the school level. Connecticut produced an impressive series of teacher-designed and teacher-tested assessments for high school mathematics and science. New York conducted a statewide manipulative skills test in science for fourth-grade students, and has officially declared its intention to move toward portfolios in state assessments. Many other states are now considering the use of performance assessments, and some are coupling new assessments with the development of standards or outcome statements. Furthermore, in some cases, even individual schools or school districts have designed and implemented performance assessments on their own, without a state mandate and without state guidance.

NATURE OF THE COLLECTION

The chapters in this collection contribute to the debate about the value and usefulness of radically different kinds of assessments in the U.S. educational system by considering and expanding on the theoretical underpinnings of reports and speculation. The papers are not an introduction to performance assessment. Introductions are available in other publications.[1]

This collection assumes readers know that *performance assessment* constitutes a variety of techniques that can be used to report directly on student achievement. It is also assumed that readers are at least familiar with the variety of topics under discussion.

These topics were chosen because they were, in 1991, among those mentioned most often in discussions of performance assessment. Today, we believe that they remain central to debates over the utility of this innovation. The topics are: (a) the technical quality of assessments in terms of reliability, validity, generalizability, and calibration with one another and with other assessments; (b) the costs of performance assessment as opposed to multiple-choice, norm-referenced tests, usually purchased from a test publisher; (c) the effect on students who have traditionally done less well in American schools, including racial and linguistic minorities; (d) how the implementation of new modes of assessment fits into the understanding of change in educational institutions; and (e) how performance assessment is utilized as an instrument of state policy. We asked our writers to examine these issues as objectively as possible, using analogies from previous research and similar techniques, if those would shed light on their own subject.

The topics provided the organizing principles for the chapters herein collected, which fall into two major categories: reviews of knowledge on the general topic, with extrapolation, by analogy, to performance assessment; and theoretical discussions based on previous research. One chapter, Easton and Koehler's description of the introduction of the Arizona Student Assessment program, is a research-based explanation of the process of adopting performance assessments.

Readers who will gain the most from this book are those who may be considering implementing new assessments in a state, district, or school. They will know what performance assessment is and how it works, but will be looking for amplification of their knowledge, perhaps in order to make policy decisions. However, we believe that the collection is capable of also deepening and expanding the understanding of all readers interested in technical considerations with regard to performance assessments.

---

[1]Among books and collections of papers providing a comprehensive introduction to performance assessment are: Vito Perrone, editor: *Expanding Student Assessment*, ASCD, 1991; Ruth Mitchell, *Testing for Learning: How New Approaches to Evaluation Can Improve American Schools*, (New York: Free Press/Macmillan, 1992); Harold Berlak, Fred M. Newmann, Elizabeth Adams, Doug A. Archbald, Tyrrell Burgess, John Raven, and Thomas A. Romberg: *Toward a New Science of Educational Testing and Assessment*, Albany NY: State University of New York Press, 1992; Joan Herman, Pamela R. Aschbacher, and Lynn Winters, *A Practical Guide to Alternative Assessment*, ASCD, 1992; Congress of the United States Office of Technology Assessment, *Testing in American Schools: Asking the Right Questions*, OTA-SET-519, Washington DC: U.S. Government Printing Office, February, 1992.

SUMMARY

Order of the Chapters

The chapters have been arranged to sequentially focus on several major topics. The first chapter presents a summary of assessment reform initiatives, alternate approaches, and concerns for successful efforts. The second chapter is the broadest of the collection, because it discusses the functions of direct assessment (performance assessment) in the educational context; the next three are concerned with technical issues; then there are two chapters from different perspectives, on the costs of performance assessment. The collection ends with a group of three chapters that deal with different aspects of the social context of assessment—change within schools, change at the state level, and the effects of performance assessment on minority students.

The following are brief descriptions of the 10 chapters in order of presentation:

"Assessment Reform: Promises and Challenges," by Nidhi Khattri of Pelavin Research Institute and David Sweet of the U.S. Department of Education's Office of Educational Research and Improvement, provides an overview of the current assessment reform initiatives at the national, state, district, and school levels. The chapter also describes the alternative approaches to performance assessments, outlines the technical issues involved in creating and implementing performance-based assessment systems, and raises concerns that must be addressed if the reform efforts are to be successful.

"Performance Assessment and the Multiple Functions of Educational Measurement," by Daniel Resnick of Carnegie Mellon University and Lauren Resnick of the Learning Research and Development Center at the University of Pittsburgh, examines the suitability of performance assessment for instruction and learning, certification, accountability, and monitoring. They conclude that direct measures of student learning are necessary for the first three purposes, but that indirect measures such as measures used by the National Assessment of Education Progress (NAEP) are appropriate for monitoring. Their discussion (a social and historical perspective that usefully provides subsequent papers with a broad context) includes an example of a Grade 4 mathematics task from the New Standards Project, of which Lauren Resnick is codirector.

"Evaluating Progress With Alternative Assessments: A Model for Title 1," by Mark Wilson, University of California, Berkeley, and Raymond Adams, Australian Council for Educational Research, extends the Resnick chapter's focus, clarifying reasons for using performance assessment, especially in a *control chart for assessment format*, which plots control over task specification against control over judgment. This graph, along with the authors' concept of a continuum of educational development, enables the reader to understand the trade-offs in choosing different kinds of assessment. Expressed in highly technical and mathematical language, the chapter makes a case for using indications of growth, based on the continuum of learning, for Title 1 assessment.

"Extended Assessment Tasks: Purposes, Definitions, Scoring, and Accuracy," by David Wiley, Northwestern University and Edward Haertel, Stanford University, is a theoretical analysis of basic concepts in measurement by performance assessment. The authors describe and define different kinds of performance assessment, such as *on-demand, portfolio, curriculum-embedded*, and discuss reliability and "evidential" validity in terms of "intents." They call for a language system that presently does not exist to ensure the accurate mapping of assessment tasks to goals contained in curriculum frameworks. They assert, finally, that validity depends on mapping and upon the accuracy of the scoring process, matched to the intent of the assessment.

"Linking Assessments," by Robert Linn, University of Colorado at Boulder and codirector of the Center for Research on Evaluation, Standards and Student Testing (CRESST), discusses the meaning of equivalence among assessments and test. The linking issue can only become more important as more assessments are developed locally, while being judged by state or national standards. Linn divides linking into two types—*statistical* and *judgmental*. Under the first heading, he provides extended definitions of equating, calibrating, vertical equating, scaling, prediction, and statistical moderation. In judgmental approaches to linking, he discusses social moderation and verification. Linn's definitions clarify the advantages and disadvantages of both techniques, as well as what might be expected from each.

"Performance Assessment: Examining the Costs," by Roy Hardy, Director of the Educational Testing Service in Atlanta, compares the costs of traditional testing and performance assessments. Those costs are examined in three categories: *development, administration*, and *scoring*. Although there is little difference in development costs, administration and material costs are significantly higher for performance assessments. Scoring costs for performance assessements also are dramatically higher. In effect, performance assessments cost between 3 and 10 times more than traditional tests, but the additional cost may be regarded as a good investment, particularly because much of the additional cost goes to teachers for their participation in scoring. In time, costs should decrease as more performance assessments become available and more efficient scoring methods are devised.

"Conceptualizing the Costs of Large-Scale Pupil Performance Assessment," by David Monk, Cornell University, in contrast to Hardy's essay, contains no figures and no direct comparisons. It is a theoretical discussion of the factors to be considered in understanding the costs of assessment. Considered in that discussion are distinctions between costs and expenditures; identification of relevant foregone benefits in order to discern costs accurately; identification of ambiguous costs and the locus of costs; and the ability to discern instances of diminishing marginal productivity. Monk recommends that alternative assumptions should be made along several dimensions in order to arrive at some combination of factors that might be a comfortable basis of policy. At a minimum, the policymaker should establish upper and lower bounds—although those bounds may seem almost ludicrously far apart.

"Change Has Changed: Implications for Implementation of Assessments From the Organizational Change Literature," by Suzanne Stiegelbauer, places the change from norm-referenced, multiple-choice "bubble" tests within the context of studies of change in schools. Reviewing the literature on change, Stiegelbauer writes that change is no longer regarded as an event, or concerned with a discrete aspect of the school. Now, change is viewed as a systemic, continuing process that should be regarded as a normal factor in the life of educators. Any innovation, such as performance assessment, can serve to begin change, but people, processes, and policies must work together to ensure that systemic structural changes will support whatever innovation is put in place.

"Arizona's Educational Reform: Creating and Capitalizing on the Conditions for Policy Development and Implementation," by Lois Brown Easton of the Education Commission of the States, and Paul Koehler of the Arizona Department of Education, can be viewed as a case history of change at the state level. Easton and Koehler analyze the political process that speedily introduced the Arizona Student Assessment Program (ASAP). They use criteria developed by Chris Pipho to show why the initiative succeeded (public information and a firm stance were major ingredients), and a framework for evaluating educational policy developed by Douglas Mitchell. They report interviews with legislators, Department of Education staff, teachers' union representatives, and school administrators, to help make the case that ASAP came along at the right time, with the right people in place.

"Performance Assessment and Equity," by Eva Baker, University of California, Los Angeles and Codirector of CRESST, and Harold O'Neil, University of Southern California, surveys what is known about effects (or expected effects) of performance assessment on minority students. The chapter presents this information in two parts. It first discusses various aspects of assessment, such as characteristics of tasks, administration, and training of raters or scorers; and it reports research on performance assessments in the industrial and military sectors. The main finding from this research is that raters or scorers tend to rate or score the performance of candidates of their own ethnicity higher than those of a different race or ethnic group. The authors predict a "rough time on the equity issue" for performance assessment, at least for the near future.

These descriptions demonstrate that this collection is open-ended. Not only could much more be said on each topic, but the topics themselves could and should be pursued as the development of assessments continues. The collection, though, raises important questions. How will education authorities at all levels deal with the costs of performance assessment? How well will minority students perform? Will states link or equate any of their assessments to the New Standards Project assessments, and is that a useful and feasible process? These and other questions generated by the papers demonstrate the need for continuing research and for watchful monitoring of reforms in educational assessment. It is our hope that our study will provide answers to some of these questions in subsequent volumes.

ACKNOWLEDGMENTS

This compendium of work would not have been possible without the capable support of several individuals. We are grateful to David Sweet, the monitor of *Studies in Education Reform: Assessment of Student Performance*, who helped us select the topics and authors for the papers constituting this book. We also are thankful to Alison Reeve, Rebecca Adamson, Raymond Varisco, Kerry Traylor, Gwen Pegram, Amy Stempel, Stephanie Soper, and Kimberly Gordon at PRI and to the editorial and production staff at Lawrence Erlbaum Associates for their help with the preparation and production of the manuscript.

In honor of Leigh Burstein's commitment and contributions to educational assessment, all royalties from this book are to go to the Leigh Burstein Memorial Fund. The fund is administered by the University of California at Los Angeles Foundation.

Washington, DC   —*Michael Kane*
June 1995   —*Ruth Mitchell*

Editors

Michael B. Kane

Michael B. Kane is Vice President for Program Development at the American Institutes for Research. He received his doctorate in education administration and organizational analysis from Columbia University Teachers College. During the past 25 years he has directed over 20 studies of education change initiatives, including the study for which this volume was prepared. He has also served in senior roles and federal and state agencies including as Associate Director of the National Institute of Education's dissemination and program improvement unit. His particular research interests focus on education change and knowledge transfer to improve schooling, particularly for at-risk populations. This is the fourth book he has authored or edited on these topics.

Ruth Mitchell

Ruth Mitchell is a partner in the Education Trust at the American Association of Higher Education (AAHE). She is Senior Consultant for *Studies in Education Reform: Student Performance*, a project conducted by Pelavin Research Institute for the U.S. Department of Education's Office of Educational Research and Improvement (OERI). She is the author of *Testing for learning: How New Approaches to Evaluation Can Improve American Schools* and the co-author with Patte Barth of *Smart Start*. She also has authored short books on the development of arts education assessment and several articles on standards and assessment.

Contributors

Raymond J. Adams

Raymond J. Adams is a Principal Research Fellow at the Australian Council for Educational Research, located in Melbourne, Australia. He completed his PhD in the Measurement, Evaluation and Statistical Analysis Special Field in the Department of Education at the University of Chicago. He currently specializes in multilevel modeling, item response modeling, and large-scale testing. In 1992, Ray was awarded a Spencer Post Doctoral Fellowship to pursue his research on multilevel item response models. In 1993, he was awarded a grant from the National Science Foundation (jointly with Mark Wilson) to develop and apply psychometric models to the use of performance assessments in large-scale testing systems. Ray is currently the psychometric advisor to the Third International Mathematics and Science Study, a comparative study of mathematics and science learning that is being undertaken in some 50 educational systems around the world.

Eva L. Baker

Eva Baker is a Professor of Educational Psychology and Social Research methods at the UCLA Graduate School of Education and Information Studies; Director of the UCLA Center for the Study of Evaluation (CSE); and Codirector of the National Center for Research on Evaluation, Standards, and Student Testing (CRESST) at UCLA. She conducts design and validation studies of performance-based assessments in the areas of history, economics, writing, science, job performance, workforce readiness, and mathematics. She served on the National Council on Education Standards and Testing and was appointed to the Secretary's Committee on the Revision of Chapter 1 Testing.

Lois Brown Easton

Lois Brown Easton is Director of Professional Development at the Eagle Rock School and Professional Development Center in Estes Park, Colorado. She also served as Director of Re: Learning Systems at the Education Commission of the States (ECS), linking the Coalition of Essential Schools and ECS to achieve systemic reform from schoolhouse to statehouse. During the time she was Director of Curriculum, she and Paul Koehler designed the Arizona Student Assessment Program (ASAP) in response to a legislative mandate entitled the Goals for Educational Excellence. She worked with policy leaders throughout the state to develop the ASAP, secure its passage into law, and implement it over a 3-year period. A middle school English teacher for 15 years, Easton earned her PhD at the University of Arizona and has been a frequent presenter at conferences, a facilitator of systems change, and a contributor to educational journals.

Edward H. Haertel

Edward H. Haertel is a faculty member of the Stanford University School of Education, where his research focuses on educational testing and measurement, including teacher assessment, policy uses of educational assessments, statistical modeling of test data, and test validation. He has served on numerous boards and committees concerned with technical and policy issues in educational assessment at the state and national levels. Dr. Haertel spent the 1994–1995 academic year as a Fellow at the Center for Advanced Study in the Behavioral Sciences.

Roy Hardy

As Director for the Educational Testing Service's Southern Field Office, Hardy is responsible for initiating, planning, and directing various testing, evaluation, marketing, service, and research programs in an area serving nine southeastern states. He specializes in test development with focus on the development of performance assessments in science and mathematics for elementary and middle school populations. He has directed developments for several national testing programs and for the statewide assessment programs of Florida, Georgia and Alabama. His background includes a Master's degree in Mathematics from Stanford University and a PhD in Educational Research from Florida State University. His publications include articles on program evaluation, test use and interpretation, instructional validity, and on practical issues in the development and implementation of performance assessment.

Nidhi Khattri

Nidhi Khattri is a Research Analyst at Pelavin Research Institute, an affiliate of the American Institutes for Research. She is the Deputy Project Director for the U.S. Department of Education-sponsored study, *Studies in Education Reform: Assessment of Student Performance.* She earned her PhD in Social Psychology from Columbia University in 1993. Her research interests include the areas of school reform, student assessment, and the effects of cooperation and conflict resolution on social relations.

Paul H. Koehler

Paul H. Koehler is the Assistant Superintendent for Academic Services of the Peoria, Arizona Unified School District. Prior to joining the Peoria District, Dr. Koehler was the Associate Superintendent of Education Services at the Arizona Department of Education for five years. He was responsible for the Department's School Improvement programs, Special Education Services, Research and Development Unit, Chapter 1, Chapter 2, Bilingual, Indian Education, Migrant, and Gifted Services, as well as state testing programs for teachers and students. He is the author of numerous articles on topics such as reading, assessment methods, and discipline and has been named one of the 100 outstanding school executives in North America.

Robert L. Linn

Robert L. Linn is Professor of Education at the University of Colorado at Boulder and Codirector of the National Center for Research on Evaluation, Standards, and Student Testing. He received his PhD in 1965 from the University of Illinois at Urbana-Champaign with a specialization in psychometrics. He is a member of the National Academy of Education. He is a former President of the Division of Evaluation and Measurement of the American Psychological Association, former President of the National Council on Measurement in Education, and former Vice President of the American Educational Research Association for the Division of Measurement and Research Methodology. He has published articles dealing with a wide range of theoretical and applied issues in educational measurement.

David H. Monk

David H. Monk is Chair of the Department of Education and Professor of Educational Administration at Cornell University. He earned his PhD at the University of Chicago, and has taught in a visiting capacity at the

University of Rochester and the University of Burgundy in Dijon, France. Monk is the author of *Educational Finance: An Economic Approach* (McGraw-Hill, 1990) as well as numerous articles in scholarly journals. He is a Senior Research Fellow at the Consortium for Policy Research in Education (CPRE) and serves on the editorial boards of *The Economics of Education Review, The Journal of Educational Finance,* and *The Journal of Research in Rural Education.* He consults widely on matters related to educational productivity and the organizational structuring of schools and school districts and is a Past President of the American Education Finance Association.

Harold F. O'Neil, Jr.

Harold F. O'Neil Jr. is a Professor of Educational Psychology at the University of Southern California. His research interests include the assessment of workforce readiness, particularly team skills, the teaching and measurement of self-regulation skills, and the role of motivation in testing. Dr. O'Neil has conducted cross-cultural research in Japan on the role of test anxiety and performance. In all of these research areas, he is interested in technology applications.

Daniel P. Resnick

Daniel P. Resnick is Director, Program in Educational Policy, Center for History and Policy, Carnegie Mellon University, and Research Associate at the Learning Research and Development Center, University of Pittsburgh. He is a historian whose work has focused on educational assessment, schooling, and literacy development. His articles and essays have appeared in *Daedalus, Harvard Educational Review, History of Education Quarterly, Phi Delta Kappan, Educational Researcher, International Review of Applied Psychology, Journal of Social History, French Contemporary Civilization,* and the *Review of Research in Education.* He has coauthored several studies of the history and practice of testing with his wife, Lauren.

Lauren B. Resnick

Lauren B. Resnick is Director of the Learning Research and Development Center and Professor of Psychology at the University of Pittsburgh. Her recent research has focused on assessment, the nature and development of thinking abilities, and the relationship between school learning and everyday competence. She is also Cofounder and Director of New Standards (formerly the New Standards Project), a consortium of 17 states building an internationally benchmarked system of standards and authentic assessments for American students. She has served on many national and international boards and commissions, including the Commission on the Skills of the American Workforce, and has chaired both the assessment committee of the SCANS Commission and the Resource Group on Student Achievement of the National Education Goals Panel. She was the founding editor of *Cognition and Instruction*, a major journal in the field, and has authored nine books and over 100 articles and book chapters.

Suzanne M. Stiegelbauer

Suzanne M. Stiegelbauer is a Professor and Program Coordinator in the Faculty of Education, University of Toronto. For over 10 years, she has been an independent consultant and workshop leader in the areas of educational research and anthropology, both in the United States and Canada. From 1979 to 1985, she was a Research Associate with the Concerns Based Adoption Model (CBAM) Program, U.S. Research and Development in Teacher Education, University of Texas, Austin. She is co-author with Michael Fullan of *The New Meaning of Education Change*.

David Sweet

David Sweet is a Senior Researcher in the U.S. Department of Education's Office of Educational Research and Improvement (OERI). Before joining OERI he was an Associate Commissioner and Division Director at the National Center for Education Statistics (NCES). He also was an Administrator in the California Department of Education's Office of Program Evaluation and Research and has taught research and statistics at the University of California at Berkeley and George Washington University in Washington, DC. He is currently pursuing several lines of research in the area of education standards and student achievement.

David E. Wiley

David E. Wiley is a Professor at the School of Education and Social Policy, Northwestern University. A statistician and psychometrician by training and early work, much of his recent research and writing has focused on public policy and program evaluation as related to educational testing, teaching-learning processes, and legislative initiatives affecting these aspects of education. He has been involved in international comparative studies of education since 1971 and recently completed (with T.N. Postlethwaite) a volume reporting findings of the second science study of the International Association for the Evaluation of Educational Achievement (IEA). He also serves on the IEA International Technical Committee. He worked with the California Learning Assessment System, the state of Kentucky, and the New Standards Project to design and implement new systems based on student performance of extended response (as opposed to multiple choice) test tasks. His current research is focused on the implementation of curricular control policies, the determinants and distribution of learning opportunities, and the integration of frameworks for the assessment of learning, ability, and performance. He received an A.B. degree from San Diego State College, and MS and PhD degrees from the University of Wisconsin.

Mark Wilson

Mark Wilson is an Associate Professor of Education at the University of California at Berkeley, specializing in the areas of educational measurement and statistics. After completing a Master of Education degree at the University of Melbourne (Australia) on the topic of variance estimation in complex sample design, he went on to complete a PhD in the Measurement, Evaluation and Statistical Analysis Special Field in the Department of Education at the University of Chicago, where his dissertation on the special considerations involved in the measurement of discontinuous structures such as "stages," won best dissertation awards in both the Department of Education and in the Division of Social Sciences. He has published several articles in refereed journals, edited three books, contributed 20 chapters to edited books, and made several presentations at meetings of professional groups. He was awarded a National Academy of Education Spencer Fellowship, and also was awarded an Office of Naval Research grant to investigate the psychological measurement possibilities of Intelligent Tutoring Systems. Recently, he was awarded a grant from the National Science Foundation to develop and apply psychometric models to study the use of performance assessments in large-scale testing systems. He has conducted workshop presentations on topics in educational measurement at the Educational Testing Service in and at annual meetings of the American Educational Research Association. He also has made invited presentations at the annual conference of the National Council for Measurement in Education, and at assessment conferences in Australia, Colorado, and Belgium. He is currently advising the California State Department of Education on its assessment system, and the National Board of Osteopathic Medical Examiners on their testing and certification system.

Chapter 1

Assessment Reform: Promises and Challenges

Nidhi Khattri
Pelavin Research Institute

David Sweet
U.S. Department of Education

Developing non-multiple-choice methods of assessing student performance has become a major, albeit controversial, part of the education reform movement currently sweeping the nation. Knowledgeable individuals on both sides of the assessment controversy have put forth arguments for and against performance assessment—arguments that are even more salient today than they were only two years ago, as the call for assessment reform has attained what can only be called a bandwagon status. In educational circles, the term *performance assessment* has, in fact, become a buzzword for change.

With the passage of the Goals 2000: Educate America Act, the assessment of student performance is, in many states, coming to the forefront of education reform. It is likely that the country will witness a proliferation of non-multiple-choice, performance-based assessments to be used not only for pedagogical, but also for accountability and certification purposes. The new legislation and the ongoing discussion about the various facets of education reform, including assessment reform, underscore the fact that we are witnessing a period of education ferment. It thus has become increasingly important to address, with intellectual and practical seriousness, questions regarding the purposes of assessments, the contexts in which assessments are implemented, their linkages to systemic reform ventures, and their technical qualities.

This introduction summarizes the history of the performance assessment movement, outlines the relationship of assessment reform to broader reform issues, and highlights the technical questions being raised about the assessments themselves. Much like the proposed assessments, the picture brought into focus is multidimensional, complex, and messy. The remaining chapters clarify and elaborate upon some of the more pressing concerns only touched upon in this chapter.

A BRIEF HISTORY OF THE PERFORMANCE ASSESSMENT MOVEMENT

Performance assessment is not an entirely new assessment strategy in American education. Essays, oral presentations, and other kinds of projects always have been a feature of elite private education; and in many classrooms, private and public, teachers for a long time have assessed student progress through assigned papers, reports, and projects that are used as a basis for course grades. On the national level, the Advanced Placement Program of the College Board from its inception has assessed students by requiring at least one written essay in addition to responses to multiple-choice questions (as well as laboratory experiments in the sciences and demonstrations in music).

What is new in the current reform movement is its emphasis on the use of performance assessments for systematic, school-wide, instructional and curricular purposes and its spread into accountability and certification. In many instances, in fact, proponents of performance assessments view assessments themselves as the lever for systemic curricular and instructional reforms at any level of the educational hierarchy. Theoretical writings, such articles by Wiggins (1989, 1991), and descriptions of programs, such as Wolf's (1989, 1991) discussions of activities in ARTS PROPEL in the Pittsburgh Public Schools, have had an enormous influence in this regard, especially on practitioners.

As discussed in other sections of this chapter, the controversy centers, not around the use of assessments for primarily pedagogical purposes, but around their use for accountability and certification—so called "high stakes" purposes. The chapter by Daniel P. Resnick and Lauren B. Resnick also details the functions of educational measurement.

Performance assessment, as the term currently is being used, refers to a range of approaches to assessing student performance. These new approaches are variously labeled as follows:

- *Alternative assessment* is intended to distinguish this form of assessment from traditional, fact-based, multiple-choice testing;
- *Authentic assessment* is intended to highlight the real world nature of tasks and contexts that make up the assessments; and

- *Performance assessment* refers to a type of assessment that requires students to actually perform, demonstrate, construct, develop a product or a solution under defined conditions and standards.

Regardless of the term used, according to Mitchell (1995), performance assessments imply ". . . active student production of evidence of learning—not multiple-choice, which is essentially passive selection among preconstructed answers" (p. 2).

Thrust for Reform

The present focus on performance assessments as a systematic strategy of public education reform owes its origins to three related phenomena, all gaining momentum during the late 1980s: (a) the reaction on the part of educators against pressures for accountability based upon multiple-choice, norm-referenced testing; (b) the development in the cognitive sciences of a constructivist model of learning; and (c) the concern on the part of the business community that students entering the workforce were not competent enough to compete in an increasingly global economy.

In 1983, *A Nation at Risk* was widely interpreted as a clarion call for school systems to tighten their curricula, and such tightening resulted in widespread testing for accountability. Most school systems came to rely upon the use of norm-referenced, multiple-choice tests for school accountability, and this phenomenon came to have a considerable amount of influence on teaching and learning in the classroom. Classroom teachers felt the pressure to prepare their students to do well on such tests and accordingly modified their approach to teaching. "Teaching to the test," thus, became an increasingly popular pedagogical strategy.

Multiple-choice tests were based on a behaviorist model of education—on the assumption that learning of almost any kind occurs in small increments, from simple to complex ideas and skills; and that discrete aspects of knowledge could be decontextually tested. The inadequacies (and, from many educators' viewpoint, pernicious effects) of such testing models were subsequently highlighted by research (e.g., Oakes, J., 1985, 1990; Cannell, 1987, 1989) causing many educators to rethink their accountability strategies.

Concurrent with such trends within the education system, the demands from outside the education system for more sophisticated thinking skills provided the fuel for the rebellion against the widespread use of multiple-choice tests. Many reformers argued, then, that multiple-choice, norm-referenced testing had assumed a disproportionate importance in the classroom, often displacing other, more pedagogically sound, practices in assessing for teaching in favor of teaching for testing.

At the same time, insights from the constructivist model of cognition began to transform educators' thinking about teaching and learning. According to this model, learning takes place when new information or experience is absorbed into or transforms preexisting mental schemata. The mind seeks to make sense of new information by relating it to prior information, thus establishing the meaning of new information within the context of old information. Furthermore, the model postulates, the search for meaning may motivate individuals to acquire further knowledge and skills. Thus, the following corollary related to this view of learning simultaneously gained currency in the reform movement: Because an individual constructs knowledge in his or her own way, a customized rather than a mass approach to education is necessary to enable him or her to achieve high standards.

Educators came to believe that, in order to strengthen all students' educational experiences and to better meet all students' needs, assessments that concurrently allow for an understanding of students' learning processes and knowledge base and that support variations in pedagogy are required. In addition, advocates of performance assessments suggest that the use of performance assessments will have salutary effects on student motivation and learning; because performance assessments stress interdisciplinary skills and use contextualized assignments (i.e., assignments that mimic the kinds of multifaceted problems one encounters outside the classroom), students are more likely to be involved in attempting and completing these assessments.

Add to these trends the voices of business and industry executives demanding that their employees be able to think creatively, solve problems, write well, work flexibly, and possess social competencies to be able to operate in groups. The Secretary's Commission on Achieving Necessary Skills (SCANS), after an extensive survey of the business community reported, "Employers and employees share the belief that all workplaces must *work smarter*" (italics added, p. v). SCANS concluded that for a workplace to *work smarter*, its employees must possess certain *competencies*, such as interpersonal skills, and *foundation skills*, such as basic skills in reading and writing and thinking. Such pressures added up to the widespread consideration of assessment reform as part of a solution to the problem of the incompetent worker.

Given this ammunition, education reformers insisted that, in order to function as a lever of education reform, assessments must: (a) be based on a generative view of knowledge; (b) require active production of student work (not passive selection from prefabricated choices); and (c) consist of meaningful tasks, rather than of what can be easily tested and easily scored. What follows are the different types of assessments that meet one or more of these requirements.

Current Performance Assessments

Performance assessments in use today can roughly be characterized as follows:

- *Portfolios* that consist of collections of a student's work and developmental products, which may include drafts of assignments;
- *On-demand tasks*, or events, that require students to construct responses—either writing or experiments—to a prompt or to a problem within a short period of time. These tasks are akin to short demonstration projects;
- *Projects* that last longer than on-demand tasks, and are usually undertaken by students on a given topic and used to demonstrate their mastery of that topic;
- *Demonstrations* that take the form of student presentations of project work; and
- *Teachers' observations* that gauge student classroom performance, usually designed for young children, and primarily used for diagnostic purposes.

All performance assessments require students to structure the assessment task, apply information, construct responses, and, in many cases, explain the process by which they arrive at the answers. (Performance assessments are never multiple-choice; but, many states [e.g., Kentucky, Maryland, Vermont] combine multiple-choice tests with performance assessments.) Student answers on performance assessments are rated using agreed upon rating criteria and standards, usually in the form of scoring rubrics, by groups of scorers or raters or by individual teachers.

In theory, this process generates a wealth of information about the student that can be used for instructional purposes. Such information might shed light on the student's understanding of the problem, his or her involvement with the problem, his or her approach to solving the problem, and his or her ability to express himself or herself. In sum, proponents argue that these assessments will motivate and involve students in the learning process itself; performance assessments will help students establish a meaningful context for learning, develop writing and conceptual skills, and, therefore, achieve higher levels of desired outcomes.

PREVALENCE OF THE PERFORMANCE ASSESSMENT MOVEMENT

A review of the prevalence of performance-based student assessment strategies is perhaps best organized by their level of initiation: national, state, district, or school. Although this taxonomy is, in some ways, artificial, it nonetheless helps us to impose order on and to understand better an otherwise unwieldy situation.

National Level

National nongovernmental and governmental involvement in assessment reform shares the limelight with state-level efforts. Several nongovernmental projects tackling assessment, curricular, and instructional reform have gained national prominence in recent years. For example, the New Standards Project (NSP) and the Coalition of Essential Schools (CES) have exerted considerable influence on education administrators and teachers across the nation and prompted a shift to performance-based assessments.

The NSP began in 1991, with the aim of reinvigorating and revamping American education (Resnick & Simmons, 1993). The crux of NSP's work involves establishing performance standards and designing curricular, instructional, and assessment strategies. The NSP Board, which guides the formulation of performance standards and assessment strategies, is composed of representatives from NSP's partner states and districts and from professional organizations, such as the National Council for Teachers in Mathematics (NCTM), the American Association of the Advancement of Science (AAAS), and the National Council of Teachers of English (NCTE). The NSP program lists 17 state and 6 urban district partners.

The NSP assessment system is being formulated for Grades 4, 8, and 10. The fully articulated system will consist of student portfolios that will contain NSP recommended matrix-sampled tasks requiring extended responses, exhibitions, projects, and other student work. The NSP piloted a number of its assessment tasks in 1992, 1993, and 1994, in its partner states and districts. Classroom teachers and content area specialists scored these pilot tests, using established scoring rubrics at national scoring conferences. NSP projected that the first valid, reliable, and fair exams would be available for use in mathematics and in English language arts by 1994–1995, in applied learning by 1995–1996, and in science by 1996–1997.

The CES also is a national force in its own right. It was established in 1984, at Brown University, as a school-university partnership to help redesign schools. Coalition members include 150 schools that are actively involved in reform.[1] The reform work of the member schools is guided by a set of nine *Common Principles*, the sixth of which pertains to assessment. The sixth principle states that students should be awarded a diploma only upon a successful demonstration—an exhibition—of having acquired the central skills and knowledge of the school's program. As the diploma is awarded

---

[1]*Coalition of Essential Schools* Information on Member Schools. Available from Coalition of Essential Schools, Brown University.

when earned, the school's program proceeds with no strict age grading and with no system of earned credits by time spent in class. The emphasis is on the students' demonstration that they can do important things (*The Common Principles of the Coalition of Essential Schools*; see Sizer, 1989). Several member schools, like Walden III in Racine, Wisconsin, and Capshaw Middle School, in Santa Fe, New Mexico, have fashioned their graduation requirements on this principle.

Performance assessments on the national level have always been a feature of the College Board's Advancement Placement (AP) Program, especially the Studio Art Portfolio Evaluation, which has no written or multiple-choice portions. The Evaluation, in fact, is an example of a well-established national portfolio examination (Mitchell, 1992).

Now, the College Board has launched another assessment development effort. The College Board's *Pacesetter* program is being designed as a national, syllabus-driven examination system for all high school students, modeled on the AP examinations, which (with the exception of Studio Art) contain both multiple-choice and partially open-response items. The *Pacesetter* design incorporated two forms of assessments—classroom assessments, scored by teachers trained to *Pacesetter* standards, and end-of-course assessments, scored in a standardized manner. Currently, 60 sites in 21 states are implementing *Pacesetter* course frameworks and associated assessments in English, mathematics, and Spanish (*College Board News*, 1995).

The most visible indication of national-level, governmental involvement in assessment reform came with the passage of the Goals 2000: Educate America Act. The GOALS 2000: Educate America Act, P.L. 103-227, was passed in 1994. As a result, Congress allocated $105 million in Fiscal Year (FY) 1994 for Goals 2000, and imposed no funding limits through FY 1999 ("Goals 200," 1994). The law formally authorizes the National Education Goals Panel (NAGB) to monitor progress toward GOALS 2000, and the National Education Standards and Improvement Council (NESIC) was to have reviewed the criteria set for evaluating student performance standards. However, the amount of funding to be allocated for GOALS 2000 is likely to be drastically reduced, and the as yet unappointed NESIC is to be abolished. NESIC's role in endorsing state-generated standards is considered too intrusive by some members of Congress (Hoff, 1995; Olsen, 1995).

As of September, 1995, 45 states had applied for the U.S. Department of Education's GOALS 2000 grants. Although states' initial applications include only general plans regarding how content and student performance standards would be set, future applications will be required to detail how student performance will be measured, in order to assess whether or not students are meeting set standards. The presence of national standards for assessment, even though voluntary, is likely to have enormous implications for the future structure of U.S. education.

In another national program, Title I (formerly Chapter 1), performance assessments, especially portfolios, stand a chance of being included as options for use beyond norm-referenced multiple-choice testing. Congress reauthorized the Title I compensatory education program in 1994. By law, states are required to use the same or equally rigorous standards and assessments they devise for GOALS 2000 for monitoring the progress of Title I students, but districts can also devise their own standards and assessments as long as they are as rigorous as those of the state. Through these requirements, Title I aims to coax states away from norm-referenced, multiple-choice tests and toward more open-ended, performance-based assessments (Olsen, 1995). The chapter by Wilson and Adams in this volume elucidates how performance assessments might be utilized for Title I (formerly Chapter 1) evaluations.

In addition to GOALS 2000 and Title I, the work of several national organizations and professional associations in developing content standards for academic areas has implications for assessment reform. The work of many of these groups (e.g., The Center for Civic Education, The Consortium of National Arts Education Associations, The National Center for History in the Schools at the University of California at Los Angeles) in establishing content standards is supported by the Federal government. Perhaps the work of the National Council of Teachers of Mathematics (NCTM), which released the mathematics standards in 1989, has been the most prominent and has had the greatest impact to date. The NCTM publications, *Curriculum and Evaluation Standards for School Mathematics* (1989) and *Professional Standards for Teaching Mathematics* (1991) are guiding the teaching and assessment of mathematics in several states and school districts across the nation. The NCTM assessments, for example, promote the evaluation of students' mathematical problem-solving and communication skills through the use of applied mathematical problems.

As previously mentioned, the SCANS reports, too, have been active in prodding schools toward more performance-based assessments. The SCANS work, in fact, is pertinent to GOALS 2000; SCANS competencies, which, among other things, emphasize interpersonal skills and intelligent use of information and technology, have a direct relationship to what students learn in classrooms. The commission envisioned setting proficiency levels for SCANS competencies and developing an associated assessment system based on demonstrating SCANS competencies through applied, contextualized problems.

State, District, and School Levels

Useful catalogues of performance assessment activity at the state and district levels include the *State Student Assessment Programs Database (1993-*

1994; see Council of Chief State School Officers and the North Central Regional Educational Laboratory, 1994) and a survey of local district activity by Hansen and Hathaway (1991). These catalogues highlight the growing popularity of performance assessments. Information about activity at the school level is more difficult to obtain, as it is circulated largely by word-of-mouth or by an occasional article.

Similarly, there are many small-scale, pilot, or research and development efforts underway that may be funded by state agencies or even by the Federal government through its national research centers and laboratories. For example, the National Center for Research on Evaluation, Standards, and Student Testing (CRESST) at the University of California at Los Angeles and the North West Regional Educational Laboratory are involved in research on and development of performance assessments. These small-scale, local-level efforts are very much a part of a national trend, but they are very difficult to catalog in a systematic fashion.

State. Developments at the state level are more dramatic than at the national level. States committed to performance assessments as public policy are slowly increasing in number. Since the mid-1980s, more than 40 states have adopted writing samples, instead of multiple-choice questions, to assess student writing ability; and in the late 1980s and early 1990s, a number of states (e.g., California, Connecticut, Maryland, Vermont) became trailblazers in the development and implementation of more innovative performance-based assessments. Currently, the most notable of these states are Vermont, Arizona, Kentucky, and Maryland. Vermont, perhaps, is the most innovative of them all, being the first to fully implement a portfolio-based performance assessment system in writing and mathematics. Kentucky and Maryland also administer performance events once a year. Other states, such as Oregon, are not far behind in designing and implementing ambitious performance-based assessment systems. However, even though there is a great deal of energy going into these reforms, public backlash in some areas has given rise to a hostile climate for such endeavors. California's bold move with its California Learning Assessment System (CLAS), for example, was vetoed in 1994 by Governor Wilson. The program ended under an avalanche of criticisms from parents that the assessments required their children to read distasteful materials, and also invaded family privacy by asking intrusive questions.

Most states experimenting with performance-based assessments are explicit in their desire and intention to use the new assessments to influence instruction in the direction of conceptual and holistic teaching and learning, in addition to being interested in program evaluation.

There is some evidence that the use of performance assessment systems has achieved the aim of influencing instruction. For example, Vermont's surveys show that teachers have changed their instructional approach to align with more project-based, holistic teaching, and Kentucky teachers have changed their instructional strategies as a result of Kentucky's system of portfolios and performance events (Kentucky Institute for Education Research, 1995; Koretz, Stecher, Klein, McCaffrey, & Diebert, 1993). However, most evidence is anecdotal and is best established for teacher performance rather than for student achievement.

In sum, states have exhibited an extraordinary variety of responses to the advent of performance assessments, from a whole-hearted embrace of portfolios to an apparent lack of interest in new assessment methods. Identifying factors that facilitate the development and implementation of performance assessments to achieve desired outcomes is clearly a challenge for future research.

District.   Assessments being developed at the district level do not seem to be as varied as those at the state level, perhaps because districts do not have a legislative mandate to fulfill. Where changes in assessment are being made, they usually result in direct writing assessments or portfolios. For example, the San Diego City school system in San Diego, California, is a hotbed of activity, as it leads the Southern consortium of the California Assessment Collaborative with money provided by the California legislature for districts to experiment with performance assessment.

The Pittsburgh Public school system, famous as the site of ARTS PRO-PEL, has a Syllabus Examination Project (SEP), 60% of which is based on percent performance assessments (Wolf & Piston, 1988, 1989, 1991). VARONA, a school district just outside Milwaukee, has portfolio assessment for all of its personnel, from students through administrators (Pelavin Associates, 1991). South Brunswick, New Jersey, Fort Worth, Texas, and Prince William County, Virginia, are other examples of districts that have embraced performance assessments.

Hansen and Hathaway (1991) attempted a systematic survey of assessments at many levels, and sent out 433 questionnaires to various institutions. They received only 110 responses, despite a follow-up mailing effort. Short of mailing questionnaires with reply-paid responses to all 16,000 U.S. school districts, a comprehensive account of district assessment practices does not, at present, seem attainable.

School.   Although schools may perceive themselves as powerless to do much in the face of state and district mandates, developing performance assessments at the school level may be easier than at the district or state levels simply because it is easier to organize change on a small scale. For example, the only graduation examinations based on performance assessments are at the school level, notably the Rite of Passage Experience (ROPE) at Walden III in Racine, Wisconsin, and the graduation portfolio at Central Park East Secondary School in Manhattan (Pelavin & Associates, 1991). Both schools are members of the Coalition for Essential Schools, which, as mentioned earlier, advocates exhibitions as replacements for norm-referenced multiple-choice tests (Sizer, 1992).

Many schools have portfolio assessments for writing, and some have them for mathematics. The use of *whole language* instructional strategy is responsible for changing much of the school-level assessment of literacy from norm-referenced multiple-choice tests purchased from publishers to teacher-designed observations or records of literacy development. The California Learning Record, for example, is an assessment developed for both informal and formal record keeping for early childhood development in literacy and mathematical ability. It is an adaptation of the Primary Language Record (PLR), which was developed by the Center for Language in Primary Education (CLPE), in London, England. Forms of the California Learning Record are being used in California, and a similar adaptation of the PLR is being promoted by the New York City Assessment Network (NYAN) in New York City schools.

In summary, while states cast a wider net and enjoy more visibility in the reform arena, quieter attempts at reform by districts and schools, too, are generating fundamental changes in education at the most basic levels.

Relationship of Assessment Reform to Systemic and Organizational Change

By its proponents, performance assessments are frequently viewed as a lever for education reform. In Smith and O'Day's terms: ". . .a major reform in the assessment system . . . is critical to education. Assessment instruments are not just passive components of the educational system; substantial experience indicates that, under the right conditions, they can influence as well as assess teaching" (p. 253). Proponents also assert that if performance assessment is effectively implemented at the school, district, or state level, it can change curriculum, teacher and student behavior, as well as the community's attitude toward schools. Leadership willing to be innovative, and a friendly political climate, appear to play pivotal roles in effective implementation; and these two broadly defined areas encompass several critical factors.

Curriculum and Assessment. The necessity of tying assessments to curriculum and instruction is one of the basic premises of assessment reform. What is new in current endeavors is the focus on equally new curriculum and broadly defined valued outcomes. Stress on cross-disciplinary knowledge, conceptually complex thinking, good writing abilities, application of mathematical and scientific concepts, and social competencies has necessitated overhauling curricular and instructional frameworks as well. To an extent, overhauling writing and math assessments has proved to be the easiest to develop at all levels. Performance-based writing assessments, especially, represent assessment reform at its most basic.

Reform of math assessments has been aided by the guidelines provided by the National Council of Teachers of Mathematics in the *Curriculum and Evaluation Standards for School Mathematics* (1989). Reforms in other areas will become easier and more widespread as guidelines become available. The National Science Foundation (NSF) and American Association for the Advancement of Sciences (AAAS), for example, have sponsored projects that address issues of science curriculum.

Work, with support from the Federal government on content standards, although controversial, is likely to influence assessment reform. Content standards in science, economics, foreign language, and other areas will have been released by the end of 1995 (Olsen, 1995, February 1). Such standards portend, of course, revisions of the current assessment system used in these content areas.

In tying assessment reform to both curriculum and instruction, individual states have followed divergent courses of action. In Oregon, for example, assessment reform and curriculum reform were undertaken simultaneously. In Vermont, on the other hand, an assessment system was instituted before the curriculum standards were articulated.

In the long run, the core educational changes are likely to be the result of a dialectic process between curriculum and assessment reforms.

Professional Development.   Professional development is crucial to reform because teachers are the deciding factor in the success performance assessments will have as a tool for reform. In fact, the importance of professional development in this or any other reform effort cannot be overemphasized (Little, 1993). In order for performance assessment to be effective, teachers expectations of their students and of their own teaching methods must change. Teachers must expect to develop their students' ability to construct answers, to think critically, and to move beyond focusing on factual knowledge. Currently, for some summative purposes, many teachers are asked to prepare their students for the administration of norm-referenced, multiple-choice tests bought from test publishers. They also are being asked to develop their students' abilities to perform well on performance-based assessments. The conflict between these two systems is probably reflected in methods of instruction and in assessing for teaching.

Performance assessment, thus, demands teachers' participation in assessment development, implementation, and scoring. Teachers must become knowledgeable about assessment design, scoring, and new pedagogical techniques. The benefits of teacher involvement in developing performance assessment is illustrated by the New Standards Project (NSP). The relative success of NSP in developing interesting assessment tasks and associated scoring rubrics can be attributed to its endeavors to build professional capacity at the local level. Teachers themselves develop assessment tasks and scoring rubrics and conduct pilot tests in their classrooms. Teachers then send their tasks to an NSP committee (and receive payment if their tasks are adopted for use by the NSP).

Teams of teachers from participating states and districts attend NSP assessment task and scoring rubrics development conferences, as well as sessions in curriculum development and portfolio design. After a prescribed number of training sessions, these teachers are designated as *Senior Leaders,* and they, in turn, offer professional development in the same activities to other teachers in their districts and states. Vermont, Oregon, Kentucky, and Maryland, among others, also are paying increasing attention to issues of professional development, largely through similar train-the-trainer professional development models.

Professional development activities are not cheap. All such activities are resource intensive when compared to traditional systems of testing. Commitment on the part of leadership to provide money, teacher release time, and materials is essential to successful implementation.

Community Support. In addition to teacher and leadership support, community support is critical throughout the entire reform process, whether or not assessment is the chosen mode of change. Without a sense of ownership on the parts of teachers, administrators, students, parents, the community, and other stakeholders, the system-wide changes required to effectively implement performance assessment will not occur. Vermont, for example, engaged in a large-scale consensus process before beginning its statewide portfolio assessments. As a result, its initiative has largely been supported by most stakeholders. On the other hand, Littleton, Colorado, had to rescind its reforms due to community opposition. The community was not kept well informed and the reforms were enacted too swiftly. In the end, community members felt that vague, nonacademic outcomes were replacing content, and that technically unsound assessments would be used to determine something as important as high school graduation.

Two chapters in this volume, Easton and Koehler's account of Arizona's assessment reform, and Suzanne Stiegelbauer's work on organizational change, provide detailed and lucid discussions of, and food for thought regarding, the issues and challenges involved in undertaking systemic change.

TECHNICAL ISSUES

Because assessment reform can no longer be considered to be a passing fad, performance assessments must pass technical scrutiny, if they are to become an accepted means of judging student performance. In fact, most major objections to performance assessments are based on a lack of faith in new methods and confidence in the technical quality of norm-referenced, multiple-choice tests, which have about an 80-year theoretical, research, and development base. Nonetheless, some reformers argue that the shift from multiple-choice to performance-based assessment systems represents a shift in the educational paradigm and, as such, must be evaluated within the framework of the new paradigm. In what ways performance assessments must be technically robust is a topic only touched upon in this chapter. Greater detail is presented in the discussion on assessment tasks by Haertel and Wiley and in the chapter on linking assessment results by Linn.

Modern day reformers view performance assessments as an integral part of teaching and learning, frequently modeling desirable instructional techniques upon performance assessments. Traditionally, educators viewed assessments as a separate, completely external event that should not influence teaching. This contrast between the two, the new and the traditional, illuminates two different conceptions of the educational process the two camps hold, the two being fundamentally incompatible (Mitchell, 1992). Thus far, this difference has not been articulated clearly in the literature, but is likely to confuse communication unless it is identified. The definition of "information" differs in each paradigm. In this sentence from a paper by Bock (1992) we see the definitions in collision: "if the system for scoring the essays produces one global rating for each exercise, the information the test conveys will compare unfavorably with the information from perhaps 50 multiple-choice items that could be answered in an equal period of time" (p. 7). The distinction between the concept of learning and the concept of measurement underlies the present dilemma with respect to the technical qualities of performance assessments.

In part, this situation may have arisen because the psychometric community continued to operate within an old model of learning, even as a change in cognitive psychology was permeating educational thinking. Mislevy (1989) wrote:

> It is only a slight exaggeration to describe the test theory that dominates educational measurement today as the application of twentieth century statistics to nineteenth century psychology. . . . It (traditional test theory) falls

short for placement and instruction problems based on students' internal representations of systems, problem-solving strategies, or reconfiguration of knowledge as they learn. Such applications demand different caricatures of ability—more realistic ones that can express patterns suggested by recent developments in cognitive and educational psychology (Abstract).

Mislevy's point is that the insights of cognitive psychology have altered the conceptions of competence and learning, and that new developments in measurement technology make a new test theory possible.

The new model of cognition and the integration of assessment into the teaching and learning processes have provoked some resistance to discussion of the technical problems presented by performance assessment. It has been difficult for psychometricians and researchers focused on terminal testing to switch to a model wherein assessment itself is viewed as an aid to learning and may even take place simultaneously with learning. Nonetheless, as others point out, validity, reliability, and generalizability have been the perennial issues with all measurement instruments and remain so with performance assessments. The three major issues are discussed briefly in this section.

Validity

A central question regarding performance assessments concerns what can be termed *pedagogical validity*. If the primary goals of performance-based assessments are to be more closely connected to the curriculum and to provide information to the teacher for instructional purposes, then how satisfactorily they are able to fulfill these goals is of central concern. A one-to-one mapping of assessment tasks to curricular areas is the most important and the fairest piece in the assessment puzzle.

Wiley and Haertel (1992) emphasized the essential connection between the goals of measurement, embodied in curriculum frameworks, and tasks meant to assess progress toward goals: "If no valid system exists for mapping tasks into the frameworks, the curricular coverage of the assessment cannot be evaluated.... The link between task selection, task analysis, task scoring, and curricular goals has to be well understood and relatively tight in order for the system to work" (p. 15). They concentrated on evidential validity and stressed that specific analyses must be performed to ensure the match between curricular goals and assessment tasks.

Wiley and Haertel sketched the types of analyses that must be carried out and concluded by underlining the importance of achieving evidential validity, since they contended that the basic reason for rejecting machine-scorable multiple-choice tests is their lack of validity, given the form of the tests and their dependence on memorization, and society's demand for complex thinking. The concept of evidential validity now can be extended to include the ideas of assessments as diagnostic tools for students' educational needs.

Consequential validity is another issue with performance assessments. Linn and Dunbar (1991) included this concept under *expanded validity*, which they saw as a major adjustment in technical theory needed to accommodate performance assessment:

> . . . serious validation of alternative assessments needs to include evidence regarding the intended and unintended consequences, the degree to which performance on specific assessment tasks transfers . . . the fairness of the assessments . . . the cognitive complexity of the processes students employ in solving assessment problems, . . . the meaningfulness of the problems for students and teachers . . . [and] a basis for judging both the content quality and the comprehensiveness of the content coverage needs to be provided. Finally, the cost of the assessment must be justified. (pp. 21–22)

The fairness issue is of particular concern if assessments are used for student certification and sorting. There must be some assurance that minority populations (who traditionally have been screened out of institutions or opportunities that would provide them with social and economic opportunities) not be inadvertently affected by assessment reform. CRESST is conducting research on the responses of minority students to performance assessments in San Diego City schools. We suspect that results will not generically apply to any and all performance assessments; much will depend on how assessments are constructed, the types of items they are composed of, and the type of curriculum they support.

Baker and O'Neil's chapter on performance assessments and equity illuminates the myriad issues that must be addressed in developing and implementing assessments that are fair and equitable.

These two approaches to validity are complementary. The two, in fact, have merged with respect to these assessments because the theoretical and ideological bases for performance assessments call for a concurrently authentic and fair psychometric system.

Generalizability and Reliability

Generalizability, including reliability, has surfaced as a major issue which must be resolved if performance assessments are to be used for individual student assessments. In addition to redefining validity, Linn and Dunbar (1991) elaborated on the concept of reliability; they argued for subsuming the traditional criterion of reliability under the transfer and generalizability criterion. Whether performance assessments sample sufficiently from the knowledge domain in question to enable fair and accurate judgments about students' achievement in that domain is a question central to assessment reform. After all, if one of the promises of assessments is to enable an understanding of students' educational needs, it must be reliably understood, in a larger sense, exactly what an assessment product indicates about a student's achievement status. In this context, then, multiple examples of student work on multiple performance tasks may be the answer to the problem of generalizability. Intertask reliability, however, has been difficult to attain.

Interrater reliability is another issue. The complexity of the assessment tasks, the myriad answers they can elicit, and the number of people used to score them, with, possibly, different frames of reference yield a very high potential for low reliability. Although cross-rater reliability is attainable through standardization of tasks, scorer training, and the establishment of explicit scoring criteria, such procedures impose certain practical constraints on these assessments.

The questions with respect to technical issues, then, are:

- How technically robust do these performance assessments need to be for high stakes sake (accountability and certification)?
- To what extent can the technical criteria be relaxed to accommodate teacher adaptation and judgment to induce effective teaching practices?

Indeed, for high stakes decisions, the assessments must be technically impeccable. This conclusion, with its emphasis on accuracy and fairness, implies that there must be serious investments in research and development to ensure assessments of high quality. On the other hand, to ensure the viability of performance assessments as pedagogical tools, investments in teachers is essential, with less attention to interrater-reliability and standardization.

The crux of these questions is whether one type of assessment system can serve multiple purposes, or whether multiplicity of purposes might subvert the goals of the performance assessment systems.

MAJOR GAPS IN CURRENT KNOWLEDGE

The performance assessment movement, in its present incarnation, has developed so rapidly that knowledge in some significant areas is simply lacking. Costs and technology represent two of those major areas.

Costs of Performance Assessments

Issues related to the financing of performance assessments are not well understood. The Office of Technology Assessment's discussion of costs in *Testing in American Schools: Asking the Right Questions* (1992) is inconclusive. A study by Pechman (1992) suggests that the costs associated with ". . . every phase of alternative assessment are alarming" (p. 24), but that they may be misleading as the benefits of professional involvement in the implementation and scoring procedures are generally not figured into the dollar amount calculations.

Getting a handle on assessment costs is difficult; and that difficulty arises for two reasons: (a) schools, districts, and state education departments do not record costs for testing and assessment as separate items, but as portions of categories such as personnel, material, and vendor costs, so that disentangling the costs of assessment is extremely difficult; and (b) the costs of machine-scorable tests and performance assessments are not comparable if professional development is taken into consideration. For example, how can the cost of developing a portfolio, which takes a year of the teacher's and student's time, be compared to the costs of a machine-scorable test, which also takes part of their time but for different purposes. The results of each process are essentially noncomparable, especially if portfolio grading is done within the context of professional development.

Charting the Course Toward Instructionally Sound Assessment, a report produced by the California Assessment Collaborative (1993), details useful budget and personnel categories for accounting for the costs of developing and implementing performance assessments. The document provides no overall dollar amounts but concludes that:

> The investment of dollars, time, and energy required to assure that performance assessment actually improves student performance are high. Although many costs are associated with initial development work, many relate to the sustaining structures and processes which will assure that assessments continue to have a positive impact on teaching and learning. (p. 110)

The chapters by Hardy and Monk contain edifying discussions on how to conceptualize costs and benefits associated with developing and implementing performance assessments systems.

Technology and Performance Assessments

The potential for applying new information and communications technology to performance assessment remains unrealized at all levels of education. At the local level, the problem presents itself as the schools' general lack of technology experience and equipment, coupled with their lack of knowledge about performance assessments. It is impossible to forge ahead with computer-based assessment when some schools have computers only in their business education departments, or worse, in their storage rooms. The old joke that in many cases children know more than do their teachers about computers and word processors is a sad reality.

Technology, in fact, offers numerous possibilities for integrating assessment into the daily life of the classroom. For example, technology applications (e.g., word processing, databases) can offer teachers a view into their students' problem-solving and thinking processes (Means et al., 1993). Electronic portfolios on a disk for each child can provide a means for ongoing assessment. This vision is appealing, but remains a dream for most school districts. (In some cases, electronic portfolios consist of work that has been scanned into the computer.)

Some organizations, however, have been instrumental in helping schools integrate technology into daily teaching and learning activities. For example, The Coalition for Essential Schools (CES) and IBM collaborated to develop an electronic exhibitions resource center. This center is intended as a resource for the CES member schools to exchange ideas about exhibitions (student demonstrations of their work) and about the CES curriculum. Such partnerships between businesses and schools are likely to be helpful in bringing technological innovations to schools and, thus, catapulting them into the 21st century.

CONCLUSION

In recent years, advocacy for performance assessments has emerged from a group of concerned educators who have linked reformed assessment strategies to needed reforms in curriculum and instruction. Because assessment reform calls for a deviation from traditional assessment strategies in more ways than one, it presents several challenges to the established organizational structure of education.

First, the challenge is to simultaneously engineer other reforms that support and enhance performance assessments. Second, the challenge is to develop assessment systems that are technically sound and pedagogically useful. Third, the challenge is to involve all stakeholders so that their informed consent provides the momentum for assessment (and associated) reforms. Judgments regarding the efficacy of performance assessment in fulfilling its promises must be based on data from the many educational systems now in the process of reform. Only when these reforms result in enhanced student outcomes will the challenge of assessment reform have been met.

REFERENCES

Bock, D. (1992). *New Standards Project: Beyond the bubble*. Unpublished manuscript.

California Assessment Collaborative (1993, September). *Charting the course toward instructionally sound assessment*, San Francisco: Author.

Cannell, J. J. (1987). *Nationally normed elementary achievement testing in America's public schools: How all fifty states are above national average*. West Virginia: Friends for Education.

Cannell, J. J. (1989). *How public educators cheat on standardized achievement tests*. Albuquerque, NM: Friends for Education.

Council of Chief State School Officers and the North Central Regional Educational Laboratory. (1994). *State student assessment programs database* (1993–1994). Washington, DC: Author.

Goals 2000 will shape state, local school reform. (1994, May 27). *Education Daily* [Special Suppl.], 27(102).

Hansen, J. B. & Hathaway, W. E. (1991). *A survey of more authentic assessment practices*. Paper presented at the National Council on Measurement in Education/National Association of Test Directors. Meeting in Chicago, IL.

Hoff, D. (1995, January 31). Goals panel looks to form its own standards council. *Education Daily*, 28(20).

Kentucky Institute for Education Research. (1995, January). *An independent evaluation of the Kentucky Instructional Results Information System (KIRIS)*. Executive Summary. Frankfort, KY: Author.

Koretz, D., Stecher, B., Klein, S., McCaffrey, D., & Diebert, E. (1993, December). *Can portfolios assess student performance and influence instruction? The 1991–1992 Vermont experience* (CSE Tech. Rep. 371). Los Angeles: Center for Research on Evaluation, Standards, and Student Testing.

Linn, R., & Dunbar, S. B. (1991). *Complex, performance-based assessment: Expectations and validation criteria*. Los Angeles: Center for Research on Evaluation, Standards, and Student Testing.

Little, J. W. (1993). Teachers professional development in a climate of educational reform. *Educational Evaluation and Policy Analysis, 15*(2), 129–151.

Means, B., Blando, J., Olson, K., Middleton, T., Morocco, CC., Remz, A. R., & Zorfass, J. (1993). *Using technology to support education reform*. Washington, DC: U.S. Department of Education, Office of Research.

Mislevy, R. (1989). Foundations of a new test theory (Abstract). Princeton, NJ: Educational Testing Service.

Mitchell, R. (1992, April). Beyond the verbal confusion over tests. *Education Week, 11*, 32.

Mitchell, R. (1992). *Testing for learning*. New York: The Free Press.

Mitchell, R. (1995). *The promise of performance assessment: How to use backlash constructively*. Paper presented at the San Francisco, CA, AERA annual conference.

National Center on Education and the Economy. (Undated). *New Standards Project*. Information Pamphlet. Washington, DC: Author.

National Council of Teachers of Mathematics. (1989). *Curriculum and evaluation standards for school mathematics*. Reston, VA: Author.

National Council of Teachers of Mathematics. (1991). *Professional standards for teaching mathematics*. Reston, VA: Author.

Oakes, J. (1985). *Keeping track*. New Haven, CT: Yale University Press.

Oakes, J. (1990). *Multiplying inequalities: Effects of race, social class, and tracking on opportunities to learn mathematics and science.* Santa Monica, CA: Rand.

Office of Technology Assessment, U.S. Congress. (1992, March). *Asking the right question: Testing in America.* Washington, DC: U.S. Government Printing Office.

Olson, L. (1995, February 1). Rules will allow district to set Title 1 measures. *Education Week, 14*(19).

Olson, L. (1995, February 8). Bills to scrap NESIC likely to hold sway. *Education Week, 14*(20).

Olson, L. (1995, April 12). Standards times 50. *Education Week, 14*(29).

Pechman, E. M. (1992). *Use of standardized and alternative tests in the states.* Washington, DC: Policy Study Associates.

Pelavin Associates and CCSSO. (1991, April). *Performance assessments in the states.* Washington, DC: Author.

Prominent educators recommend wide use of Pacesetter. (1995, February). *College Board News, 23*(3), 1, 2.

Resnick, L., & Simmons, W. (1993, February). Assessment as the catalyst of school reform. *Educational Leadership, 50*(5), 11–15.

Secretary's Commission on Achieving Necessary Skills. (1991, June). *What work requires of schools: A SCANS report for America 2000.* U.S. Department of Labor: Author.

Sizer, T. (1989). Diverse practice, shared ideas: The essential school. In H. J. Walberg & J. J. Lane (Eds.), *Organizing for learning: Toward the 21st century.* Reston, VA: National Association of Secondary School Principals.

Sizer, T. R. (1992). *Horaces' school.* Boston: Houghton Mifflin.

Smith, M. & O'Day, J. (1990). Systemic school reform. *Politics of Education Yearbook.*

Wiggins, G. (1989, May). A true test: Toward more authentic and equitable assestment. *Phi Delta Kappan, 70*(9), 703–713.

Wiggins, G. (1991). Standards, not standardization: Evoking quality student work. *Educational Leadership, 48*(5), 18–25.

Wiley, D. & Haertel, H. (1992). *Extended assessment tasks: Purposes, definitions, scoring, and accuracy.* Paper prepared for the California Assessment Program.

Wolf, D. P., & Pistone, N. (1989, April). Portfolio assessment, sampling student work. *Educational Leadership, 46*(7).

Wolf, D. P., & Pistone, N. (1991). *Taking full measure: Rethinking assessment through the arts.* New York: College Board.

Chapter 2

Performance Assessment and the Multiple Functions of Educational Measurement

Daniel P. Resnick
Carnegie Mellon University

Lauren B. Resnick
University of Pittsburgh

Education reformers recognize the novel characteristics and functions in the combination of projects and exhibitions, portfolios, and sit-down examinations that comprise new ways schools are being encouraged to assess students. In comparing current assessments to traditional, standardized tests, advocates have stressed the directness of the contemporary measures, the ways in which they encourage applications of knowledge, their strong relationship to curriculum, their power to motivate student work, and the ways in which they can assist teachers to help students learn. With language rooted in description, advocates have advanced the innovative features of newer assessments and plainly illustrated what sets those assessments apart from traditional, standardized tests.

Still, performance assessments, as they are more widely adopted by states and districts and as they are more effectively integrated into ongoing state and district testing programs, might be considered just another kind of test. This is not surprising, because it is perhaps inevitable for performance assessments that become part of a mandated state or district testing program (subject to control and review by administrators) to be described and understood in established ways that underline their resemblance to what is already in use. Such a conservative effect of the diffusion process for technologies makes a great deal of sense, because sit-down examinations, for example, whether of the new or old form, demand design of development and trial schedules by measurement specialists; communications with superintendents, principals, and teachers; appropriate security procedures, technical review of results, and some form of public reporting. In the face of such commonalities, for administrators, the novel features of the new assessments are likely to recede from view, just as the revolutionary technology of the automobile and the opportunity it presented for restructuring social life vanished for a time beneath the simplified rubric of a horseless carriage.

Within the psychometric research community, there is unlikely to be resistance to this assimilation of new assessments to old practice. For researchers, as Fitzpatrick and Morrison argued more than 20 years ago, "There is no absolute distinction between performance tests and other classes of tests" (1971, p. 238); and the research community is right, as it thinks of the broad concerns for reliability, validity, and related criteria that all assessments are expected to respect.

Are there, then, major differences between the old and the new assessments? Has there been an exaggeration of difference, tied to the rhetoric associated with the advocacy of performance measures? In this chapter, these related questions are explored in two major sections: First, we look at measures and consider the difference between direct and indirect ways of gauging performance; and then we consider the purposes of assessments, noting the roles of old and new measures in a historical and policy context. Second, we review the social context, school environment, and support required for various direct measurements of each of the four basic functions, or purposes, of assessment: instruction and learning, certification, accountability, and monitoring. Our goal is to reconceptualize the purposes for which assessments are used and to examine the implications of those purposes.

ASSESSMENT AS MEASUREMENT

Perhaps it should be stressed at the outset of this discussion that both old and new assessments constitute a means of measurements that capture samples of student work for different purposes. As measures are examined more closely, a distinction can be drawn between those that are direct and those that are indirect. Measurement theory recognizes this distinction and acknowledges that each type has functional strengths and weaknesses, depending on its purpose and its representation and sampling of student work. For some purposes (particularly monitoring), we will argue that indirect measures are entirely appropriate, but for instruction and learning and certification and accountability, the analysis indicates that direct measures are essential.

Direct and Indirect Measures

Direct measures are those that capture performances that are valued—that people care about. When students are asked to write a memo, solve mathematical problems, carry out an experiment, or troubleshoot mechanical and electrical failures, they are being asked to demonstrate what they know and to perform in a way that the public can recognize and identify as valuable, not just in schools, but also in society at large. Because this is true, direct measures often are called "authentic" (Wiggins, 1991). Authentic measures demand an active performance by the test taker that someone inside the school and outside (in a science lab, a business organization, a library, a shop, or a production plant) ought to be able to do. Thus the test taker demonstrates the practicality of her or his performance.

Indirect measures are those for which students cannot study. Intelligence tests are classic examples of indirect measures. The knowledge and know-how such tests try to sample are not an explicit part of a school program, and student scores on those kinds of measures are very little affected by short-term preparation and effort. Measures of this variety may be used when evaluators wish to gather evidence about a school program without introducing new objectives to direct the work of students and teachers, the goal being to preserve as much neutrality with respect to the school program as possible. Because direct measures run the risk of changing the nature of the data, the goal of indirect measures is to gather data that have not been at all influenced by the use of any measure.

Scores on indirect measures can be good predictors of student performance on direct measures, under very limited conditions. For example, an indirect measure that samples a student's editing skills, but requires no writing, may be a good predictor of writing skill. However, performance on indirect measures will correlate well with performance on direct ones if, and only if, the knowledge and skill sampled by a direct measure remain a central part of the student's program.

Correlations of this kind, then, are unstable. If the indirect measure is successful as a predictor at the outset and takes the place of the direct measure, the substitution may remove incentives for the student and teacher to assign time and value to the activity that was once prized and directly measured. If students and teachers try to gear instruction to improving performance on the indirect measure, the indirect measure will no longer predict performance on the direct measure; and because the tendency within school environments is for teachers and students to want to improve performance on whatever measures affect promotion, graduation, and other forms of school success, indirect measures will affect student and teacher effort and lose any correlation they may have had with performance on direct measures. Thus, because standardized indirect measures of editing skill claim success in predicting writing ability, the time actually spent on classroom writing may decline. Eventually, then, indirect measures will cease to be a good predictor of writing.

Successful correlation of indirect with direct measures also depends on the nonintrusiveness of whatever indirect measure is used. Even if successfully nonintrusive, indirect measures raise serious ethical questions. Is it fair to hold students accountable for matters they cannot directly work on? Is it socially and morally acceptable to introduce measures for performance that cannot be used to motivate and encourage student work? How should we judge the bias of tests that students cannot see and that cannot help them to organize their work?

We argue that, for purposes of instruction, certification, and accountability, our public education system needs direct measures, because those alone offer hope of raising the level of student achievement, particularly in the area of instruction and learning. Performance assessments, for teachers, for students, and for the lay public, have a power to communicate the goals of instruction and learning that indirect measures cannot claim.

Historical and Policy Context

Although direct measures of performance have never disappeared totally from our public schools, a decline in their use began in the 1920s under the influence of popular, relatively inexpensive, and indirect standardized tests. Direct measures were preserved as the dominant form of assessment only in areas that seem unrelated to one another: the arts, including music and dance, and sport, shop, and driver education. The not-so-mysterious something that those areas of a school program share, of course, is a belief that human judges are required to certify the quality of what is learned, along with a kind of "show me" attitude on the part of those judges, and a sense that students need to see and to experience examples of excellent work in order to do that work well themselves.

With the decline and compartmentalizing of direct measures, indirect measurement of student outcomes continued to be widely encouraged as a sign of progressive administration and as an aid to efficiency. There is a correlation, for example, between the growth of education and the use of measurements. A case in point is the rapid expansion of school enrollments between 1880 and 1925, which increased school attendance. Simultaneously, attention was focused on the need to continue building and expanding schools and the need to keep costs under control (Callahan, 1962). The need for speed in making decisions about building and the costs of education can be appreciated if one considers that, between 1880 and the outbreak of World War I, the portion of the age group in high school quintupled, and the outlay for public schooling tripled. Attention to measurement followed from this movement for swift cost-efficiency.

For schools to become cost-efficient, it was thought, they had to develop programs that were adapted to the understood abilities of students, and means had to be found to move students along with their age group. Retention of a high portion of students at the same grade level for two or more years, once thought of as the necessary consequence of maintaining high standards, came to be regarded as a failure of public policy and administration (Ayres, 1909).

Our present preoccupation with measurement for purposes of accountability and monitoring owes a great deal to the way in which the political and social goal of efficiency was addressed by the measurement community in the Progressive Era (1900–1917) (D. P. Resnick, 1982). By the 1920s, it was common for students to advance with their age group and to be placed in programs where they were believed less likely to fail. Homogeneous grouping became common practice in elementary programs, and separate tracks came to define the new comprehensive high school. Entrance examinations to public high schools, still quite common before 1910, disappeared except in schools with specialized programs. Such examinations, it was believed, constituted an unacceptable barrier to educational access. The focus on access, tracking, and low failure rates thus helped to establish a large market for measurement instruments that could be used to assign students to various programs.

Pencil-and-paper intelligence tests, for which students could not study and for which they were not taught, were widely used for assignment to programs and tracks (Tyack, 1974). Although there were more than 200 achievement tests available for primary and secondary schools by 1918 (Monroe, 1918), the intelligence tests, tied to no specific curriculum, were seen as the most useful for classifying students. In 1923, Lewis Terman's intelligence test for Grades 7 to 12, for example, sold more than one half million copies (Chapman, 1988).

School use of intelligence tests followed the introduction of the Army's Alpha and Beta tests to classify 1.7 million American army recruits in World War I (Kevles, 1968; Yerkes, 1921). A survey of all cities of 10,000 or more population in 1925 (Deffenbaugh, 1926) indicated that two thirds of the reporting cities used group intelligence tests to place students in homogeneous groups in elementary schools, more than half in junior high schools, and 41% in high schools.

The use of indirect measures of learning, however, was promoted by far more than the vogue of intelligence tests in the 1920s, or by the need for measures to support homogeneous grouping patterns, so well described by Oakes (1985, 1992; Oakes, Ormseth, Bell, & Camp, 1990) as a persisting and dominant feature of our elementary, middle, and high schools. Two other factors influenced the development of indirect measures. The first was the dependence on textbooks to define course content and performance standards and, with that, the inchoate national market for school tests. The second and perhaps more basic factor was the way in which knowledge itself was defined.

Publishers who introduced achievement tests before World War I (e.g., the World Book Company) found no common curriculum that crossed the boundaries of districts and states. Textbooks marketed by different publishers generated curriculum. If achievement tests were marketed to serve the needs of only the purchasers of a single text, tests would enjoy only restricted sales. Thus, the search for wider markets, associated with greater profits, encouraged publishers to develop achievement tests that were not overly dependent on a particular teaching program.

The achievement tests that subsequently were introduced called for knowledge that could be accounted for by students who approached the subject in many different ways or perhaps not at all. Less removed from the curriculum of the classroom than intelligence tests, standardized achievement tests were nonetheless unrelated to any particular teaching program and were not expected to mobilize and direct learning activity in the classroom.

The generally accepted concept of knowledge during the developmental period of American testing also encouraged test features (now associated with indirect measures) that we have characterized elsewhere as decomposition and decontextualization (Resnick & Resnick, 1992). The psychologists who fought against abstract and deductivist theories of knowledge in the period from 1900 to 1925 favored tests they saw as direct measures of sampled elements of mathematical knowledge. However, they seem to us (after the cognitive revolution of the 1970s) random bits of knowledge—collections of bits and pieces of knowledge, without coherence or context.

The ground-breaking work of Edward L. Thorndike is a good example of this difference in "seeing." Thorndike developed a theory of knowledge as a collection of bonds (Thorndike, 1922). In Thorndike's view, connection-making and practice in using right habits (in which drills play a positive role) help to establish reasoning in arithmetic. A theory of sampling, influenced by what Thorndike calls a sociology of arithmetic (Thorndike, 1922), was needed to determine which bonds should be present in what was taught and tested; but he was not uncomfortable with the kind of computational basics found in the standardized achievement tests of the period following World War I. For Thorndike, those basics were not indirect measures of mathematical thinking but direct examples of the essential bonds in arithmetical reasoning.

The cognitive researchers of the last 20 years perceive knowledge, knowing, and learning differently; and that change in perception represents a paradigm shift that, for a new set of reasons, calls into question earlier testing practice. What was a direct representation and sampling of knowledge in test protocols of Thorndike's day now appears only partially successful, often indirect, and missing the essential construction, context, process, complexity, and applications that define contemporary knowledge and the process of knowing (Brown, Campione, Webber, & McGilly 1992; Resnick & Resnick, 1992). Contemporary research has enriched our understanding of what it means to have direct measures for the improvement of instruction and learning.

PURPOSES OF ASSESSMENT AND DIRECTNESS OF MEASUREMENT

Having reviewed essential features of direct and indirect measures within a historical and policy context, we now turn to the functional use of such measures in school environments. Learning improvement, we argue, is the first of the four reasons for which schools seek to measure the work of their students. Although the other reasons include certification, accountability, and monitoring, for us and for increasing numbers of parents and lay people, learning improvement has the highest and most urgent priority.

Learning Improvement and the School Environment

Since Thorndike's day, we have learned a great deal about how indirect measures work when they are allowed to define the goals of instruction and learning. The work of Shepard (1989, 1991) is especially relevant in this regard, for her research on high-stakes tests indicates that, when promotion or retention, school grouping, federal funding, and the social ranking of schools are expected consequences of school testing, teachers and students will spend large amounts of time on classroom practice designed to help students improve their performance on the indirect measures. Such practice has the effect of destroying the predictive validity of such tests as indicators of how students would perform on the intended curriculum of the classroom because simply put, the predictive validity of tests depends on their correlation with performance on direct measures of learning. As previously noted, when learning is driven out by a preoccupation with teaching oriented to indirect measures, indicators are useless as predictors of learning.

If there are high stakes involved for students and teachers, indirect measures mobilize the energy of the classroom for practice on learning activities that are routinized. Indirect measures do not help students to understand and deal with complexity, nor do they test or encourage the use of what is generally called higher order thinking.

Higher order thinking requires effort and involves dealing with complexity, judgment, and uncertainty (L. B. Resnick, 1987a). No single step in reasoning is sufficient to identify or resolve a problem. This kind of thinking involves a recognition that human judgment is central to decision making, that choices have to be made and defended, that contexts affect the meaning of problems and the responses to them; and there is always uncertainty. Therefore, the right answer to a question or a situation is often highly dependent on how a question is posed. Responses and arguments have to be developed by persons facing the challenge of uncertainty; and in that challenge, effort counts. Resourcefulness must be wedded to perseverance, for in complex environments, answers do not come easily.

Higher order thinking is needed to deal with the difficult problems of science, society, and the workplace. After all, problems are most likely to motivate student effort and have a resonance beyond classroom walls. Ergo, problems must be interesting, not only for schools and established subject areas but also for scholars, workers, and citizens at large. We believe that direct measures of learning can provide an opportunity to display the complex thinking we seek to foster, and that direct measures can have a positive effect on learning in general and on achievement in the classroom.

A group of 17 states has joined the New Standards Project (NSP)[2] to develop direct measures and to pilot them in school districts across the country in order to build a professional development program and raise expectations for what all children can learn.

A Practical Task as Direct Measure. New Standards assessment tasks are intended to be direct measures of learning. Perhaps the best example of this is a mathematics and literacy exercise for fourth graders, known as the *Aquarium Task.* First piloted in 1992, it remains a useful illustration of how a direct measure can capture complexity.

The task works as follows: In a letter from the principal, it is announced that the fourth-grade classroom will be getting a 30-gallon aquarium. The

---

[2]The New Standards Project, codirected by Lauren Resnick of the Learning Research and Development Center at the University of Pittsburgh and Marc Tucker of the National Center on Education and the Economy in Rochester, NY, and Washington, DC, was launched in 1991, with the support of The Pew Charitable Trusts and the John D. and Catherine T. MacArthur Foundation. Its state partners are Arkansas, California, Colorado, Connecticut, Delaware, Iowa, Kentucky, Maine, Massachusetts, Missouri, New York, Oregon, Pennsylvania, Rhode Island, Texas, Vermont, and Washington.

students in that classroom have the responsibility of buying fish for the tank. The class will receive $25 to spend on fish and a *Choosing Fish for Your Aquarium* brochure. The brochure provides the necessary information about the size of each type of fish, how much each costs, and the special needs of each fish. The students are instructed to choose as many different kinds of fish as possible and then to write a letter explaining which fish were chosen. In the letter, the students must indicate how many of each kind of fish were selected and the reasons they were chosen, demonstrate that the fish will not be overcrowded in the aquarium, and prove that the purchases maintain the limited budget of $25.

Mathematically, the aquarium task problem is one of optimization. For the students who first worked on it, it also was a practical and complex problem in planning an aquarium for the class.

In their comments on the task, students wondered how anything that was so much fun could be a test. Teachers, on the other hand, were often surprised that their students could do anything so complex. After many decades of worksheets in classrooms, assessments that involve single-step operations, and little interest in the evidence of how students solve complex problems, it is not surprising that both teachers and students often are unprepared for direct measures that have such a positive impact on learning.

How can direct measures like this, avowedly administered in a first phase pilot to no more than six thousand students, affect the opportunity to learn? Three critical features are necessary for such measures to have a substantial impact on classroom learning: (a) the visibility of large numbers of examples; (b) high performance expectations for students; and (c) positive consequences for student effort. To establish a large number of examples of complex direct measures of this kind, a network of producers—teachers, math educators, and entrepreneurial developers—has been established around the country by the NSP. Publications are being organized that display exemplary tasks and student responses, and there are plans to develop a large number of such materials for public display in annual releases.

A reasonable criticism of direct measures of this kind is that they are too narrowly effective in orienting student efforts. If students cannot study for indirect measures, direct measures risk focusing student efforts on tasks that are too restrictive. One way to deal with this criticism, which calls attention to the problem of generalizability for single complex tasks, is to increase the number of tasks students and teachers can inspect and deal with. Another method is to integrate complex tasks into cumulative records of student work, so that teachers work with students, under guidelines, to produce projects and portfolios of work they broadly sample from the actual curriculum of the classroom, without confining prescriptions.

A second feature of direct measures is high performance expectations. Openly disclosed rubrics serve teachers as scoring guides. Every one of the tasks that is released by the NSP will be accompanied by the rubrics used for scoring the task. In order for the high performance standards represented in such tasks to affect what teachers expect of students in the classroom, teachers have to be able to internalize those standards through discussion with their peers and to use rubrics for scoring in professional conferences. New Standards has taken a leadership role in arranging such conferences and in generating professional development opportunities.

Without incentives for students to engage in the kind of challenging work that complex tasks represent at any grade level, it is unlikely that direct measures for assessment will fully produce the desired effect on learning. Thus, in addition to the visibility of examples and clear standards for student performance, some coupling with opportunities for further schooling and for integration into the workplace is needed. The intention of this is to call for more effort from students on behalf of their own learning, which requires a close linking of within-school and out-of-school opportunities.

In many of the NSP's state partners, a demand for better student work is itself coupled with a redefinition of key elements of modern education, including: (a) the requirements for a high school diploma; (b) initiatives to make cumulative work through the high school relevant to entrance into colleges and universities; (c) the issuance of certificates of accomplishment to mark the transition into the last years of high school programs; and (d) the programs that combine the last years of high school with community college and on-site apprenticeship programs.

Direct Measures and Equity. Efforts to use direct measures to promote learning have a strong equity component. Such measures demand that all students be held to the same standard of performance so that they can apply effort to reaching realistic goals. With the indirect measures now used, the performances of students are compared with one another, even within the same classroom, rather than with an overall achievement criterion. A system that tends to compress performance for minorities and the poor into a bottom quartile is inherently inequitable. But setting a higher hurdle will not necessarily, by itself, produce changes in effort and in learning. Although such a hurdle is necessary, it is not sufficient to achieve desired learning results. A social compact also is necessary.

If students produce effort, they should be assured that there are teachers who can help them and that they are provided with the necessary classroom resources, as well as more time, when needed. Furthermore, public administration officials and parents must join together and agree to provide resources to make achievement possible. All students now have an equal right to go to school; the right to achieve should be just as explicit.

Certification as a Measure of Learning

Certification for completion of school studies currently proceeds largely without the use of any form of assessment. The high school diploma is the most commonly used certification of school completion, and it is almost universally awarded on the basis of numbers of courses and course units completed. No external assessment is required. The diploma is not useful, however, to either employers of high school graduates or institutions of higher education. In the case of the former, it is rare to find employers who look at documentation for the diploma in the high school transcript (Bishop, 1989). Course labels, moreover, are far from transparent, and grading standards are perceived as highly variable. Although most higher education institutions want evidence of the completion of secondary studies, they do not use the secondary school certificate to establish qualification for entrance. Instead, most require an independently administered selection test (SAT or ACT). Some institutions also require achievement tests in different subject areas, such as science or math, to be independently administered.

Minimum competency testing represented an experiment in the use of indirect measures to establish eligibility for the award of a diploma. However, this use of indirect measures is now largely deemed unsatisfactory (D. P. Resnick, 1980). In vogue during the 1970s, minimum competency tests were used in more than half of the states to establish that young people had minimally adequate verbal and mathematical skills. What minimum competency meant in practice, however, was questioned by the public at large. Such tests, which are difficult to study for, did not offer explicit criteria for acceptable achievement; and success was generally described in terms of placement in a certain distribution—doing better than others—without reference to a quality criterion.

Many educators and employers now believe certification must be treated as integral to the agenda of improving learning and instruction and not simply as a by-product of school attendance. That integration requires the engagement of both employers and postsecondary institutions.

Involvement with certification has been more visible in the business sector than in higher education. However, the self-interest of both sectors in transforming the certification process to help with recruitment will most likely make them active partners in the process of school reform. At the same time, the pressure exerted will encourage public schooling to develop graduates with a capacity for reflection and the experience of being productive (Bishop, 1989; Marshall & Tucker, 1992; L. B. Resnick, 1987b).

Accountability and the Education System

In accountability, as elsewhere, the function for which a particular kind of measure is used suggests a view of the social system in which that measure

operates. Public education is nestled in a complex set of social and institu-
tional relationships that are seen as two rival views of how schooling should
operate. The dominant view of the system is that it should be hierarchical
and administrative. It is a view that comes to us from the 1920s, a time in
which information indicators were treated as essential measures of accountability. In that early first model, authority was exercised from the top down.
It was thought that bureaucrats in states and districts needed only data to
do their jobs. With information about per capita funding, numbers of
classrooms, teacher pools, student enrollments, and graduation requirements, bureaucrats could formulate an accountable system.

The current version of that first model of accountability occurs if states
provide their share of resources and establish certain minimal requirements
for graduation. Districts, in turn, establish the hiring process for teachers and
administrators and provide their own share of resources. Schools administer
and deal with the curriculum. As long as there is no breakdown in this process,
it is assumed to contain self-accountability. Teachers, students, and parents, it
can be observed, are treated as passive elements within this system (Darling-
Hammond, 1988). As voters and as members of various pressure groups,
teachers and parents can intervene intermittently to influence resource allocations, but they cannot change the administrative nature of the system.

Accountability in what we term a more comprehensive second model
requires information that can bond parents, teachers, and students to the
learning goals of the entire system. If this bonding should not occur, there will
be a serious dysfunction in the system, no matter how much information is
provided on the subject to or through bureaucrats. Direct measures of the kinds
we have proposed for learning can, in this model, also serve for accountability.
It is difficult to conceive of how this bonding can occur without direct communication among all concerned about the expectations for learning in the system;
it is not easy to imagine how expectations can be shared without discussion of
persuasive examples of exactly what students are learning.

Thus, without denying that gross indicators of resources, staffing, and
enrollments play a role in efficient administration, we argue for nothing
less than a reconceptualization of the role of direct measures of learning in
accountability, coupled with a reconsideration of the role of teachers and
parents in the public accountability process. This argument for accountability in public education joins other efforts to clarify the purposes of
government and to reinvent our public institutions and the way they
function (Osborne & Gaebler, 1992).

Monitoring and Appropriate Indirect Measures

Monitoring is an area in which indirect measures are the appropriate
instrument, although it is the only function of the four described for which

this is true. Indirect measures are those that do not intrude upon classroom goals and that can offer information valuable to policymakers. Indirect measures, we are certain, can be used in this way, and we offer the United States' experience of the National Assessment of Educational Progress (NAEP) as a case in point.

The NAEP was introduced 30 years ago to serve as a kind of report card for American education. In its first 20 years, the NAEP focused on the school performance of 9-, 13-, and 17-year-olds and, more recently, on Grades 3, 9, and 11. At first, testing periodically by a light sampling in reading, writing, mathematics, and science, the NAEP aggregated results for the nation as a whole, as well as for large regions. More recently, the NAEP produced reports that indicate state-level performance. The NAEP provides indicators of how well schools are doing in the area of academic learning; and it is our only national monitoring system.

Through the background data it collects, the NAEP can focus on the relationship among policy variables, at the national and state levels, as well as on student performance. Although its sampling is not designed to provide information that can help with classroom decision making, it can focus on input variables that are relevant to national and state policymakers.

The weakness of the NAEP is that it cannot mobilize the energies of teachers, students, and parents to change performance in classrooms and schools. That also is the corollary of its strength. By seeking a space outside the curricular goals of the classroom, the NAEP can gather information on environments wherein students and teachers have yet to feel the impact of the movement for higher expectations. At the same time, the NAEP can offer an independent judgment on how well the movement for reform is proceeding in states where higher expectations through performance assessment have become a policy commitment.

By gathering information on background variables that policymakers at the national and state level are capable of influencing, the NAEP may also contribute to the progress of the reform movement. Data can be collected about the educational background of teachers, teacher salaries, instructional time, textbooks, class size, homework, and the like. By relating these components to student performance, the NAEP can direct public attention to variables that, under certain conditions, do make a difference to total performance.

Over time, results of the NAEP's indirect measures should show trends in student learning that resemble those that emerge from direct performance measures. To make this possible, measures in the NAEP will have to draw on the same body of content standards (generated by professional bodies such as the National Council of Teachers of Mathematics) that a state partnership such as New Standards has. If, under such conditions, trend data show differences in performance on direct and indirect measures, some public accounting must be made. Only in this way can the public be assured that the funds expended for assessment as monitoring have been well spent.

DIRECT MEASURES AND THE SOCIAL SYSTEM FOR LEARNING: SUMMARY

In this review of the differences between direct and indirect measures and of the way in which the different functions of testing call for different kinds of instruments, we have highlighted the extent to which direct measures are critical to three of the basic uses of testing—instruction and learning, certification, and accountability. Anticipating an acceleration of the effort to assimilate direct and indirect measures, we have focused on the power of direct measures to stimulate and support a social system that works toward learning improvement. Direct measures, by their nature, generate an understanding about the act of learning. Direct measures also help to lift the secrecy about classroom process that indirect measures so often support.

Indirect measures, in our view, have only a small role to play in encouraging learning and in certifying what young people demonstrably know, although we do contend that indirect measures used under appropriate conditions are important in establishing meaningful monitoring systems. The power of indirect measures is intended to be predictive, rather than motivational or mobilizing, in nature. Assumptions about predictive value, in turn, rest on theories of correlation. If success on indirect measures defines performance goals for the classroom, those measures will predict success in the classroom curriculum. Indirect measures, however, are not stable predictors of student learning. Their heavy use over time, as we have argued, has driven out the very performances they were expected to predict. Ergo, indirect measures must be used with great care.

CONCLUSION

There is an urgent need to generate public support for public schools. To gain that support, the public has to be shown more about the learning that goes on in classrooms. For this reason, the power of direct measures has been underlined, not only for purposes of instruction and learning, where they are enjoying a growing acceptance, but also for purposes of certification and accountability. The kinds of reporting required for the use of direct testing in these areas are not yet clear, but there is little question that in various quarters there will be considerable effort expended over the next few years to determine what kinds of reporting are most effective in enlisting support for the enterprise of holding public schooling to high standards.

It is possible for indirect measures to function differently in school environments that have (a) clear inherited traditions of learning, (b) clearly articulated standards, (c) a well-trained teaching corps, and (d) highly motivated students. In such conditions, the occasional use of indirect measures of learning, and even their regular use for accountability, might have little impact on classroom practice. Indeed, there are pockets of American schooling—occasionally in inner cities, more often in sub-urbs—where, at a site level, a counterculture of resistance to indirect testing has been sustained. In those sites, administrators have established supportive environments for innovative teachers; and those teachers do not ask their students to spend endless classroom hours practicing on worksheets and multiple-choice tests. Instead, they seek to assure that learning takes place and are, therefore, the first to support the high expectations of performance examinations, portfolios, and projects.

Equity demands, however, that one high standard be set for all students, so that every student will have the opportunity to work toward a common goal of achievement in learning. It is not possible to make the same standards explicit for all children, without using direct measures. We anticipate that those measures, tied to the open display of learning for students, teachers, and parents, will help our transition from a school culture without clear criteria for excellence to one of clear application and achievement.

Direct measures, by themselves, cannot assure the passage to such a culture of high expectations, but direct measures have an important role to play in that passage. Transforming the existing school culture into one of high expectations requires the commitment of teachers and students, families and communities, and all other concerned groups. In the social system described in this chapter, the ambitions and intentions of all actors will play a determining role in the future of the nation's education system.

REFERENCES

Ayres, L. P. (1909). *Laggards in our schools: A study of elimination and retardation in city school systems.* New York: Russell Sage Foundation.

Bishop, J. (1989). Why the apathy in American high schools? *Educational Researcher, 18*(1), 6–10.

Brown, A., Campione, J., Webber, L., & McGilly, K. (1992). Interactive learning environments. In B. R. Gifford & M. C. O'Connor (Eds.), *Changing assessments: Alternative views of aptitude, achievement and instruction* (pp. 121–211). Boston: Kluwer Academic Publishers.

Callahan, R. (1962). *Education and the cult of efficiency: A study of the social forces that have shaped the administration of the public schools.* Chicago, IL: University of Chicago Press.

Chapman, P. D. (1988). *Lewis M. Terman, applied psychology, and the intelligence testing movement, 1890–1930.* New York: New York University Press.

Darling-Hammond, L. (1988, Winter). Accountability and teacher professionalism. *American Educator, 8–43.*

Deffenbaugh, W. S. (1926). *Uses of intelligence and achievement tests in 215 cities. U.S. Bureau of Education, City School Leaflet No. 20.* Washington, DC: U.S. Department of the Interior.

Fitzpatrick, R., & Morrison, E. J. (1971). Performance and product evaluation. In E. L. Thorndike (Ed.), *Educational Measurement, 2nd ed.* (pp. 237–270). Washington, DC: American Council on Education.

Kevles, D. J. (1968, December). Testing the army's intelligence: Psychologists and the military in World War I. *Journal of American History, 55,* 565–581.

Marshall, R., & Tucker, M. (1992). *Thinking for a living: Work, skills, and the future of the American economy.* New York: Basic Books.

Monroe, W. S. (1918). *Existing tests and standards. Seventeenth yearbook of the National Society for the Study of Education. Part 2.* Bloomington, IN: Public School Publishing Company.

Oakes, J. (1985). *Keeping track.* New Haven, CT: Yale University Press.

Oakes, J. (1992, May). Can tracking research inform practice? Technical, normative and political considerations. *Educational Researcher, 21*(4), 12–21.

Oakes, J., with Ormseth, T., Bell, R., & Camp, P. (1990). Multiplying inequalities. *The effects of race, social class, and tracking on opportunities to learn mathematics and science.* Santa Monica, CA: Rand.

Osborne, D., & Gaebler, T. (1992). *Reinventing government: How the entrepreneurial spirit is transforming the public sector.* Reading, MA: Addison-Wesley.

Resnick, D. P. (1980). Minimum competency testing historically considered. *Review of Research in Education, 8,* 3–29.

Resnick, D. P. (1982). History of educational testing. In *Committee on ability testing, national academy of sciences, ability testing: Uses, consequences, and controversies* (Vol. 2, pp. 173–194). Washington, DC: National Research Council.

Resnick, L. B. (1987a). *Education and learning to think.* Washington, DC: National Academy Press.

Resnick, L. B. (1987b). Learning in school and out. *Educational Researcher, 16*(9), 13–20.

Resnick, D. P., & Resnick, L. B. (1992). Assessing the thinking curriculum. In B. R. Gifford & M. C. O'Connor (Eds.), *Changing assessments: alternative views of aptitude, achievement and instruction* (pp. 37–73). Boston: Kluwer Academic Publishers.

Shepard, L. (1989). Why we need better assessments. *Educational Leadership, 46*(7), 4–9.

Shepard, L. (1991, April). *Effects of high stakes testing on instruction.* Paper presented at the Annual Meetings of the American Educational Research Association and the National Council on Measurement in Education, Chicago, IL.

Thorndike, E. L. (1922). *The psychology of arithmetic.* New York: Macmillan.

Tyack, D. (1974). *The one best system: A history of American urban education.* Cambridge, MA: Harvard University Press.

Wiggins, G. (1991, February). Standards, not standardization: Evoking quality in student work. *Educational Leadership,* 18–25.

Yerkes, R. (Ed.) (1921). *Psychological examining in the United States Army. Memoirs of the National Academy of Sciences, XL, Part 2.* Washington, DC: U.S. Government Printing Office.

Chapter 3

Evaluating Progress With Alternative Assessments: A Model for Title 1

Mark Wilson
University of California, Berkeley

Raymond J. Adams
Australian Council for Educational Research

Title 1 (formerly called *Chapter 1*) is the major U.S. Federal funding for education. It targets schools with concentrations of disadvantaged students. Evaluations that rely on one form of assessment, particularly standardized multiple-choice tests, are inadequate. New views of learning require assessments that focus on constructed understandings, and especially on changes in those understandings. These changes cannot be assessed with our present testing technology. As an alternative, we suggest the development of a coordinated assessment and evaluation system focused on student progress. The assessment component of the system, which we call an *assessment net*, is composed of: (a) a framework for describing and reporting the level of student performance along achievement *continua*; (b) the use of diverse indicators based on observational practices that are consistent both with the educational variables to be measured and with the context in which that measurement is to take place; and (c) a measurement model that provides the opportunity for appropriate forms of quality control. The evaluation component of the system takes as raw material the location of schools, or other groups of students, on the continua and the progress that they make along those continua. This information is evaluated by taking account of the conditions in which the education takes place

39

and the scope of the educational interventions made available by Title 1 funding. The development of such a system draws upon the emerging tehnologies of multilevel modeling, item response modeling and curriculum framework specification, as well as alternative assessment practices. In this chapter, the authors delineate how these technologies can be combined to provide an approach to evaluation that we believe is suitable to Title 1.

Because this proposed system relies on new technologies, it is not yet ready for implementation. We suggest, however, that investigations of the practical aspects of the system and its implementation would provide a valuable method of evaluating student progress in Title 1.

One of the motivations behind these suggestions is an acute awareness that the vast expenditures on Title 1 evaluation that have been made to date have not only yielded little information that has proven valuable in an evaluation sense, but also that these expenditures have made little or no contribution to Title 1 instruction. In fact, if one considers the amount of educational time that Title 1 students have spent on standardized multiple choice tests which might have been spent on valuable instruction, one might be tempted to conclude that these expenditures to have had a negative impact on the instruction of Title 1 students.

The authors believe not only that the system described in this chapter will provide valuable evaluation information, but also that the implementation of such a system will have salutary influence on instruction. When teachers learn and use good rating systems for assessing their students' actual performances, there is an important opportunity for the development of teachers as educators. The integration of their judgments into the assessment net, providing as it does for professional interaction and feedback, is another important opportunity for development. Moreover, the recognition of the importance of teacher contribution to the evaluation of students is an affirmation of the professionalism of Title 1 teachers. It is only in such an atmosphere of mutual professional respect that the important work of reforming Title 1 can take place.

AN ASSESSMENT NET

To date, work in the area of performance assessment has addressed a small portion of what one might call an *assessment system* (Linn, Baker, & Dunbar, 1991). Attention has focused largely on the area of observational design, with specific emphasis on instructional validity (Wolf, Bixby, Glenn, & Gardner, 1991). To take an example, a recent issue of a journal concerned with measurement in education was devoted to performance assessment, yet only one article by Stiggins and Plake (1992) dealt substantively with issues outside the area of information gathering. The problem seems to be that the complexity of performance assessment poses serious challenges to both the philosophical foundations (Shepard, 1991) and the technology (i.e., the measurement models) used in standard educational and psychological measurement; and we do not yet have a comprehensive methodology that encompasses performance assessment.

In contrast, the more traditional rival to performance assessment, standardized multiple choice testing, is part of a coherent system of assessment (APA, AERA, & NCME, 1985) albeit one that we believe is flawed. The traditional system ensures quality control by addressing issues of test construction, test piloting, reliability and validity, and reporting formats. The authors' eventual aim is to build a competing system that has the coherence of the traditional approach but addresses new issues that have been brought forward by the performance assessment movement.

Frameworks

The assessment net begins with the idea that what should be assessed is student progression along the strands, or continua, of the curriculum. This progression must be part of a shared understanding on the part of the users of the net. That understanding must include the notion of progression, an agreed upon set of important continua, an agreed upon set of discernible levels of performance along the continua, and an acceptance that this progression is a tendency but not an absolute rule.

A *framework* is a set of continua within a defined curriculum area, along which are defined levels of performance and along which students would be expected to progress. The continua extend from lower, more elementary knowledge, understanding, and skills to more advanced levels. The levels describe understanding in terms of qualitatively distinguishable performances along the continua.

The idea of a framework is not new. Related notions are: The California Frameworks (e.g., California State Department of Education, 1985), the Australian National Curriculum Profiles (Australian Education Commission, 1992), and the UK National Curriculum strands (Department of Education and Science, 1987a, 1987b). For example, Fig. 3.1 illustrates five levels from the "Processes of Life," one strand from the national science curriculum for the UK.

Another example is the California Framework in mathematics (California State Department of Education, 1985) which is composed of continua in number, measurement, geometry, patterns and functions, statistics and probability, and algebra. Within each of these strands are defined four broad levels of performance: Grades K-3, 3-6, 6-8, and 9-12. Within each strand at each level is defined a list of goals. For example, according to the California State Department of Education (1985) within the geometry strand, at the base level one of the goals is: "Use visual attributes and

Level 6

- know that respiration is a process in which energy is transferred to enable other life processes to occur.
- know that water, light, energy, and carbon dioxide are needed for photosynthesis and that oxygen is a by-product.
- understand the factors necessary for the well-being of young children.
- know about the physical and emotional changes that take place during adolescence, and understand the need to have a responsible attitude to sexual behaviour.
- understand the risks of alcohol, solvent and drug abuse and how they affect the body.
- understand the processes of human conception.

Level 5

- know that living things are made up from different kinds of cells.
- understand malnutrition and the relationships between diet, exercise, health, fitness and circulatory disorders.
- know that in digestion food is made soluble.
- understand the way in which microbes and lifestyle affect health.
- be able to describe the functions of major organs.

Level 4

- be able to name the major organs and organ systems in flowering plants and mammals.
- know about the factors which contribute to good health and body maintenance, including the defence systems of the body, balanced diet and avoidance of harmful substances.
- understand reproduction in mammals.
- be able to describe the main stages of flowering plant reproduction.

Level 3

- know that the basic life processes, feeding, breathing, movement and behavior, are common to human and other living things.
- be able to describe the main stages in the human life cycle.

Level 2

- know living things reproduce their own kind.
- know that personal hygiene, food, exercise, rest and safety, and the proper and safe use of medicines are important.
- be able to give a simple account of their day.

FIG. 3.1. The processes of life strand for the UK National Science Curriculum (Department of Education and Science and the Welsh Office, 1988).

concrete materials to identify, classify, and describe common geometric figures and models, such as rectangles, squares, triangles, circles, cubes, and spheres. Use correct vocabulary" (p. 24).

At the three to six level, one of the goals is: "Use protractor, compass, and straightedge to draw and measure angles and for other constructions" (p. 27).

And at the six to eight level, one of the goals is: "Describe relationships between figures (congruent, similar) and perform transformations (rotations, reflections, translations, and dilations)" (p. 32).

Each level is associated with a set of special concerns and emphases for that particular period of schooling, such as, at the base level, an emphasis on concrete materials and classification.

Essentially, the levels defined within a continuum will be in most cases a convenience. They must summarize a segment of the continuum in a useful way, but the boundaries between the levels could probably be defined differently without affecting their usefulness. The concrete meaning of the levels will reside in the way students are observed and rated.

Information Gathering

New views of student learning demand that we use information gathering procedures that extend beyond the tradition of standardized multiple choice tests. During the last decade, much work has been done to achieve this in the field through procedures variously called authentic, alternative, or performance assessment. The term *performance assessment* is somewhat narrow, and the term *authentic performance* overly positive, hence we will use the term *alternative assessment*.[1] The key features of such assessment have been described by Aschbacher (1991) as follows:

- Students perform, create, produce, or do something that requires higher level thinking or problem solving skills (not just one right answer);
- Assessment tasks are also meaningful, challenging, engaging, instructional activities;
- Tasks are set in a real-world context or close simulation;
- Process and conative behavior are often assessed as well as product; and
- The criteria and standards for performance are public and known in advance. (p. 276)

Many of these features are not new (Stiggins, 1991). For example, 40 years ago, Lindquist (1951, also quoted in Linn, Baker, & Dunbar, 1991) wrote

. . . it should always be the fundamental goal of the achievement test constructor to make elements of his test series as nearly equivalent, or as much like, the elements of the criterion series as consequences of efficiency, comparability, economy, and expediency will permit. (p. 152)

---

[1] But see chapter 10 by Baker & O'Neil for a different view of this expression.

However, it is probably fair to say that in the interim, concerns with efficiency, comparability, economy, and expediency have predominated. Multiple choice tests have been widely advocated because of their positive features with regard to such criteria. It is probably time that the pendulum swung back so that more attention is paid to tasks that are valued because of their close alignment to the criteria of interest.

The alternative assessment movement has reminded us that there are many information gathering formats that we should be using. In order to facilitate discussion of these formats, the simple notions expressed in Fig. 3.2 are used to discuss approaches to gathering information. It is not suggested that this figure provides a complete formula for describing all assessment types but rather we find that it assists in conceiving of and describing several aspects of assessment that are relevant to the arguments in this chapter.

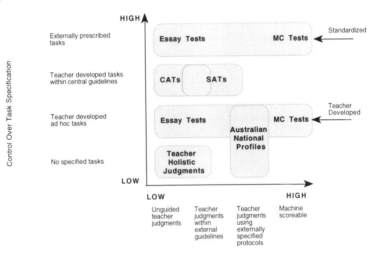

FIG. 3.2.   Notions to discuss approaches to gathering information.

In this figure, the vertical dimension indicates variation in specification of assessment tasks. At the high end of this dimension is assessment that is undertaken using externally set tasks which will only allow students to respond in a prescribed set of ways. Standardized multiple choice tests are an example of the high end, whereas short-answer items are not quite at this extreme because students may respond in ways that are not predefined. The low end of this dimension is characterized by a complete lack of task or response specification. Teachers' holistic impressions of their students belong at this end of the task control dimension. Lying between these two extremes are information gathering approaches such as teacher-developed tests and tasks which are adapted from central guidelines to local conditions.

The horizontal dimension, control over judgment, is used to indicate variation in approaches to judgment. The extremes are typified by machine scoreability at the high end and unguided holistic judgments at the other. Between these, we consider variations in terms of the expert status of the judge and the degree of prescription of judgment protocols.

Fig. 3.2 illustrates some examples of assessment formats that can be arrayed along these dimensions. At the top of the figure are standardized tests of various sorts. Multiple choice (MC) tests are represented at the right hand side because they can be machine scored, but essay tests can be judged in a variety of ways, so they occupy a broader range on the left. The same horizontal classification can be used for teacher-developed tests but they appear lower on the task specification dimension. In the bottom left had corner are teacher-holistic judgments, which might, for example, be made from memory without reference to specific tasks. The extension of the shaded region to the right allows the possibility of teacher knowledge of general guidelines being incorporated into the judgment.

Another region on the figure is exemplified by the Australian National Profiles (Australian Education Council, 1992) in which teachers are provided with carefully prepared rating protocols that they may use with ad hoc examples of student work or on the basis of their accumulated experience of students. Curriculum embedded tasks such as the UK Standardized Assessment Tasks (SATs; Department of Education and Science, 1987b) and the Victorian Common Assessment Tasks (CATs; Stephens, Money, & Proud, 1991) are externally specified project prompts that are locally interpreted to suit student needs and then scored by teachers. Within the CATs, control over the scoring varies from unguided teacher judgments to local (teacher) judgments within external guidelines. Typically SATs involve a tighter control over judgment and have therefore been placed a little further to the right.

Assessments that are placed in different locations on the figure are often valued for different reasons. Figure 3.3 for example, indicates that assessments that occur in the upper right hand corner are typically valued because they are perceived to have greater reliability. That is, they are composed of standardized tasks that: (a) are the same for all students, (b) can be scored using objective criteria, and (c) are congruent with existing psychometric models. Alternatively, assessments in the bottom left hand corner are typically perceived to have greater instructional validity. That is, they are closer to the actual format and content of instruction, are based on the accumulated experience of teachers concerning their own students, and

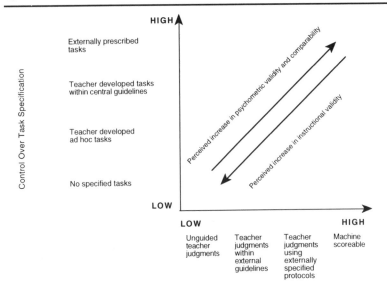

FIG. 3.3. Assessments perceived to have greater reliability.

allow maximum adaptation to local conditions. The problem is that it is desirable to have the positive features of both of these forms of assessment, but, as the figure illustrates, no single assessment format can encompass them.

The idea of the assessment net is to attempt to use information from assessments at a variety of locations on the figure, so that we can capitalize on the opportunity that some assessments might provide for enhancing validity, and that others might provide for increasing reliability.

An example of appropriate use of an assessment net is provided by the student assessment system that was designed for California students (California Assessment Policy Committee, 1991). This is composed of the following three types of assessment activities:

• *Structured On-Demand Assessments* include most forms of traditional examinations. These might range from fifteen minute quizzes (of perhaps multiple choice type, or possibly an open-ended format), to extended activities that could take up to three class periods and would be more in the performance assessment mode. The distinguishing feature is that, although they derive from the framework in the same way as a student's regular instruction, they are organized in a more test-like fashion, with uniform tasks, uniform administration conditions, and without the possibility of in-depth instructional activity occurring while they are taking place. The on-demand assessments would typically be either scoreable in a manner that involved little judgment on the part of the scorer, or would be scored by expert judges. This class of assessment information would reside at the top right hand corner of Fig. 3.2.

• *Curriculum-Embedded Assessments* are intended to be seen as a part of the regular instruction by students. They would be chosen, however, from among the best of the alternative assessments, collected, tried out, and disseminated by teams of master teachers. They would typically be scored by the instructing teacher herself, although the results may need to go through certain types of adjustment for particular uses. This class of information would reside somewhat towards the middle of Fig. 3.2.

• *Organic Portfolio Assessments* include all materials and modes of assessment that a teacher or student decides should be included in a student's record of accomplishments. This could be composed of an enormously varied range of assessment formats and instructional topics. Teacher judgments as to the relationship between these records and the levels in the frameworks will be the major form of assessment information derived from the portfolios. This class of information would find its place in the bottom left-hand corner of Fig. 3.2.

These various modes are located in different parts of the control chart, and hence, each makes a useful contribution to the entire assessment. What is needed, however, is a way to integrate them and ensure quality control.

Quality Control

A quality control procedure is necessary to coordinate the information (scores, ratings, and so on) that comes from the assessment net. In particular, procedures are necessary to: (a) examine the coherence of information gathered using different formats, (b) map student performances onto the continua, and (c) describe the structural elements of the net (items and raters) in terms of the continua. The traditional elements of test standardization, such as validity and reliability studies, and bias and equity studies, must also be carried out within the quality control procedure. To meet these needs, we propose the use of generalized item response models (sometimes called item response theory). Generalized item response models such as those described by Adams and Wilson (in press), Kelderman (1989), Linacre (1989), and Thissen and Steinberg (1986) have now reached levels of development that make feasible their application to many forms of alternative assessment. The output from these models can be used as quality control information and to obtain student and school locations on the continua, which may be interpreted both quantitatively and substantively.

The general methodological approach taken here is one that is based on Rasch-type models. The motivation for the choice of item response models and, more particularly, Rasch-type models is that:

- A latent continuous variable is an appropriate metaphor for many important educational variables;
- We need maximum flexibility to use different items, raters, and other variables for different students if we are to reap the promised benefits of novel assessment modes;
- We need a measurement approach that is self-checking—in this case it is termed *fit assessment*;
- We need a simple building block for coherent construction of complex structures; and
- We need a model that can be estimated efficiently from basic observations such as counts.

Although it is not appropriate to give the full details of the model, some of its key elements are briefly described to illustrate how it might be used to meet the flexibility requirements of alternative assessments. A detailed description of the unidimensional version of this model and the marginal maximum likelihood algorithm used to estimate its parameters is given in Adams and Wilson (in press), a multidimensional version is described in Adams, Wilson, and Wang (in press), and an extended application is described in Wilson and Adams (1995).

We begin by considering a test composed of I items indexed by i, where each item has K_i response alternatives. That is, the observed response of any student to Item i can be allocated to one of the K_i mutually exclusive categories. Here the term *item* is used generically; in a given context, the items may be much more complex than the traditional multiple choice items that we are used to. For example, where there is a series of questions all based on a common piece of stimulus material, and with possibly a complex dependence structure among themselves, the items could be the entire set of questions (e.g., a testlet), and the response categories could be all distinct response strings to the whole testlet (see Wilson & Adams, 1995). A second example would be provided by a set of tasks which have been scored by a group of raters where the item could be a rater-task pairing.

The vector $x_{ni} = (x_{ni2}, x_{ni3}, \ldots, x_{niK_j})'$ is used to denote the responses of Person n to Item i, with a "1" placed in the category in which he or she responded, and "0"s elsewhere. Note that a response in the first category (which we are using as reference category), is denoted by a string of zeroes. By collecting the item vectors together as $x_n = (x'_{n1}, x'_{n2}, \ldots, x'_{nK_i})$, we can formally write the probability of observing the response pattern as:

$$f(x_n; A, B, \xi | \theta) = \frac{\exp x'_n (B\theta + A\xi)}{\sum_{z\epsilon\Omega} \exp z'(B\theta + A\xi)} \tag{1}$$

where A is a design matrix that describes how the elements of the assessments (e.g., raters and tasks) are combined to produce observations, $\xi = (\xi_1, \xi_2, \ldots, \xi_p)'$ is a vector of the parameters that describe those elements, B is a score matrix that allows scores to be assigned to each performance, and $\theta = (\theta_1, \theta_2, \ldots, \theta_d)'$ is a vector of student abilities, or locations on the framework continua. The summation in the denominator of Equation (1) is over all possible response patterns, Ω, and ensures that the probabilities sum to unity. The model is applied to particular circumstances by specification of the A and B matrices.

For example, consider the simplest unidimensional item response model, the Simple Logistic Model (SLM), otherwise known as the Rasch model (Rasch, 1960/1980). In the usual parameterization of the SLM for a set of I dichotomous items there are I item difficulty parameters. A correct response is given a score of one, and an incorrect response is given a score of zero. Taking a test with just three items, the appropriate choices of A and B are:

$$A = \begin{bmatrix} 1 & 0 & 0 \\ 0 & 1 & 0 \\ 0 & 0 & 1 \end{bmatrix} \text{ and } B = \begin{bmatrix} 1 \\ 1 \\ 1 \end{bmatrix} \tag{2}$$

where the three rows of A and B correspond to the three correct responses, the three columns of A correspond to the three difficulty parameters, one for each item, and the single column of B corresponds to the student location on the continuum.

If the A and B matrices given in (2) are substituted into (1), it can be verified that this is exactly the Rasch simple logistic model (see Adams & Wilson, in press). The estimated parameters that result from the application of the model would be a collection of item locations and person locations on a continuum.

More complicated item response models may be expressed using equally straightforward matrices. For example, the Partial Credit Model (PCM; Masters, 1982), is designed for assessment situations with multiple levels of achievement within each item. Following the notation of Andersen (1973), each item is described by a set of parameters, one for each response category. For an instrument with, say, three items and three categories in each, the categories scored 0, 1, 2, the **A** and **B** matrices are:

$$\mathbf{A} = \begin{bmatrix} 1 & 0 & 0 & 0 & 0 & 0 \\ 0 & 1 & 0 & 0 & 0 & 0 \\ 0 & 0 & 1 & 0 & 0 & 0 \\ 0 & 0 & 0 & 1 & 0 & 0 \\ 0 & 0 & 0 & 0 & 1 & 0 \\ 0 & 0 & 0 & 0 & 0 & 1 \end{bmatrix} \text{ and } \mathbf{B} = \begin{bmatrix} 1 \\ 2 \\ 1 \\ 2 \\ 1 \\ 2 \end{bmatrix} \tag{3}$$

The matrices have six rows, two for each item—recall that the responses scored zero do not appear in the matrix because they are used as reference categories. The A matrix is an identity matrix indicating that each response to each item is modeled by a unique response parameter. The B matrix contains the scores allocated to each of the responses and has one column, corresponding to a single ability dimension.

An Example of a Continuum. The estimated item and person parameters from this model can be used to map student performance in a manner similar to that illustrated for the simple logistic model. Figure 3.4 illustrates such a continuum developed in the Testing Students' Science Beliefs project (Adams & Doig, 1991; Adams, Doig, & Rosier, 1991) which mapped student understanding of "Force and Motion."

Figure 3.4 is a map of the continuum that has been constructed from the calibrated item difficulties for a unit that assesses student conceptions of force and motion. The unit was a pseudonewsletter about skateboarding in which students were shown illustrations of skateboards and skateboard riders in a variety of contexts and were asked to provide written answers to questions that were asked about each illustration. The answers to the questions were rated into a small number of levels. The data reported in Fig. 3.4 resulted from administration of the unit to 559 Year 5 students and 479 Year 9 students in schools in Victoria, Australia. The map has a vertical scale—the numerical expression of the continuum—that represents increasing difficulty, and in the middle panel the difficulty thresholds for items are plotted. In this panel, the notation 'x.y' is used to indicate the difficulty of achieving Level y in Item x. The left side of the figure indicates the distribution of student scores over the continuum. The map relies on the fact that the measurement model produces person ability estimates and item difficulty estimates that are expressed on a common scale. If an item and a person are located at the same position on the scale, then we have

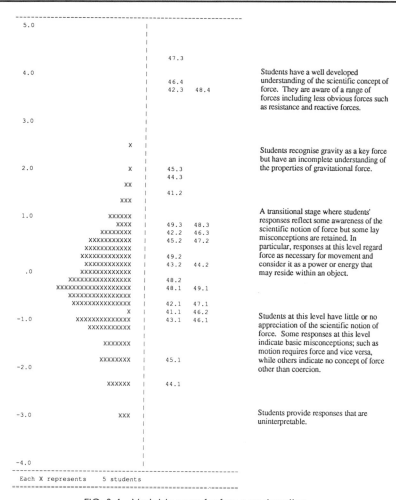

FIG. 3.4. Variable map for force and motion.

estimated that the person has a 50% chance of being able to successfully attain that level of the item or below.

In the right hand panel of the map is a description of increasing student competence with respect to force and motion—this is the substantive expression of the continuum. This description allows a substantive interpretation of the numerical location that is estimated for each student by the measurement model. For example, a student at the position denoted by 2.0 on the numerical continuum would typically be expected have an understanding of force and motion like that described by the adjacent description on the substantive expression of the continuum, that is, a recognition that gravity is a key force, but an incomplete understanding of the properties of gravitational force. The student would be expected to have not yet attained the understandings indicated by the description above 2.0, and would be expected to have previously attained the understandings indicated by the descriptions below 2.0.

If more data are collected from these students at a subsequent testing, then a second location is obtained for each student on the continuum. Hence, progress can be measured using the locations on the numerical continuum, and we can interpret it using the levels on the substantive continuum.

An Example Involving Raters.   As a final illustration of the flexibility of the measurement model, consider a more complicated example that may be more typical of alternative assessment. Students are set two problem solving tasks, and two judges rate the student's performances into one of four categories. Category one represents no strategy and is assigned a score of 0, categories two and three represent alternative but less sophisticated strategies and are both scored 1, while the fourth category represents a superior strategy and is scored 2. A model that allows estimation of the difficulty of the tasks as well as the relative harshness of the raters, and places the students on a single continuum is given by the following A and B matrices:

$$
\mathbf{A} = \begin{bmatrix}
1 & 0 & 0 & 0 & 0 & 0 & 0 \\
0 & 1 & 0 & 0 & 0 & 0 & 0 \\
0 & 0 & 1 & 0 & 0 & 0 & 0 \\
0 & 0 & 0 & 1 & 0 & 0 & 0 \\
0 & 0 & 0 & 0 & 1 & 0 & 0 \\
0 & 0 & 0 & 0 & 0 & 1 & 0 \\
1 & 0 & 0 & 0 & 0 & 0 & 1 \\
0 & 1 & 0 & 0 & 0 & 0 & 1 \\
0 & 0 & 1 & 0 & 0 & 0 & 2 \\
0 & 0 & 0 & 1 & 0 & 0 & 1 \\
0 & 0 & 0 & 0 & 1 & 0 & 1 \\
0 & 0 & 0 & 0 & 0 & 1 & 2
\end{bmatrix} \text{ and } \mathbf{B} = \begin{bmatrix}
1 \\ 1 \\ 2 \\ 1 \\ 1 \\ 2 \\ 1 \\ 1 \\ 2 \\ 1 \\ 1 \\ 2
\end{bmatrix} \tag{4}
$$

A and B have 12 rows, corresponding to the three possible non-zero scores for each of the four items (rater-task combinations). The first six rows are for the tasks rated by rater 1 while the last six rows are for the tasks rated by rater 2. The first six columns of A correspond to task parameters analogous to those in Equation (3), and the last parameter is a rater harshness parameter, in this instance estimating how the harshness of rater 2 compares to that of rater 1. The rows of the B matrix are simply the item scores, and since we are again assuming a single continuum, B has only one column.

The preceding situation models only variation in rater harshness. This is a simplistic view of how raters may vary. Raters may also vary in the way that they use the response categories, in that some may have a tendency to give more extreme responses, while others may prefer the middle categories. This, and many other possibilities could be modeled through different choices of **A**. The most general approach would involve the estimation of a separate set of item parameters for each rater.

In the case of multiple raters, maps like that illustrated in Fig. 3.4 could be constructed for each rater, or they could be constructed for the average rater. In a quality control context, the ideal would be to use this approach to help raters align their judgments. When this alignment process has resulted in a sufficiently common map for all raters, we would need only a single map. In the case of large numbers of raters, the model can be respecified under the assumption that the raters have been sampled from a population, and the model would estimate characteristics of the rater population, and, most importantly, the degree of variation between raters.

In applying this model to an assessment net, we will need to apply the procedure to mixed item formats. The technique described generalizes quite readily to such situations, and allows the specification of different weights for different formats. For example, a teacher's end-of-year rating would occur in the model as one item, and this would need to be weighted according to beliefs about the relative importance of the summary end-of-year rating compared to ratings on specific tasks.

Quality control information is also available in the assessment net. The standard techniques for assessing reliability, validity, fairness, and equity using item response models are available due to the pedigree of the measurement model (Hambleton, Swaminathan, Cook, Eignor, & Gifford, 1978; Lord, 1980; Wright & Masters, 1982).

AN EVALUATION SYSTEM

The measurement model provides measures of the changes that students within schools have made along the continua. Background characteristics for those students and the contextual characteristics of the schools that they are in will influence the magnitude of this growth. Some school characteristics might be: average SES of the students in the school, geographical location of the school, and racial characteristics of the school body. Because these characteristics are beyond the control of the school, and because they are likely to influence the performance of students within the school, it would appear unreasonable to only compare the measured growth. The evaluation system must incorporate the possibility of taking into account such influences in comparing schools. In this section we refer to "schools," but the same arguments and procedures would apply to other groupings of students.

The authors propose a hierarchical model that uses the student measures from the measurement model (Raudenbush, 1988) to estimate how the progress of students in each school compares to students' progress made in similar schools. Suppose that θ_{nst} is the measured location of Student n in School s at Time t. Changes in location over time can be modeled using a linear growth trajectory specified as:[2]

$$\theta_{nst} = \mu_{ns0} + \mu_{ns1}t + e_{nst} \tag{5}$$

where μ_{ns0} is the mean for Student n in School s at Time $t = 0$, μ_{ns1} is the mean gain for Student n in School s over unit time interval, and e_{nst} is the residual for Student n in School s at Time t. The residual is the amount by which the individual student measure at time t varies from the predicted student measure at Time t.

Considering now the between student level, we model the school means and school means gain using:

$$\mu_{ns0} = \beta_{s0} + u_{ns0}, \quad \text{and} \tag{6}$$
$$\mu_{ns1} = \beta_{s1} + u_{ns1},$$

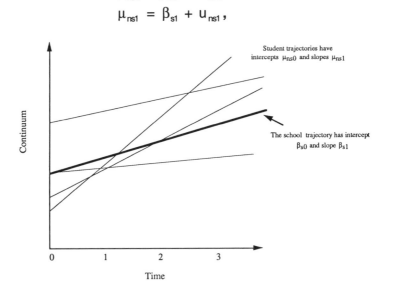

FIG. 3.5. Hypothetical student trajectories and the trajectory of their school.

---

[2]The restriction to a linear trajectory is an unnecessary one. Given sufficient time points, more complex growth trajectories also can be modeled. For clarity of presentation, we have restricted ourselves to the linear case.

where β_{s0} is the mean of all students in School s at Time 0, β_{s1} is the mean gain for students in School s, u_{ns0} is the residual for Student n in School s at Time 0, and u_{ns1} is the residual gain for Student n in School s. A hypothetical set of individual student growth trajectories and their school growth trajectory is shown in Fig. 3.5. The intercepts of the student trajectories with the vertical axis correspond to the μ_{ns0} values and the μ_{ns1} values describe the slopes of the student trajectories. β_{s0} and β_{s1} have analogous interpretations for the school trajectory.

We could now model the school means at Time 0 and the school mean gains as:

$$\beta_{s0} = \gamma_{00} + \varepsilon_{s0} \qquad (7)$$

$$\beta_{s0} = \gamma_{00} + \varepsilon_{s0}$$

where γ_{00} is the grand mean at Time 0, and γ_{10} is the grand school mean gain. The school mean at Time 0 and the school gain for each school can then be compared to averages over all schools. This is illustrated in Fig. 3.6. The difference between the intercepts of the two trajectories in the figure indicates the difference between the School s at Time 0 and the average of all schools, and the difference between the slopes of the two trajectories indicates the difference between the gain of School s and the average gain. We call these differences the *raw effects* of School s.

Given the preceding discussion, however, we would not only wish to

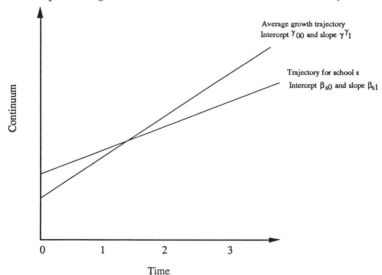

FIG. 3.6. A hypothetical school trajectory compared to the average school trajectory.

interpret the school locations and gains, β_{s0} and β_{s1}, and the comparison of these values to the average, but also interpret school gains adjusted for certain agreed characteristics. Suppose that the characteristics for School s are represented by $W_{s1}, W_{s2}, \ldots, W_{sK}$. Then we model the school means at Time 0 and the school mean gains as:

$$\beta_{s0} = \gamma_{00} + \gamma_{01} W_{s1} + \gamma_{02} W_{s2} + \cdots + \gamma_{0K} W_{sK} + \varepsilon_{s0} \qquad (8)$$
$$= \gamma^*_{00s} + \varepsilon_{s0} \text{ and}$$
$$\beta_{s1} = \gamma_{10} + \gamma_{11} W_{s1} + \gamma_{12} W_{s2} + \cdots + \gamma_{1K} W_{sK} + \varepsilon_{s1}$$
$$= \gamma^*_{10s} + \varepsilon_{s1}$$

where γ_{0K} is the extent of the influence of W_{sK} on the school location at Time 0, and γ_{1K} is the influence of W_{sK} on school gains. If the characteristics W_{iK} are centered at the average for all schools, then γ_{00} is the grand school mean at Time 0, and γ_{10} is the grand school mean gain. γ^*_{00s} is the predicted location at Time 0 for schools with the same characteristics as Schools s, and γ^*_{10s} is the predicted school gain for schools with the same characteristics as Schools s. The adjusted effects of individual School s are the differences between the mean of Schools s and Time 0 and mean gain for School s and the values that would be predicted for schools with equivalent characteristics. The adjusted effects are given by

$$\hat{\varepsilon}_{s0} = \beta_{s0} - \gamma^*_{00s} \qquad (9)$$
$$\hat{\varepsilon}_{s1} = \beta_{s1} - \gamma^*_{10s}$$

That is, ε_{s0} is the estimated difference of initial performance of School s from the average performance of all schools, adjusted for school educational environment variables, and ε_{s1} is the estimated difference in the progress of School s from the average progress of all schools, adjusted for school educational environment variables.

In Fig. 3.7, we have plotted the growth trajectory for School s, the average growth trajectory for all schools, and the predicted growth trajectory for schools with characteristics equivalent to those of School s. The adjusted school effects are reflected in the differences between the first and third of these trajectories. In this hypothetical case, note that the raw effects, shown in Fig. 3.6, indicate that School s had a higher initial mean than the average but lower gains. The adjusted effects, shown in Fig. 3.7, indicate that School s

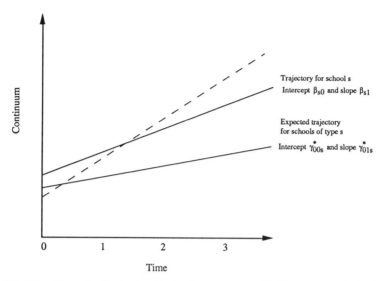

FIG. 3.7. A hypothetical school trajectory compared to the average trajectory adjusted for school characteristics.

has initial mean and gain that both exceed expectations for schools with equivalent characteristics.

The γ_{0K} and γ_{1K} in Equation (8) can be interpreted as indicating the general effects of the school characteristic W_{sK} among the set of schools, and the residuals ε_{s0} and ε_{s1} can be interpreted as indicating the unmodeled effects for each school, including both the particular school characteristics effects for School s and effects of other school characteristics not embodied in the general model.

The use of residuals in the manner described in this example should be treated with caution. As Goldstein (1991) warned, the residuals have large errors compared to the regression coefficients, and this error must be taken into account when interpreting the residuals. For example, one would not be advised to rank schools according to their residuals, although one might find it acceptable to use the residuals to screen the school into classes for further examination. Also, the magnitude of the residuals is affected by the choice of the W (controlling) variables, implying that the controlling variables need to be chosen a priori. Thus it is necessary to examine the raw gains as well as the residuals.

Note also that this model does not include any student-level controlling variables such as SES, gender, or race as this makes the interpretation far more complex (i.e., an extra two βs for each student-level controlling variable would need to be estimated and interpreted for even the linear growth trajectory). However, if these variables are included, then the possibility is introduced of comparing how the progress of students in each school compares to similar students' progress in similar schools. This might be useful from two perspectives: First, the influence of the school on the growth of particular groups of students can be examined; and second, individual characteristics of students within each school can be controlled for in estimating school level growth trajectories.

CONCLUSION

The methods suggested are based on existing technologies. Some, such as frameworks and alternative assessment, can hardly be said to be new. Others, such as the complex measurement models and multilevel modeling are quite new (although both now have programs available to implement them). Nevertheless, these methods need adaptation to the tasks and conditions of Chapter 1 evaluation. What is needed is a concerted research effort that investigates the design and function of an evaluation system such as that described in this chapter, perhaps starting with just a few states where alternative testing practices are widely enough disseminated to no longer be a novelty. The authors believe that such an investigation would yield positive benefits even before the system itself was fully functional, in the sense that even small parts of the system could operate independently and be educationally useful. For example, the assessment net would provide very useful instructional and quality control information, as described in this chapter, even without application to evaluation of progress. Similarly, a focus on progress in evaluation, even if applied to data that have not been fully validated as they would be in an assessment net, would make for more useful Chapter 1 evaluations.

REFERENCES

Adams, R. J., & Doig, B. (1991, November). *Surveying students' science beliefs*. Paper presented at the Assessment in the Mathematical Sciences Conference, Geelong, Australia.

Adams, R. J., Doig, B., & Rosier, M. (1991). *Science learning in Victorian schools: 1990*. ACER Research Report No. 41. Hawthorn, Australia: ACER.

Adams, R. J., & Wilson, M. (in press). A random coefficients multinomial logit: Generalizing Rasch models. In G. Engelhard & M. Wilson (Eds.). *Objective measurement: Theory into practice III*.

Adams, R. J., Wilson, M., & Wang, W. (1995). The multidimensional random coefficients multinomial logit model. Manuscript submitted for publication.

Andersen, E. B. (1973). Conditional inference for multiple choice questionnaires. *British Journal of Mathematical and Statistical Psychology, 26*, 31–44.

APA, AERA, & NCME. (1985). *Standards for educational and psychological tests*. Washington, DC: Authors.

Aschbacher, P. R. (1991). Performance assessment: State activity, interests, and concerns. *Applied Measurement in Education, 4*(4), 275–288.

Australian Education Council. (1992). *Mathematics profiles, Levels 1–6*. Melbourne, Australia: Curriculum Corporation.

California Assessment Policy Committee. (1991). *A new student assessment system for California schools*. Sacramento, CA: Author.

California State Department of Education. (1985). *Mathematics framework for California public schools, kindergarten through grade twelve*. Sacramento, CA: Author.

Department of Education and Science. (1987a). *Education reform: The government's proposals for schools*. London: HMSO.

Department of Education and Science. (1987b). *National curriculum task group on assessment and testing: A report*. London: HMSO.

Department of Education and Science and the Welsh Office. (1988). *Science for ages 5 to 16*. London: Author.

Goldstein, H. (1991). Better ways to compare schools? *Journal of Educational Statistics, 16*(2), 89-91.

Hambleton, R. K., Swaminathan, H., Cook, L. L., Eignor, D. R., & Gifford, J. A. (1978). Developments in latent trait theory: Models, technical issues and applications. *Review of Educational Research, 48*, 467–510.

Kelderman, H. (1989). *Loglinear multidimensional IRT models for polytomously scored items*. Paper presented at the Fifth International Objective Measurement Workshop, Berkeley, CA.

Linacre, J. M. (1989). *Many faceted Rasch measurement*. Unpublished doctoral dissertation, University of Chicago, Chicago.

Linn, R. L, Baker, E. L., & Dunbar, S. B. (1991). Complex, performance-based assessment: Expectations and validation criteria. *Educational Researcher, 20*(8), 15–21.

Lord, F. M. (1980). *Applications of item response theory to practical testing problems*. Hillsdale, NJ: Lawrence Erlbaum Associates.

Masters, G. N. (1982). A Rasch model for partial credit scoring. *Psychometrika, 47*, 149-174.

Rasch, G. (1980). *Probabilistic models for some intelligence and attainment tests*. Chicago: University of Chicago Press. (Original work published 1960)

Raudenbush, S. W. (1988). Educational applications of hierarchical linear models: A review. *Journal of Educational Statistics, 13*(2), 85–116.

Shepard, L. A. (1991). Psychometricians beliefs about learning. *Educational Researcher, 20*(6), 2–16.

Stephens, M., Money, R., & Proud, S. (1991, November). *Comprehensive assessment at senior secondary level in Victoria*. Paper presented at the ACER Conference on Assessment in the Mathematical Sciences, Geelong, Australia.

Stiggins, R. J. (1991). Facing the challenges of a new era of educational assessment. *Applied Measurement in Education, 4*(4), 263–273.

Stiggins, R. J., & Plake, B. (Eds.). (1991). Special issue: Performance assessment. *Applied Measurement in Education, 4*(4).

Thissen, D., & Steinberg, L. (1986). A taxonomy of item response models. *Psychometrika, 49*, 501–519.

Wilson, M., & Adams, R. J. (1995). Rasch models for item bundles. *Psychometrika, 60*(2), 181–198.

Wolf, D. P., Bixby, J., Glenn, J., & Gardner, H. (1991). To use their minds well: Investigating new forms of student assessment. *Review of Research in Education, 17*, 31–74.

Wright, B. D., & Masters, G. N. (1982). *Rating scale analysis: Rasch measurement*. Chicago: MESA Press.

Chapter 4

Extended Assessment Tasks: Purposes, Definitions, Scoring, and Accuracy

David E. Wiley
Northwestern University

Edward H. Haertel
Stanford University

Wide-ranging use of extended assessment tasks in the form of performance exercises, curriculum-embedded assessment tasks, and portfolio-based measurement bring forward new issues for both measurement theory and testing practice. The intent of this chapter is to sketch some of these issues and to point the way toward their resolution.

Throughout this chapter, a particular frame of reference is elaborated. The authors' perspectives are shaped by an ongoing research program intended to reshape the conceptual underpinnings of testing (e.g., Wiley, 1990; Haertel & Wiley, 1993). Although this research program is only just begun, the results generated have led to new insights, many of which are incorporated in this paper. The entire perspective as it is now understood will not be elaborated here. However, because of its newness and some of the concepts used, occasional asides will be taken, especially to orienting perspectives or newly defined concepts. Some of these definitions may seem either obvious or unusual. However, they are intended to give some common ground for understanding.

One such perspective relates to testing. In our view, testing is an activity that is intended to reveal (uncover, estimate, assess, evaluate) skills, conceptions, abilities, or knowledge of the individuals being tested. The use of such estimates may be to compare individuals to one another or to a criterion, for the purpose of making a decision about subsequent opportunities or requirements in education, therapy, social life, or work. On occasion, they also may be used to evaluate a portion of the learning systems of which the individuals are a part. This is accomplished by giving an individual one or more tasks to perform. The manner in which the tasks are performed and the outcomes that eventuate may be used to infer the individual's state[1] with respect to the particular skills, abilities, or knowledge being tested. Test theory is the systematic formalization of the concepts and practices of testing.

This perspective places abilities, tasks, and their interrelations at the heart of testing and test theory. In our view, abilities (capabilities, skills, knowledge) are characteristics of individuals that allow them to successfully perform tasks. These are acquired through learning. Some individuals may acquire particular abilities more readily than others, depending on other characteristics including prostheses, bodily characteristics, environmental supports, or prior learnings. One important characteristic of abilities however, is their transferability. That is, abilities must enable successful performance on more than one task, otherwise they could not be distinguished from the performance itself.

The current basis for test theory derives from Spearman and Thurstone (e.g., Thurstone, 1947). It assumes that the skills and abilities[2] underlying test performance are understandable as quantitative variables. These variables, in the context of most recent psychometric models, are termed *latent traits* and are characterized in terms of *item response theory*. The position taken here is that this perspective is well adapted to current testing practice but not to the new kinds of assessment exercises and instruments now being considered. Current practice involves test forms or instruments composed of many dichotomously scored (assumptively homogeneous and to a large extent interchangeable), multiple-choice test items. The continuity assumptions used in traditional test theory are suited to such a testing practice. These assumptions imply that the appropriate way to estimate ability is by aggregating individual task performances so that finer differentiations in

---

[1]The term *state* is used to denote the particular level or profile of ability or skill possessed by the individual. In complex test tasks, performance results from the particular combination of ability levels. In the absence of measurement error, this state would completely determine the individual's performance path (process) and resulting outcome (product).

[2]In this chapter, the terms *ability* or *capability* encompass all of what is commonly classified as knowledge or skills, both procedural and conceptual, as well as motivational or other dispositional attributes determinative of task performance.

continuous skill levels are identifiable. Latent trait models produce estimates of these levels that are closely related to traditional total test scores,
but have more attractive statistical characteristics.

The new kinds of test tasks to be undertaken by students are distinguished in a number of ways from traditional multiple-choice test tasks.
They are more complex, take longer to perform, attempt to measure multiple, complex, and interrelated skills and capabilities, and employ scoring
rules that are more variegated and (currently) more labor intensive. Measurement theory appropriate to these kinds of task collections cannot treat
them as even approximately interchangeable; it must extract information
from performances that are partially overlapping, and that inform inferences about complex interrelated sets of skills. Thus, it requires methods
for extracting multiple information elements from single task performances
and integrating them across tasks into complex aggregates. Methods for
evaluating the accuracy of such methods must distinguish differences in
the skills underlying performances on distinct tasks, which traditional
methods have to treat as replicates within homogeneous categories. However, these methods still must address the issues of aggregation and generalizability of results.

In order to accomplish this, it is essential to broaden and deepen the
fundamental characterizations of skill, capability, and knowledge, as well
as their relationship to task performance. The complex tasks that are
beginning to emerge as a part of the new assessment paradigm cannot be
adequately handled without a thorough revision and extension of our
underlying conceptual structure. This revision must clearly elucidate distinctions among ability, learning, and performance, together with clear
linkages among them.

As frameworks for the scientific understanding of learning have
evolved, there has been increasing emphasis on the small-scale processes
by which task performance capabilities are acquired and, consequently,
on the fine-grained structures of the specific abilities of which they are
constituted. As these processes and structures are elaborated, their combinations better represent the kinds of complex learning that take place in
schools. Evolving frameworks juxtapose the individuals' learning experiences and their states of ability when they enter those experiences. The
interaction of ability patterns with learning experiences results in new
learning (i.e., transitions to new ability states). Current test theory seems
ill-equipped either to address these specific abilities or build on them for
further understanding of aggregate abilities. Latent traits seem to be
averages of many abilities whose fine structure is not taken into account.
In addition, the interrelations which constitute structure are correlational,
not contingent or prerequisite in nature. Perhaps this is why it is so difficult

to see most aggregate abilities as anything other than hazy collections with arbitrary boundaries.

Clearly, the only way to improve this situation is through an elaboration and articulation of the fine structure of abilities. By this it is not meant that some ultimately differentiated set of skills must be identified. What is required, at least in the short term, is a way of defining the subskills involved in task performance at a level and in a way that scoring can be accomplished and capabilities identified which contribute to the performance of more than one task without retreating to the assumption that several tasks are functionally equivalent. If this is to be appropriately accomplished, a new conceptual framework must be established.

LEARNING GOALS

Learning Goals Versus Teaching Specifications: Systems and Tasks

Curriculum is usually defined in terms of the goals that are to be addressed by a learning system. Such goals refer to what is desired or intended to be learned by pupils, that is, what pupils should become capable of doing after completing instruction. In contrast, teaching specifications, whether phrased in terms of syllabi, lesson plans, or specifications for learning activities, address what instruction must, should, or may take place. These specifications are often phrased as guidelines and linked to goals, but usually take the form of examples of relevant instruction which are not fully analyzed in terms of the total set of goals. In short, we frame educational goals in terms of abilities to be acquired, but we frame instruction in terms of activities (tasks) to be carried out.

During this century, pupil learning goals have increasingly been phrased in psychological terms. That is, doing has been defined in terms of task performance and capability has come to mean knowledge, skill, or ability. Teaching specifications, on the other hand, are usually phrased in social organizational terms. They focus on activities, mostly defined in terms of what teachers should do with pupils; less frequently, in terms of pupil participation in instruction. Thus, although goals refer most directly to the attributes successful students should come to possess, the operational focus of goals actually contains the activities in which the students participate.

The structure of interrelations among goals is complex. First, some capabilities are prerequisite to others. (This is not to say that in any curriculum there are not arbitrary orderings of the skills to be acquired, only that there exist some abilities that cannot be acquired before certain others.) Second, capabilities are usually thought of as groupable. For example, both *decoding* and *reading* are skills or abilities, as are *linear equation solving* and *algebra.*

Typical school tasks aim at (i.e., require or promote) more than one ability in terms of their conception or selection. Because activities in which pupils participate most often have more than one goal, their goal characterization must be multiple. This multiple-goal aspect of activities refers to more than the kind of hierarchical capability grouping described in the previous paragraph. It also recognizes that actual tasks draw upon multiple capabilities that do not bear obvious hierarchical relations. For example, mathematics tasks may require reading. This multiple characterization is most obvious at the system level.

Curricular guidelines or *specifications* often contain descriptions of exemplary or mandatory learning activities. Although instructional specifications are intended to guide teachers about what they should do, specifications may relate to the kinds of tasks pupils are expected to undertake, their sequence and durations, the materials used, the teacher's exposition and monitoring, and so forth. Similarly, when test tasks are grouped or categorized, it is often not with respect to the goals that they are intended to assess, but instead the features of the tasks or the presumed performance components. In short, test specifications are often made in terms of task features rather than ability targets or goals.

Thus, as the activity to be categorized becomes narrower in space, time, and participation, the goal system often becomes more obscure. It is much easier in the narrow to characterize such an activity in terms of what the teacher or the pupils actually do rather than specifying the collection of microgoals intended. The point here is not that task groupings are useless or irrelevant; they are useful and relevant for both the organization of instruction and the creation of tests. The issue is that these kinds of category systems should not be confused with goal characterizations or specifications. Conceptual distinctions between tasks and goals must be maintained.

Learning Goals and Assessment Modes

The basic reason that such profound changes are taking place in the American system of testing and assessment is dissatisfaction with the validity of multiple-choice test instruments. There are at least three reasons for this dissatisfaction. First, there is broad agreement that in many multiple-choice tests, significant performance advantages accrue to individuals who have acquired so-called test-taking skills. Multiple-choice formats allow individuals to eliminate options by using skills that are ancillary to the measurement intent of the test. This induces a fundamental invalidity in scores of many individuals. This lack of validity is often hard to detect with standard psychometric techniques because the ancillary skills are positively correlated with the skills that form the measurement goals of the test.

A second reason for distrust of multiple-choice test validity is the tendency for test constructors to allocate most of the test's items and response time to tasks that draw more on recall and recognition than on reflective and multistage cognitive processing. The reason for this allocation is twofold: (a) complex tasks are more difficult to construct, and (b) the scoring constraints imposed by multiple-choice responses limit the amount of information extracted from task responses. The latter constraints, together with increases in response time, make the amount of consistent information contributed by such tasks small in relation to that provided by several less complex multiple-choice items.

Last, the goals of assessment have changed. The educational reform movement and the perception that students have not become sufficiently qualified for economic productivity has led to a reassessment of education goals. In addition to the more complex cognitive processing abilities referred to above, there is now a greater emphasis on building capabilities for work on tasks of significant length and complexity—tasks which require days or even weeks of effort, often with others in team endeavors. In standard testing paradigms, the amount of time devoted to testing is insufficient to evaluate the skills developed in these lengthy learning activities. For these reasons, the traditional multiple-choice testing paradigm carried out with short, fixed-length tests given at specific time points is perceived as inadequate. Moreover, assessment is now believed to be a primary influence on what is taught. Consequently, assessment, in political and curricular control terms, is viewed as a tool for bringing about policy changes in schooling.

The changes just discussed mean that students perform longer, more complex tasks, and that scoring procedures change so that more information, of a more complex nature, can be extracted from student responses. In order to accommodate these demands several ideas have been put forward. They involve (a) replacing multiple-choice tasks with those that require pupil-constructed responses; (b) increasing the complexity and length of tasks which students perform; (c) relaxing the traditional requirement that students take tests on demand; (d) ensuring that many of the tasks used to characterize students' abilities and skills are embedded in the instructional process; and (e) incorporating project work as testing tasks, both individually and in portfolios of cumulative accomplishment. To the extent that the criticisms of traditional testing have been taken up in political debate, these new assessment strategies have provided an important impetus for educational reform.

In order to discuss these issues, some terms need to be defined:

On Demand.   The basic concept of on-demand testing is that the student is required to participate in a prescheduled test session. That is, the test is given at a specific time under specified circumstances and the student has no choice about the timing of the testing event. Sometimes the scheduling aspect is implicitly supplemented by the notion that the test is externally imposed, that is, that the testing requirement and the testing instrument did not come out of the particular instructional process in which the student has participated.

Performance Exercise.   This term is variously interpreted. For some, it simply means an assessment task that is not in a multiple-choice format. For others, such an exercise must involve an interaction with the environment beyond a mere paper-and-pencil response to a visual stimulus. Often a performance exercise involves a product, such as a written passage, a construction, a proof, or a multipart solution. For the purposes of this chapter, the authors use the former definition and consider a performance exercise to be any task given to an individual to perform, for which the recorded response is not solely a single choice among a small number of pre-specified alternatives. Given this definition, anything from a simple open-ended version of a multiple-choice item to a year-long major project could be a performance task. Also, there is no prejudgment about the cognitive or other processes that might be involved in successful or unsuccessful task performance. Thus, it might be that a complex performance task has a multiple-choice response version that involves virtually the same cognitive processes. More specifically, however, there is an expectation that performance tasks typically involve more complex cognitive and performance structures than most multiple-choice items. In addition, in many performance exercises, the processes of performance, products of performance, or both, are available for evaluation and therefore complex scorings of performance are possible. These might involve graded response categories, subtask evaluation, or multiple-aspect scoring (defined later in this chapter).

Embedded.   The concept of embedded is, in part, in opposition to the idea of on-demand testing. Embedded tasks are those that are incorporated into the regular instructional process, either to promote or to evaluate learning. The idea behind this concept is that the tasks form a natural part of the instructional process rather than being considered an external or foreign element. One motivation for embedding tasks is that they do not take time away from the instructional process and thus do not place an extra burden on teachers and students. Embedded tasks could be of three types: (a) They could be externally provided assessment tasks, but incorporated by the teacher into his or her instruction; (b) they could be developed or selected as assessment tasks by the teacher or teachers in the school as a regular part of the instruction; or (c) they could be learning tasks used in the instructional process but evaluated as measures of accomplishment.

Cumulative. Cumulative refers to the state of the learner's accomplishments as it changes over time, through learning. Assessment tasks undertaken at different points in the school year should reflect changes in this state. This point is particularly important for the use of portfolios as measurement devices because they collect performance products and outcomes from across the school year. Some key issues (around which there is as yet no consensus) relate to the role of the timing of products in both the definition of what is to be measured and in the actual scoring. The learning status of a student at an intermediate point in the school year is useful for a teacher to know for planning instruction. However, if a portfolio can only be completed and is only formally evaluated at the end of the year, then this information does not come to the teacher as a part of the portfolio evaluation, even though it might be available to the teacher as a consequence of the task performance that was incorporated into the portfolio. Given an end-of-year cumulative evaluation, there seem to be only two kinds of possible foci for individual assessment: evaluation of the learner's state at the end of the year, or evaluation of the learner's progress through the year. The use of these two evaluations for decisions about the student would seem to differ, depending on which decisions are made, by whom, and for what purpose.

Culminating. Culminating assessments are directed to the learner's state at a break point in the instructional process, such as the end point of a segment of instruction (e.g., end-of-course or end-of-grade or end-of-level assessment). Often these assessments take place after instruction has been completed. However, there seems to be little difference between post segment assessments and the assessments that may enter into a portfolio at or near the end of the term.

Portfolio. A portfolio is a collection of task performance products, which could include records of performance at various stages of task completion as well as a final performance product. Thus, a portfolio might contain an annotated bibliography created at an earlier stage of a project as well as the final outcome, such as a completed paper. The component tasks in a portfolio could vary in length of time required for completion, from a few minutes to weeks or months. As the term has been used in recent discussions, portfolio implies a collection of student work assembled over a lengthy period, often the entire school year. In designing portfolios, some specifications must be made, however weak, about the kinds of materials to be included, how many of each kind, and what criteria a set of materials must meet in order to be included. Scoring is more complex than for a single task in that the portfolio as a whole is the focus of evaluation. Scoring may be accomplished by evaluating the component products separately and combining these evaluations or by a holistic assessment of the entire collection. As noted earlier, a portfolio could be used for a culminating assessment or an assessment of growth or change over the duration of its definition.

What Kinds of Tasks Can Be Used for What Kinds of Goals? Although in principle it may be possible to measure highly complex skills with multiple-choice items, it is seldom done, in part because the multiple-choice format limits the information that can be obtained about task performance. Although the responses to multiple-choice tasks are restricted to a relatively small number of alternatives, a task that engages a number of skills in a complex interdependent way only yields a highly aggregate categorization of responses. Ergo, a highly complex multiple-choice task would take up considerably more response time than a more typical multiple-choice item, but would produce only a similarly limited amount of performance information.

On the other hand, when the same or a similarly complex task is viewed as a performance exercise, it is common practice to collect information on the solution process as it evolves toward a successful outcome. Also, in many performance tasks, the product is an entity that may be scored with respect to multiple parts and with multiple criteria. This implies that more information can be obtained, but, of course, at a higher cost.

An even more important point concerns the knowledge, ability, and skill that is to be measured. Skills differ in the way they can be accurately assessed. Complex and integrative skills about which detailed information is desired require performance information that can differentiate distinct skills and exhibit how they jointly contribute to successful task performance. It seems unlikely that some skills, such as those that require considerable integration of subcomponent performance elements into larger complexes, can be assessed in short periods of time.

Because different kinds, lengths, complexities, and scorings of tasks are required to measure different kinds of skills and abilities, care must be taken in evaluating particular measurement strategies. This is especially true with respect to validity. If, for example, some goals (desired abilities) cannot (or cannot without considerable research and development investment) be assessed with certain narrower kinds of tasks (e.g., multiple-choice tasks), then in order for the full set of goals to be evaluated, the kinds of tasks used must include some that can assess the attainment of those valued goals.

Curricular Goal and Measurement Intent. In the next section, the authors discuss how assessment tasks can be aligned to frameworks and other written specifications for curricular goals. In order for such alignment to take place, the skills and abilities that a task is intended to measure must be specified. It is the concept of intent that links curricular goals to tasks. This linkage can be accomplished because that which is intended at both levels is a specific set of abilities or skills. Linkage is greatly facilitated by a framework for characterizing abilities in which the relation of narrow, specific abilities (say, the level of specificity at which intents of specific learning activities are conceptualized) to broader, more general abilities (say, the level at which goals are presented in State Frameworks) may be made explicit.

The authors distinguish between the intent of a measurement and the ancillary abilities that contribute to successful task performance. In statistical terms, both the intent of measurement and the ancillary abilities are dimensions of measurement. For example, test taking abilities contribute to performance on multiple-choice tests such as the SAT. Individual differences in such skills constitute part of the reliable variation in scores on any test. However, such abilities are not part of the measurement intent of these tests. From the authors' perspective they detract from validity or, to put it the other way around, add to the invalidity of a test. Ancillary abilities, their distribution over test tasks and their relations both among themselves and with the characteristics intended to be measured, are critical to an adequate conception of test validity. From this perspective, test validity must be assessed by examining all of the dimensions which contribute to test performance. The invalidity in measurements characterized by Messick (1989) as "construct-irrelevant variance" is in this terminology, measured abilities (skills) that are ancillary—not included in the intent of measurement for a particular test or test application. Validity, then, should be measured by an index that reflects the degree to which the test measures (a) what is intended, as opposed to (b) what is not intended, or (c) what is unsystematic or unstable.

A test is not simply valid or invalid. Instead a score or measurement resulting from the test is made up of components. Some combination of these (the valid part) constitutes the intent of the measurement. The remaining parts, both stable and unstable, are invalid. Because the stable undesired components are, in general, co-related to the intended component, simple correlational indices do not accurately reflect the validity of the measurement. Thus, the key to the distinction between invalidity and valid multidimensionality is intent.

It has become conventional in discussions of test validity to assert that a measurement procedure is not in itself valid or invalid, only a test interpretation. The authors would agree that some critical aspects of validity can only be evaluated in the context of a specific testing application, but would argue that the intents of most measurements are almost entirely constant across applications, and therefore, that a very large part of validity or invalidity does inhere in the measurement procedure itself. Moreover, an accounting of the ancillary abilities a measurement requires can clarify the range of situations in which it can be expected to lead to valid interpretations. To take a trivial example, an algebra test that requires some degree of English language proficiency (here regarded as ancillary) will not be valid if used with test takers lacking the necessary language skills, unless some special accommodation can be made to either reduce the dependence of the test on the lacking abilities or to provide additional supports in the testing situation. Obviously, within this framework a sharp specification of the intent is essential before validity can be assessed. Note also that a specification of significant ancillary ability requirements can ground the investigation of issues of test bias.

Tasks are, by definition, goal oriented. One must distinguish, however, between the goal pursued in a particular task (i.e., the performance goal, from the perspective of the person undertaking it), and the goal(s) pursued by the person giving the task (i.e., the measurement goal). (See the next section, Assessment Tasks, for further discussion of the performance goal.) The measurement goal follows from the learning goal, as discussed above. In the context of assessment, it is the set of assessment goals for which we use the word *intent*.

The measurement intent, however vaguely it may be specified, has several important consequences for the measurement process, including the following:

- *Task creation or selection*, which involves:

    Specifying the specific performance goals of a task,

    Specifiying the circumstances of measurment, and

    Specifying the *charge*—communicating the task requirements to the person undertaking it; and
- *Performance Assessment and Scoring*.

As described, tasks cannot generally be conceived as unifocal (i.e., assessing only a single ability). Tasks, and the performances they stimulate, form a part of a structure which links (hypothetical) abilities for task performance with the (potential) performances of particular tasks. This structure involves multiple abilities and multiple categories of tasks. And the relationship between these abilities for task performance and the task categories is not one-to-one. That is, task performances eventuating in a given task category reflect multiple abilities, whether that task performance category is the choice of Response D on a multiple-choice item or a particular profile of dimensional ratings derived according to the complex scoring rubric for a performance task.

This complexity occurs because (a) tasks and performance goals cannot be found which precisely match the measurement intent, (b) the circumstances of measurement bring into play additional abilities that are not explicitly part of the goals, and (c) the communication of the task requirements may be inaccurate or misunderstood. Thus, some of the abilities that were intended may not be present or may not be weighted appropriately in the performance and its assessment, and other abilities not part of the intent may form a part of the performance or its assessment. All of these will result in multidimensionality and, as this will most often be unintended, invalidity.

Learning Goals and Ability Specifications. An ability is a human characteristic that is required for successful task performance. At the simplest level, ability can be identified with the capacity to perform a single class of tasks. In this case, since an ability must encompass characteristics which bear on more than a single performance, the concept implicitly incorporates a relational structure linking a focal task to similar tasks, which require the same ability for successful performance. In its simplest form, this relational structure corresponds to the equivalence class set up by the task specification.

However, in order to be an ability, a human characteristic must not only differentiate successful from unsuccessful task performance, it also must apply to some tasks or classes of tasks and not to others. That is, particular abilities must be defined so that they subdivide tasks and classes of tasks into two subgroups—those to which the ability applies and those to which it does not. Also, once the ability concept is thought to apply beyond a narrow equivalence class of tasks, then since formally different tasks, by definition, are conceived as having different ability requirements, some tasks must require more than one ability. That is, the subdivision of tasks by abilities also implies a subdivision of abilities by tasks. A given task subdivides abilities into those that are required to successfully perform it and those that are not.

The most difficult part of any measurement process involves the specification of its intents in a fashion that leads to effective measurement outcomes. There is little guidance for this key part, especially as new, complex tasks are incorporated into the process. The traditional multiple-choice procedures are colored by the subtest homogeneity paradigm. That is, subtests are given labels that, at least functionally, describe types of items rather than abilities. Where test specifications within subtests are created, they mix these item type specifications with skill specifications that don't easily link to curricular goal frameworks. These frameworks, where they exist, are seldom linked to subtask labels except by the assertion of the test constructors. Regardless of the validity of this traditional test specification technology, it gives little guidance to the process of specifying measurement intents for extended assessment tasks.

Perhaps in consequence, the new extended assessment tasks have been relatively diffuse in specifying what is to be measured. Often there is an attempt to attach tasks to curricular frameworks, but this has been unconvincing, largely, perhaps, because there is no "language system" for doing so. The need for such a language system is clear because test tasks are specified at a much greater level of detail than the formal specifications in frameworks. The strategy suggested by Haertel and Wiley (1993) involves (a) clarifying the relation between tasks, their performance structures, and the abilities underlying the performance in a general, definitional way; (b) developing task analyses that preliminarily identify underlying abilities with subtask and aspect structures (see "Assessment Tasks"); (c) linking such components of other tasks into a network of task relations anchored by the identified abilities; and (d) iterating this process to develop a refined set of abilities, which can then be used to construct new tasks.

The policy issues in this lack of specification are significant. If no valid system exists for mapping tasks into the frameworks, the curricular coverage of the assessment cannot be evaluated. In addition, without the detailed linkages, the scoring process for individual tasks remains impoverished and will likely produce scores that are neither valid nor comparable. The links among task selection, task analysis, task scoring and curricular goals have to be well understood and relatively tight in order for the system to work. This is just as true for goals that are tailored to individual schools and classrooms as for goals that are statewide.

In the long run, this gap will have to be filled. This will take place in at least three ways. First, the frameworks must be elaborated. This elaboration need not be directly oriented to test tasks; better would be an orientation to more elaboration of the goals themselves—both richer description and finer differentiation. Second, tasks must be more extensively analyzed in terms of their performance requirements. By devoting analytic effort to understanding, subdividing, and distinguishing relevant aspects of task performance in terms of target abilities and skills, an infrastructure will be laid which will be commensurate with the elaboration of framework goals. Finally, the linking of the elaborated goals to this developed infrastructure needs to be an explicit activity. These linkages would allow refinement of scoring to increase validity and enable the evaluation of the total collection of assessment tasks in terms of the frameworks.

ASSESSMENT TASKS

The Uses of Tasks

Tasks can, for some purposes, be roughly grouped into three categories: life, learning, and test (cf. Wiley, 1990). These groups are overlapping, as the categories refer more to context, setting, or use than to the nature of the tasks themselves. Thus, writing an essay could be a normal life activity of a newspaper columnist, a school assignment intended to teach writing, or a part of a college entrance examination. To the extent that the skills exercised and the processes used in the writing of such an essay are similar, these tasks would not differ in the abilities which their performances reflect.

Life tasks, for our purposes, are the commonplace segments of goal-oriented life activities of individuals, where the formal learning and formal evaluation aspects of these tasks are secondary to other facets of their goals. Learning tasks are those whose primary function is to acquire an ability to perform similar or related tasks (i.e., to learn a skill). Test tasks are those whose purpose is to establish whether or not an individual possesses such an ability.

In educational work all three kinds of tasks are central. Abilities to perform life tasks constitute the primary goals of educational systems. The specification and performance of learning tasks fulfills the process of education in terms of curricular design and instructional implementation. And test tasks channel the delivery of instruction by diagnosing and confirming the abilities of students. Recently, the distinctions among these rough categories have been (deliberately and appropriately) blurred. Often the recent demands for "authentic" tasks have been taken to mean that learning and test tasks should simulate life tasks. The notion of "embedded" implies that the gap between test task and learning task has been narrowed.

The Definition of a Task and a Task Performance

As set forth in Haertel and Wiley (1993), a *task performance* is a human activity that has a performance goal; a beginning, an end, and therefore, a (possibly variable) duration; and which can be evaluated with respect to success in attaining its goal. The *performance goal* is the goal toward which the task performance is directed (the goal set for the test taker), as opposed to the learning or assessment goal that a task formulator might have in using the task to further learning or make inferences about ability. This goal is not an intended ability; it is a desired end state. The process and the products of the performance must be characterizable in relation to the performance goal. This might only mean that performance is judged to be either satisfactory or not, or it might imply an elaborate multicriterial evaluation.

A task specification sets the conditions under which a task performance can take place. It allows a task to be defined in such a way that it can be performed more than one time by more than one person or group. For example, an open- and a closed-book examination might have the same goals of successful performance for the individuals taking the examinations, but the specification of conditions is sufficiently different that the two would commonly be judged as distinct tasks.

Typically such a specification would address the following:

- The environment or circumstances within which the task performance will take place, including:
  Physical environment,
  Timing,
  Tools, equipment, physical resources, etc. to be made available,
  Information to be made available; and
- Any communications directed to the person performing the task, perhaps including:
  Delineation of its goal, including the evaluation criteria,
  Performance (i.e., the circumstances within which it is to be performed),
  The tools which could be used to perform the task.

A task specification sets up an equivalence class of task implementations or realizations, such that a realization belongs to a specification's equivalence class if and only if its conditions match those of the specification. It is this framework that allows two different individuals to perform the same task, or permits more than one performance of the same task by a single individual. A full task definition includes both the task goal and the task specification, thereby providing the context for both the performance and its evaluation. A task performance ensues from implementing the definition.

Structures

Both tasks and abilities may be structured. *Structure*, for our purposes here, means subdivisions of a group of entities. Entities within the same subdivision are considered more similar than those in different subdivisions. Structures can be complex; subdivisions may be partial, may be further divided, may be overlapping, or may be recombined. In other words, structures need not be simple partitions or hierarchies.

Structure is conceptually essential because once tasks are successfully performed it seldom makes sense for them to be done again. We desire learning to enable learners to successfully perform new tasks that are structurally linked to the tasks undertaken in the learning process. So, we traditionally group similar tasks into equivalence classes within which tasks are considered to be structurally identical. As already argued, however, the simplicity of this kind of structure may be suitable when many similar tasks (e.g., objective paper-and-pencil test questions) are used, but not when there are only a few distinctive ones (e.g., complex performance assessments). The critical issue here is that some (perhaps more complex) structure is needed if we are to validly characterize future performance on novel tasks. A formulation in terms of task performances alone, not grounded in a framework for their requisite abilities, can offer no formal basis for generalization to tasks outside the overall set of learning or test task specifications.

Much current educational work, especially that linked to testing, is premised on the direct correspondence of abilities and tasks. Thus, tasks often are hierarchically organized into content domains and skills. These are usually defined by identifying them with a class of task-ability pairs without explicitly distinguishing whether the skill category system applies to the tasks or to the abilities. The issue here is not whether ability distinctions can be unlinked from task distinctions. They clearly cannot. Because skills are abilities to perform tasks, they are linked by definition. The main point is that joint structures of abilities and tasks do not consist of simple one-to-one correspondences of task and ability.

In the instructional context, there is no essential difference between learning and test tasks. All are classroom activities or components of such activities. They only differ in the intent of their use. Learning tasks require particular clusters of abilities for their successful performance. The instructional intent is to select learning tasks that require both the abilities to be learned (targets) and abilities already acquired (prerequisites), and that permit the learning of the target abilities during task performance. Test tasks traditionally do not have learning goals, but they do require particular clusters of abilities. Their primary function is to assess whether abilities necessary for successful performance have been acquired.

Individual task implementations themselves, as well as tasks themselves, may be joined and subdivided. Thus a task such as mowing the lawn may be temporally divided into preparatory, operational, and cleanup subtasks (i.e., by subgoal, or for other purposes, each of those subtasks could be treated as a complete task in itself). Such subtask analysis is one way in which subskill definitions evolve. Alternatively, several individual mowing task implementations might be merged conceptually into a whole summer's mowing activities. Task episode *poolings* and *dividings* are conceptually distinct from aspects of a structural system of classification which might, for example, abstractly group hedge trimming with lawn mowing into a gardening category.

Structures imposed on ability conceptions are based on distinctions among tasks and, therefore, on task structures. But historically, as psychologically based inquiry has proceeded, these structural ability distinctions have departed from the holistic life task categories that form the traditional base for task structures. There is still a fundamental linkage, however, especially in educational settings. Test tasks assess the skills that learning tasks are supposed to produce and these skills, in turn, constitute the abilities to perform the life tasks which are the goals of schooling.

As was discussed, these linkages are not necessarily one-to-one. For example, the development of skill concepts has often proceeded by analyzing holistic task performance into components (e.g., Sternberg, 1977). Thus, many learning tasks are focused on component skills required for a variety of life tasks. And test tasks frequently diagnose subcomponents of abilities that are the intended outcomes of learning tasks. This, as discussed, has been taken to the extreme in many multiple-choice items.

Task Performance Goals

Let us return for the moment to the issue of task performance goals. The fact that these goals can vary in complexity has significant consequences and raises some important conceptual distinctions. In fact, the elucidation of performance goals leads the way toward linking these goals to the learning and assessment goals of the task.

A task can have a single performance goal with several different aspects, or it can have several subgoals. These are distinguished by two related characteristics: time order and goal dependence. A subgoal—as opposed to a goal aspect—can be attained discretely. The activities directed toward it

can occupy a time subduration distinct from other parts of the task performance. The performance can then result in the successful attainment of a
subgoal prior to success on other subgoals. That is, subgoals imply subtask
performances (Haertel & Wiley, 1993).

Goal aspects, as distinct from subgoals or subtask structures, refer to
distinctive features that cannot be broken into subdivisions to be performed
separately. An example is the traditional pursuit rotor task for investigating
psychomotor learning, which involves a spinning plate with a spot on it
that conducts electricity. The person performing the task has a stylus that
can make electrical contact with the spot, and the task performance goal is
to keep the stylus in contact with the spot as much of the time as possible.
Performance can be evaluated with respect to a number of distinct aspects:
contact time, average distance of stylus from the spot, smoothness of
performance, and so on. These aspects all reflect the individual's performance capabilities, but they cannot be segmented into subtasks.

Many complex performance tasks—tennis, for example—have both aspects and subgoals. Tennis includes aspects such as backhand and forehand
performance, which are integrated into the overall game performance. It
would be misrepresenting the game to treat these as subtasks. On the other
hand, the *serve* could be characterized as a subtask. (Clearly, such distinctions for some tasks may be somewhat arbitrary.)

Implications for Task Analysis and Scoring.   When a task is analyzed into subtasks and aspects via the goals and the performance segments, the result is a mapping of different abilities into differentiable parts
of the performance. This allows the multiple learning or assessment goals
specified for the task to be more closely aligned with its internal structure,
that is, its subtasks and aspects. This kind of task analysis makes clear the
available information from the task performances about the target abilities.
This has important implications for scoring, which are explored next.

Performance Records.   The scoring of task performances is always
based on scoring records of some kind. However, the criteria for what is
included in a scoring record are quite varied. For example, in a multiple-
choice task, only the response category chosen by the respondent is recorded. There are no mechanisms for recording the process stages or the
preliminary products of the task. In experimental work, eye movements
have been recorded, but this is not feasible under ordinary testing conditions. In computer administered multiple-choice test tasks, it is possible to
gather information on search and intermediate processing depending on
how the computer program and the task are structured.

In some tasks, process versus product distinctions are made in distinguishing parts of scoring records. As just noted, in traditional multiple-choice tasks, no process information is recorded and the response category chosen is considered the product. In some types of mathematics problem solving tasks, the answer is often considered the product and the steps leading to the answer are considered part of the process. In this case, depending on the definition of a successful solution, process information may be used in scoring. For example, if the performance goal is to exhibit the logic of the solution, computational errors may not result in a lower score. These judgments obviously require process information to be recorded and incorporated into scoring. Essay writing is another example. In most cases the essay itself is considered the product. However, in many instructional processes of writing, drafts receive comments or even preliminary grades. If the measurement intent included "ability to revise," these preliminary products could be used for grading. (This relates to the cumulative vs. culminating nature of task and scoring, discussed earlier.)

Another interesting example is a lengthy end-of-course project. In a vocational education curriculum, for example, the final examination might consist of a product design and construction of a prototype based on the design. In this case, it is not clear that the distinction between process and product would be fruitful. Alternative scorings might focus (a) only on the prototype as product; (b) on the design as process and the prototype as product (i.e., using the design as a template to evaluate the product); (c) on the design and the prototype as products; or (d) on the design and the prototype as products, with intermediate prototype construction information recorded to adjust the product scoring in a way similar to computation errors in the mathematics example. Obviously, there are many other alternatives.

The primary implication seems to be that careful consideration needs to be given to which abilities are to be measured. Carefully crafted decisions must be made about which aspects or subtasks are relevant in which ways to the scoring. From our perspective, the issues in the design of scoring rubrics are:

- Deciding what skills or abilities are to be measured;
- Deciding what aspects or subtasks of the task bear on inferences about those abilities;
- Assuring that the recording of performance adequately reflects those aspects or subtasks;
- Designing rubrics for those aspects or subtasks; and
- Creating procedures for merging aspect and subtask scores into a final set of scores organized according to the skills or abilities initially set forth as the intents of the measurement.

SCORING

Assessment Operations and Processes

Measurement is not a unitary concept. It involves six central and separate operations and processes, each of which must be carefully expounded. The six, followed by subcomponents, are:

1. *Task Analysis or Construction*
   - Specifying measurement intents
        overview
        intertask and subsidiary task review
        sequencing issues for skill identification
        implicit/explicit decisions
        list and description of intents
   - Stipulating ancillary abilities
        general nature and range of ancillary abilities
        abilities to be assumed available to all examinees
        abilities not to be entailed by the task
        accommodations (e.g., for handicapping conditions)
   - Subtask identification
        segmentation of subtasks
        identification of subtask contingencies
        subtask map
        review of implicit and explicit decisions
   - Aspect specification
   - Aligning subtasks and aspects with intents
        skill analysis of subtasks
        skill review and respecification of aspects
        revision of intent list and description
        mapping of subtasks and aspects to abilities
   - Design of environment
        physical environment
        timing
        tools
   - Design of communication (charge)
        review of role of communication
        performance goal delineation
        evaluation criteria
        environment description
        script construction

2. *Designing Performance Records*
- Technology review in relation to intents
- Subtask and aspect review
- Form design (note linkage to communication design)

3. *Creating Scoring Rubrics*
- Review of subtask map
- Review of intent list and description
- Review of performance records
- Design rubrics
  aspects
  subtasks
  linkage map
  scoring forms
  scoring instructions
  specification of training issues

4. *Administering Performance Tasks*

5. *Implementing Scoring Procedures*
- Collecting performance records
- Organizing scoring process
  locations
      primary scoring
      secondary and moderation scoring
  timing
  scorer selection and training
  within-location on-site training and instructions
      grouping
      activity specification
      time sequence
      scoring form use
      scoring process evaluation records
- Transmission of scoring forms and evaluation records

6. *Data Processing Design*

Of the six processes, only the first, third, and fifth will be discussed here. The second, *designing performance records,* was briefly discussed earlier. The fourth, *administering performance tasks,* and the sixth, *data processing design,* are beyond the scope of this chapter.

Task analysis or construction is the most complex and the most important measurement process, as it underlies each of the other steps. Specification of measurement intents is the first part of this step. This requires an overview of the goal structure of the instrument(s) to be used in the assessment as a whole. Decisions must be made about which of the curricular goals appropriate to the test population will be addressed in the assessment, which means deciding which particular tasks or subcollections of tasks are to be used to measure which goals. It also requires sequencing decisions about tasks and subtasks and interdependencies among them.

These latter decisions are critical to effective use of tasks and appropriate measurement of skills. For example, some tasks allow the person responding to work out a general strategy for solution of a problem and then implement that strategy. If the strategy chosen is not effective, then some of the implementing skills might not be evaluable. One solution might be to supplement the original task with one in which the strategy is provided or scaffolded. This would allow a controlled and equitable way of evaluating the implementing skills, although care would have to be taken concerning the introduction of additional ancillary abilities required to comprehend and apply the additional assistance provided. The ultimate outcome of the first part is a list and description of each of the skills intended to be measured by the task.

The second part of task analysis is subtask identification. This involves specification (segmentation) of subtasks, identification of contingencies among subtasks (i.e., how the products of one subtask are required for initiation of another), and setting out a map (graphical representation) of subtask relations together with a review of the original intent list to see if it needs revision. A similar analysis is required of aspects.

The next part is to look at each subtask and aspect separately. A separate skill analysis is performed for each. These, in turn, may result in further revision of the overall lists of task intents and a mapping of subtasks and aspects to abilities. This is the most important feature for scoring, as it determines what performance path and end state correspond (in the absence of measurement error) to each possible profile of relevant abilities. Design of the task environment and communications to the task performer follow that which has been outlined in "Assessment Tasks."

The scoring rubric design is based directly on the task analysis. Aside from reviewing the intent list and subtask maps and aligning these with the performance record, the links among them must be used in designing scoring forms. These forms should be as explicit and directive as possible about subtasks and aspects, which should be separately scored and recorded on forms that correspond closely to the organization of the information in the performance records. If holistic scoring is desired, it should be treated as a separable aspect and its logical relationship to other aspects and subtasks should be analyzed. Pilot testing should allow empirical interrelations among the particularistic and holistic aspects to be estimated. Instructions should be designed to make all elements of the forms explicit. Judgments should be, insofar as possible, dichotomous, with any gradings calculated later from the recorded judgments. Training issues should be brought forward at this stage so that issues of meaning and clarity of the required judgments will be a common basis for forms, instructions, and training.

Scoring procedure implementation has only two aspects. One is design of the gross social organization of scoring process. This means deciding on rater stratification (respondents' teachers, teachers in respondents' schools, teachers in other schools, experts, etc.) and qualifications, on how and where raters should be grouped, on the timing and sequencing, on the training process off-site, on the rater selection and sampling processes, and on transmission of the scoring forms and other data.

The second aspect is the micro-organization of the rating process itself. This includes instruction and on-site training, grouping of scorers for interaction, assignment of performance records to scorers, scoring activity specification and sequencing, quality control, and evaluation provisions. Some of the issues in micro-organization include aids to scoring, exemplary performance records as models for rating or classification, computer-assisted review of records and computer ratings (replacing or supplementing printed rating forms), on-site auditing, and moderation of judgments.

Scoring Judgments Versus Standards Judgments

No two distinct skills or abilities have any natural relationship to one another except in so far as the learning of one is (partially or completely) contingent on the prior learning of the other. Without such contingencies, curricula could be constructed which result in the acquisition of either skill without the other. Because the learning of skills and concepts is partly constrained by such contingencies and partly constrained by the curriculum and the instructional process, definition of standards will always be a mixture of our understanding of the learning process and our values.

If two skills are of a kind, or close together in some sense (e.g., addition and multiplication), then contingency relations are more likely. It seems reasonable, for example, that given the mathematical relations between addition and multiplication of integers, that there may be some contingencies once the microstructures of this kind of ability are elucidated. On the other hand, if science abilities are to be compared with mathematics abilities, then contingency relations are much weaker, especially in terms of the abilities and skills taught in elementary and secondary school. Even less related are abilities in history with those in mathematics. Thus, while our understanding of mathematics learning might lead us at a given grade level to judge multiplication skills as meeting a higher standard than addition skills, such a basis would be unlikely for judgments with respect to a common standard between, say, multiplication skills and knowledge or concepts related to the Boston Tea Party. Clearly, complex value judgments are required that incorporate knowledge of the existing curricula and instructional practices and desired changes in them, framed against the background of the whole system.

Implicit in most state-level discussions is that standards are graded. Ability assessments (scores as defined above) must be transformed into a graded set of categories representing ordered valuations of the skills. Also implicit is that these levels or grades are meaningfully comparable across different abilities and different aggregations of abilities. Because most of the comparisons will not be of narrowly defined skills, judgments of level or grade equivalence or discrepancy are complex, incorporating judgments about the relative educational and societal importance of distinct constellations of skills attested by different patterns of performance on different tasks.

In this kind of process it is important that two distinct judgments be separated. The first is the judgment about skill level, which comes out of the scoring process. The scoring judgments here should not be linked to standards. The criterion for these judgments is their accuracy as measures of definable ability and skill levels, unleavened by standards judgments. In this sense their validity and reliability can be assessed without mixing in the judgments of what history skills are equivalent in value to what mathematics skills. From our perspective, this accuracy issue includes comparability of scores.

The second judgment process is one that maps or transforms estimated skill levels into standards grades. These judgments should not be part of the process of scoring. They should be made in the context of a separate procedure that links scores to standards grades or levels. Ideally, a correspondence table, based on validated expert judgment about the correspondence of scoring outcomes to standards, should be generated by a careful selection of persons from a well defined, relevant population of judges. This table should be computerized and the transformation applied to the scores at the end of the scoring process. The table makes the results of deliberations about the worth of alternative learning outcomes explicit. It should be published and documented so that it can be critiqued and improved over time. This process will also allow adjustments in standards as achievement improves. Note that it is the scores that should be comparable over time, not the standards levels.

On the other hand, when judgments are to be merged across ability or skill categories, it is most important that the standard levels be merged rather than the scores unless there is great confidence that by doing the merger, the judgment will be unequivocally viewed as technical rather than value laden. That is, once the value-laden transformation is made to standards levels, the comparability of the levels is already legitimated. Thus, there is no problem in combining the levels except for weighting. Weight judgments are easy to describe and criticize, so this should not be a serious problem. As far as combination algorithms are concerned, the easiest to understand and to compute is simply an average of the vectors of 0s and 1s of grade assignments (a 1 for the assigned grade and a 0 for the other grades). These can be averaged over skills and persons; the aggregation is consistent because of the linear additive form of the average. The result is a vector of proportions which is interpretable as the proportion of skills that the individual possesses at each grade or the proportion of individuals in each grade.

ACCURACY OF SCORES

In this section, we treat issues related to the accuracy of scores and standards levels. The term accuracy is chosen specifically to cover, at least in part, the traditional concerns of validity and reliability in educational and psychological measurement. By choosing accuracy as an organizing framework for validity, we use Messick's (1989) terminology, and focus primarily on *evidential* as opposed to *consequential* interpretation of test results. Thus, in Wiley's (1990) terms, we de-emphasize the uses of test scores in ways that do not relate directly to what they are intended to measure in order to emphasize the meaning or interpretation of test scores in terms of intents. This focus is chosen in part because these unintended uses may be difficult to anticipate and in part due to limitations of space, not because we do not acknowledge the importance of such unintended uses of scores. In treating reliability, we take the position that standard measures can be seriously misleading. We are concerned that the assumptions underlying them are not as appropriate for traditional modes of scoring tasks as has been accepted, and have serious defects for new scoring modes.

Reliability

There is a problem with distinguishing reliability from validity when the transition is made from multiple-choice to extended assessment tasks. In the multiple-choice context, error has been defined in terms of variations among items within tests or forms. The view of tests as having single scores calculated by summing dichotomous item scores (or the approximately equivalent latent trait versions) has placed the framework for evaluating reliability within the context of homogeneity. Even the extensions of reliability (e.g., generalizability) have only modified the homogeneity framework by stratification of tasks within tests. But within strata, regardless of how highly cross-classified, tasks are still assumed homogeneous.

The problem with this approach is that, within homogeneous task collections, performance variations among tasks with different skill requirements are considered as measurement error. This may be appropriate when the tasks really are homogenous and the desired score is some kind of simple aggregate or total of scores on individual assessment tasks, but it is not appropriate when assessment task performances are evaluated in complex fashions and the resulting scores of individual tasks are combined into multiple (multivariate) composites. To reflect the complexity of these task performances, traditional simple aggregations of dichotomies or graded responses are not likely to be adequate. Consequently, the underlying theory of reliability (or generalizability) indices such as Cronbach's coefficient alpha is no longer as useful in describing the consistency of relevant summaries. This lack of homogeneity among tasks is likely one of several reasons why simply rated performances of complex tasks are often inconsistent with seemingly similar tasks.

In operational terms, the most important guidance that can be given is to insist that performance records be adequately designed to reflect the important (intended) skills. Second, ambiguity in the criteria for scoring must be minimized. For both of these issues, the distinction between task-based scoring categories and skill-based categories is critical. Formal task analyses relating performance records to performance structures to skills must be undertaken. These are the only bases for assuring adequate scoring records and minimizing ambiguity of scoring criteria. Third, the scoring criteria must be communicated and understood by the scorers. This means careful attention to training, instructions, and exemplars. It also means that score recording forms must be well matched to the desired criteria. Discussion of some of these issues can be found in Haertel (1992).

Validity

In the introduction to this section, we indicated that we would focus on evidential, rather than the consequential, basis of validity, to use Messick's (1989) terminology. In fact most of the recent discussions of validity in the context of performance tasks and large scale assessment have concentrated on the consequential side. Examples include Baker, O'Neil, and Linn (1993) and Linn (1991). We hope to redress the lack of discussion on evidential issues in the following discussion.

This chapter opened with a summary of the strong critique of multiple-choice tests that has emerged in the educational community in recent years. That critique was linked to two issues: (a) the inadequacy of basic, underlying conceptions of ability and skills as they have dominated thinking

about testing; and (b) the increasing societal focus on the kinds of conceptual, analytic, and problem-solving abilities that multiple-choice tests, historically, have had difficulty capturing.

In our focus on evidential issues, we developed the notion of learning
goals as intended capabilities and carried this through with (a) an analysis
of task definition and structure; (b) a framework for the specification of
abilities and skills; and (c) a structural linkage between task performance
and ability, which formed the basis for scoring the new kinds of extended
assessment tasks. From this perspective, one fundamental validity issue is
defined at the task level and specifically concerns the performance-ability
link (Point c) and its implications for scoring. A second validity issue
concerns curricular goals. Given the criticism that multiple-choice tests are
not adequate for measuring the abilities required to perform complex tasks,
and given the great effort that has been made to form curricular frameworks
for guidance of educators in bringing about these skills, a high standard is
set for any statewide assessment in terms of the skills actually to be assessed.
Acknowledging the skill coverage limitations of traditional testing in the
light of current goals, how successful have we been in extending our reach
by substituting new kinds of tasks?

From this perspective, the logic of analyzing the validity of an assessment
is twofold. First, the match between measurement intents of the whole
collection of assessment tasks (or subtasks) and the appropriate collection
of curricular goals must be assessed. Only when this match is clear will the
second step, the validity of the performance scorings for the manifest
measurement intents of particular tasks, become interpretable. The first
issue is the validity of the task collection's intents for the curricular goals;
the second is the validity of the task scorings for the task intents.

The first (match) issue is sketched at the end of the first section of this
chapter, "Learning Goals." In probing this aspect of validity, there are three
sequential tasks to be performed:

•*Clarifying and Articulating the Measurement Intents of Each Assessment
Task.* The current system for doing this is unstructured and leads to vague
and ambiguous task specifications. A language system needs to be
designed for specifying tasks' ability intents. This system requires a basic
vocabulary for describing and distinguishing knowledge from skills from
conceptual structures from abilities to use tools and materials from
coordinating and organizing abilities. These vocabulary elements should
form a multiple-feature taxonomy from which descriptors can be taken and
combined to form goal-focused task specifications. The formation of this
vocabulary system requires subject-matter and psychological expertise.
The vocabulary then needs to be applied to specific tasks to generate
descriptions of what the tasks are intended to measure. Clearly, this is an

iterative and interactive process, in that the task analyses conducted for the scoring process contribute to the vocabulary development and vice versa.

•*Articulating and Refining Curricular Goals in Terms of Desired Abilities.* These goals need refinement and clarification before they can be smoothly linked to the kinds of task descriptions advocated earlier. The vocabulary development discussed earlier should greatly aid in this refinement. The result of this process could be conceived as a map of the intended curriculum.

•*Matching Refined Versions of Curricular Goals to Intents of Assessment Tasks.* This matching should produce a correspondence of tasks to curriculum by means of ability-acquisition intents. The correspondence will be many-to-many rather than one-to-many or one-to-one, as each task will have multiple intents and each (refined) goal will be reflected in multiple tasks.

Once the first approximation to these three tasks has been completed, both the frameworks and the assessment can be evaluated for adequacy of coverage. This evaluation should result in revision of both. It should also clarify, on a systematic basis, the issue of which modes of assessment may be used to assess which goals. To fully address this issue, of course, the validity of task scores must be elucidated. However, the map and the systematic task-goal-curriculum correspondence will give an essential first vision of coverage issues and guide initial task development resource allocation decisions.

The second issue, task and scoring validity in relation to manifest measurement intents, also has three primary foci. These are:

•*Analysis of Task (Performance) Structures.* This addresses the issue of whether the performance structure of a task allows the identification of the target (intended) abilities. Tasks must be analyzed with respect to subtasks and aspects of performance and must be linked together to provide an infrastructural description of the task demands and resulting performance potentials (see "Accuracy of Scores"). As indicated previously, this is likely to be most difficult for tasks in which pupil choice in performance alternatives is wide (e.g., essays with relatively open topic specifications or portfolios).

•*Design and Specification of Performance Records.* Scorers cannot assess abilities and skills that are not revealed in the performance records used for scoring. A great deal more effort must be exerted to assure that all intended abilities contributing to a given performance are made manifest in the scoring records. It may be that pupils must be asked structured questions about their performance process and its products in order to accomplish this. Note that such analytic rationalizations may significantly reduce interpretive ambiguity in the scoring process.

• *Improvement of the Scoring Process.* Several issues related to the validity of scoring were discussed in "Scoring." These included organization of the scoring process, instructions, training, scoring exemplars, etc. From our perspective, however, the most critical issue has to do with the specification of measurement intent. If sufficient effort is not put into task analysis (in particular, clarifying the measurement intents of each task), performance records cannot be made adequate and meaningful scoring cannot be achieved. Only after task analysis has resulted in useful performance records can the scoring process be improved. Once this stage is reached, the results of task analyses are still critical. They must form the basis for training, for formulating instructions, for organization of the process, and must undergird the construction of scoring exemplars.

The process of establishing the validity of extended assessment tasks is crucial to the success of any modern assessment program. In the current circumstance of rapid movement to new models of assessment, which themselves are motivated almost solely by the prospect of significant enhancement of validity, this must be our primary task.

REFERENCES

Baker, E. L., O'Neil, H. F., & Linn, R. L. (1993). Policy and validity prospects for performance-based assessment. *American Psychologist, 48*, 1210–1218.

Haertel, E. H. (1992). *Issues of validity and reliability in assessment center exercises and portfolios.* (Report No. S-1). Stanford, CA: Stanford University School of Education, Teacher Assessment Project.

Haertel, E. H., & Wiley, D. E. (1993). Representations of ability structures: Implications for testing. In N. Frederiksen, R. J. Mislevy, & I. Bejar (Eds.), *Test Theory for a New Generation of Tests* (pp. 359–384). Hillsdale, NJ: Lawrence Erlbaum Associates.

Linn, R. L. (1991). *Technical considerations in the proposed nationwide assessment system for the National Educational Goals Panel.* Paper prepared for National Educational Goals Panel.

Messick, S. (1989). Validity. In R. Linn (Ed.), *Educational Measurement* (3rd ed., pp. 13–103). New York: American Council on Education/Macmillan.

Sternberg, R. J. (1977). *Intelligence, information processing and analogical reasoning: The componential analysis of human abilities.* Hillsdale, NJ: Lawrence Erlbaum Associates.

Thurstone, L. L. (1947). *Multiple factor analysis.* Chicago: University of Chicago Press.

Wiley, D. E. (1990). Test validity and invalidity reconsidered. In R. E. Snow & D. E. Wiley (Eds.), *Improving Inquiry in Social Science* (pp. 75–107). Hillsdale, NJ: Lawrence Erlbaum Associates. Also as *Studies of educative processes*, No. 20, Northwestern University, 1987.

Chapter 5

Linking Assessments

Robert L. Linn
University of Colorado at Boulder

Comparisons between the results obtained from one test or set of assessment tasks to those of another are often desired; and the comparisons themselves can take a variety of forms and serve substantially different purposes. The nature of the linking that is needed, the inferences that are justified, and the degree of precision that is required also vary with the uses that are to be made of the comparisons.

The following list of examples, while not comprehensive, illustrates the variety of situations for which comparisons might be desired. The types of linking appropriate for each situation appear in parentheses.

• Different versions of a college admissions test are administered on different dates, but the scores from the various versions are treated interchangeably. (equating)

• New versions of a state test used to certify high school graduates are introduced each year. There is a desire to assure that the requirements in one year are equivalent to those of previous years. (equating)

• A short form of a longer test is administered and the results are used to estimate the scores that individual students would obtain on the longer form of the test. (calibration)

• Scores on different, grade-appropriate forms of a test administered in grades 3 and 5 are compared to assess student growth on a scale common to both forms. (calibration, also referred to as vertical equating)

• A state assessment identifies the percentage of students whose performance is in one of four categories (from *needs remediation* to *outstanding*), according to preestablished performance criteria. The state would like to compare the percentage of its students who are placed in each of the four categories to the corresponding percentages for the nation as a whole. (calibration)

• State results from the administration of the National Assessment of Educational Progress (NAEP) are obtained at Grades 4 and 8 in mathematics as part of the Trial State Assessment in 1992. The state wants to compare the percentage of students exceeding the three NAEP achievement levels (basic, proficient, and advanced) at Grades 4 and 8 to those scoring above selected points on the state's own assessment in subsequent years. (equating, calibration, or prediction, depending upon the similarity between NAEP and the state assessment)

• A state wants to express scores obtained by individual students on the state's mandated assessment in terms of the NAEP achievement levels. (equating, calibration, or prediction, again depending upon the similarity between the two assessments)

• The National Education Goals Panel wants to compare the performance of U.S. students to the performance of students in other countries by linking NAEP results to the results of international assessments. (calibration or prediction, depending upon the similarity between the NAEP and the international assessment)

• An assessment system consists of extended-response questions scored locally by teachers and a standardized test with objectively-scored questions (e.g., multiple-choice or short-answer questions that are scored right or wrong) administered to all students under controlled conditions. The standardized test is used to adjust for between-school differences in the teacher-assigned scores on the extended-response questions. (statistical moderation)

• Achievement tests are offered in a variety of subject areas. Students may elect to take the tests in any of three areas. Student scores obtained from different combinations of tests are compared during the college admissions process, or for the award of honors. (statistical moderation or scaling)

• Student performance on an achievement test administered in one grade is used to predict level of achievement in the following year. (prediction)

• A group of states develops a series of performance-based assessments that use portfolios of work, projects, and on-demand performances. States, districts, and individual schools and teachers have considerable latitude in the choice of the specific tasks included in the assessment. Scoring heavily relies on the professional judgments of teachers and on a system of spot checks and verification. Nonetheless, it is expected that the performance of individual students, schools, school districts, and states will be compared to a single set of national standards. (social moderation)

Other examples could be listed, but these suffice to illustrate most of the range of applications of linking. Some of the examples involve the comparisons of one student with another or of individual students to a fixed standard, while others involve the comparison of distributions. Some comparisons may be used as the basis for important decisions about individuals or institutions, whereas others are primarily descriptive. Such distinctions have important implications for the degree of precision required of a comparison and for the technical design of an assessment system.

STRONG AND WEAK FORMS OF STATISTICAL LINKING

The word *linking* is a generic term. It covers a variety of approaches (e.g., anchoring, benchmarking, calibration, equating, prediction, projection, scaling, statistical moderation, social moderation, verification) that attempt to make results of one assessment comparable to those of another. Some terms have well established technical meanings and associated technical requirements, but others do not. In the remaining sections of this chapter, we will clarify the terminology and show the correspondence between the approaches identified and the demands for accountability illustrated earlier.

Mislevy (1992) characterized three levels of correspondence among tests that are in current use by testing companies (see also Beaton, 1992; Linn, 1993): *equating, calibration,* and *projection.* Equating is the strongest form of linking and has the most stringent technical requirements; projection is the weakest of the three categories. The Mislevy categorization and description of requirements for the three levels is consistent with the best current technology and thinking on statistical approaches to linking.

Two additional categories of linking discussed by Linn (1993) and by Mislevy (1992) also deserve consideration. *Statistical moderation* has been used in some other countries (notably Australia) to improve the comparability of scores assigned to examination results by different teachers. It employs a more controlled, external examination to improve the comparability of locally scored examinations. Statistical moderation also has been used as a means of improving the comparability of scores obtained on tests in different subject areas.

The former purpose is closely aligned with the goal of procedures used to scale College Board Achievement Tests, though no claim is made that achievement tests in different subject areas are equivalent. Because the procedures are different, however, we will refer to the linking of College Board Achievement Tests as *scaling.* In addition to these statistical approaches, there are approaches that are primarily judgmental in nature and rely only secondarily on statistical analyses. There also are hybrid approaches that use a combination of statistical and judgmental procedures.

First the major statistical approaches are discussed, using the Mislevy terminology for the first two categories (equating and calibration), but substituting the possibly more familiar term *prediction* for the condition they refer to as *projection*. Because the strength of comparisons that rely on statistical moderation or scaling fall somewhere between calibration and prediction, they will be considered before prediction is discussed. Then other approaches that are primarily judgmental in nature are considered.

Equating

Equating is the best understood and most demanding type of link of one test to another. If two tests (or other types of assessments) satisfy the assumptions of equating, then the results can be used for any of the illustrative comparisons listed earlier. Equated scores can be used interchangeably. Any use or interpretation that is justified for scores on Test X also is justified for the equated scores on Test Y.

Lord (1980) noted that, for a linking to be considered equitable, the choice of a particular version or form of a test must be a matter of indifference to all concerned. The 1985 *Standards for Educational and Psychological Testing*, adopted by the American Educational Research Association, the American Psychological Association, and the National Council on Measurement in Education, acknowledges that the form of a test should be a matter of indifference as a goal of equating. The *Standards* (AERA, APA, NCME, 1985) also noted, however, that this goal can only be approximated in practice.

> Ideally, alternate forms of a test should be interchangeable. That is, it should be a matter of indifference to anyone taking the test or anyone using the results whether Form A or Form B of the test was used. Of course, such an ideal cannot be attained fully in practice. Even minor variations in content from one form to the next can prevent the forms from being interchangeable, since one form may favor individuals with particular strengths, whereas a second form may favor those with slightly different strengths. (p. 31)

Despite these caveats, the ideal of equating can be adequately approximated if care is taken in the design of alternate forms to assure that they are as similar as possible in terms of content coverage, administration conditions, numbers and types of items or tasks, and the types of cognitive demands that are placed on students. It is likely to be more difficult to approach the goal of equating with assessments consisting of a relatively small number of tasks than with tests involving a relatively large number of tasks, because the relative weight of each task increases as the number of tasks decreases.

Procedures that help evaluate the adequacy of an equating are available. Judgments about the comparability of content coverage and the types of tasks required on two assessments may be supplemented by a variety of statistical comparisons. For example, strict equating requires that the forms be equally reliable and that they have the same relationships with other measures (e.g., another test, grade-point average). The correspondence between equated scores needs to be symmetrical. That is, the single table or correspondence can be used to go from scores on Test X to those on Test Y and vice versa. In addition, the equating should not depend on the group of students used to compute the equating function. Except for sampling error, the equating function should be the same for any subgroup of students (e.g., boys and girls, racial and ethnic minorities, region of the country, program of instruction). Finally, an equating should not be time dependent—it should not matter whether the equating is based on data obtained in 1990, or data obtained in 1995.

A number of designs and techniques for analyzing data are used to equate tests. A discussion of specific designs is beyond the scope of this chapter. See Angoff (1984), Petersen, Kolen, and Hoover (1989), and Skaggs and Lissitz (1990), and references in those articles for detailed discussions of these issues. However, we do need to mention one type—anchor test design—because *anchoring* has been used to describe a type of linking.

Anchoring

Anchor test equating of Forms X and Y involves the administration of what is called an anchor test, U, together with Form X to one group of students and U together with Form Y to another sample of students. The anchor test can increase the precision of the equating and be used to adjust for differences in the proficiency of the samples of students taking Forms X and Y. How well an anchor test works depends on the relationship of the anchor to the two forms to be equated. Ideally, the anchor should have a strong and equivalent relationship to both X and Y. If the anchor test has a stronger relationship to one form, the two forms cannot strictly be equated. This point will be considered below in discussing the use of an anchor to link assessments that differ substantially in their characteristics and in what they are attempting to measure.

Calibration

The third example in the introduction referred to the comparison of scores on a short, generally less reliable, form of a test to those on a long form. Although one might wish that two such forms could be equated, it can readily be demonstrated that the standard of indifference cannot be achieved in this situation. This is not simply a limitation of classical test theory or of traditional notions of reliability that depend upon an *individual differences* conception of measurement. The conclusion applies equally well to criterion-referenced conceptions of measurement that compare each individual's performance to a fixed standard, without any regard to how others perform. This is illustrated by the following example:

> A basketball league wishes to award certificates to the player who can make 75% of his or her attempted free throws. Players are "tested" with either a "short form"—4 attempts—or a "long form"—20 attempts. Player 1 is a consistent 60% free throw shooter; Player 2 is a consistent 90% shooter. Assuming that each attempt in a free throw test is independent of every other attempt, the probabilities of getting certified using the short test are .48 for Player 1 and .95 for Player 2. The probabilities for the long test are .10 for Player 1 and .99 for Player 2. Clearly, the choice of test form is not a matter of indifference to the two players. Player 1 has a much better chance of being certified with the short test, whereas Player 2 has a somewhat better chance of being certified if the long test is used. For a player whose level of proficiency is below the standard, the chances of passing due to a lucky streak are much better with 4 attempts rather than 20.

Although the example demonstrates that the short and long tests cannot be equated, they can be calibrated in ways that support some useful comparisons, for calibration provides a means of comparing scores on tests that satisfy somewhat less stringent requirements than those for equated tests. As was noted by Mislevy (1992), calibration still assumes that two tests measure the same thing but they may be designed to assess performance at different levels (e.g., a reading test designed for third-grade students and one designed for fifth-grade students) or with different degrees of reliability (e.g., short and long forms of a test). Calibration of tests designed to measure performance at different developmental levels is frequently referred to as *vertical equating*. Calibration is a better description of this type of linking, however, because tests designed for different developmental levels generally will not satisfy the requirements for a true equating.

A proper calibration will give the right answer to some questions, but not others. For example, Mislevy (1992) noted that when Tests X and Y are not equally reliable, a calibration that transforms Y-scores to the X scale can be constructed to give the right answer to the question, "For what X-value is this person's score most likely?" However, the correct transformation for the above question will " . . . in general, give wrong answers to other questions—especially about characteristics of the distribution of proficiencies in groups (e.g., What proportion of the students in this population are above 300 on the X-scale?)" (p. 3).

A different calibration could be devised to support the right inference for the latter question, but that calibration would not simultaneously give the answer to the former question. If, as in the fifth example in the introduction, the goal is comparison of the percentage of students in a state who exceed certain levels of performance to the national percentage of students who exceed the same levels, then the calibration procedures need to be designed to match that particular purpose. Achieving the purpose of the fifth example will not at the same time achieve the goal of the seventh example, which requires that the performance of individual students be expressed in terms of the NAEP achievement levels.

It should be stressed that a calibration that achieved either the goal of the fifth example or that of the seventh example is possible only if the state assessment and the national assessment to which it is to be calibrated measure essentially the same thing. It is important that the two assessments be well matched for (a) the content coverage, (b) the cognitive demands placed on students, and (c) the conditions under which the assessments are administered.

The importance of matching content coverage is underscored by recent research on *customized tests*. Customized tests were introduced in the 1980s, by several test publishers in an effort to meet expanded demands for tests serving different purposes, without increasing the overall testing burden. There are a number of variations on customized testing, but generally it involves the modification of a norm-referenced achievement test (NRT) to meet state or district specifications. The modification might mean (a) adding some locally constructed items to an NRT; (b) substituting locally constructed items for some of the NRT items; or (c) substituting an entire locally constructed test for an NRT, combined with the use of equating or calibration to report scores in terms of the NRT metric.

Research on customized tests has shown that the validity of normative interpretations of customized tests depends heavily on the degree to which the content of the customized test and the NRT match. Disproportionate representation of content areas, the addition of content not found on the NRT, or the elimination of some of the NRT content can distort the normative comparisons. See, for example, Linn and Hambleton (1991) and Yen, Green, and Burket (1987).

Statistical Moderation

Statistical moderation is a term less familiar in the United States than in some other countries. As Wilson (1992) noted, the term statistical moderation has been used to describe two different situations in which comparison of results obtained from different sources is desired. In one common situation, statistical moderation means the use of an external examination to adjust teacher-assigned grades. The process used in some countries to adjust scores on examinations in different subject areas or to compute a total score for students taking examinations in different subjects also is referred to as statistical moderation. See, for example, Keeves (1988).

The use of an external examination to statistically moderate locally assigned scores is conceptually straightforward. If moderation takes place at the school level, the locally assigned scores at each school are simply transformed so that the mean and standard deviation of the transformed scores is equal to the school means and standard deviations on the external examination (McGaw, 1977; Wilson, 1992). This type of statistical moderation does not change the relative standing of individual students within a school on the locally assigned scores. It does, however, change the between-school results on the locally assigned scores. All the locally assigned scores at School A might be increased, for example, while all those at School B might be decreased. Students with the highest scores in School B before statistical moderation would still have the highest within-school scores after moderation. However, their standing in comparison to students from School A would be better before than after moderation.

The external examination in the above example serves as an anchor test. Locally defined tests and locally assigned scores would be adjusted to match the within-school average and spread of performance on the anchor test. The utility of such an approach depends heavily upon the relevance of the anchor test and its comparability to the locally defined tests. If the anchor test and the locally defined tests measure different types of achievement and if the locally defined tests differ from one another, then this type of statistical moderation is problematic. Paradoxically, if the locally defined tests were equivalent to each other and to the external anchor test, there would be no need for anything other than the external test.

The second type of statistical moderation is used for comparisons among students who take different combinations of achievement tests. It adjusts scores for differences in means and standard deviations of students taking different tests, resulting in scores on an apparently common metric, even though Student A may have taken examinations in mathematics, physics, and English, while Student B took examinations in history, political science, and English.

Clearly, the inferences that are justified for equated scores or even for calibrated scores cannot be justified simply because the scores are reported on a common metric and adjustments have been made using statistical moderation. The particular set of achievement tests to be taken obviously does matter to the above two hypothetical students. Preparation for the history test by Student B is unlikely to be very helpful if the student is suddenly told that he or she will have to take the mathematics test. In other words, although comparisons are made between students based on their statistically moderated scores on different combinations of tests, the scores cannot be considered equivalent in any rigorous sense.

Scaling

The more familiar counterpart to the latter form of statistical moderation is the procedure used to scale College Board Achievement Tests. Because students choose the particular Achievement Tests they take, it cannot be assumed that the subpopulation taking one achievement test is equivalent to that taking another. Consequently, the differences in average scores on two achievement tests may be due to (a) the relative difficulty of the tests, (b) unequal levels or academic preparation of the groups taking the tests, or (c) some combination of the two.

One indication that at least part of the variation in average performance on different Achievement Tests may in fact be due to academic preparation is that groups vary greatly in their average scores on the Verbal and Mathematical sections of the Scholastic Aptitude Test (SAT). Donlon and Livingston (1984), for example, reported mean SAT verbal scores ranging from 495 for students taking the Level I Mathematics Achievement Test, to 565 for students taking the European History and World Culture Achievement Test. Means on SAT mathematics scores had an even wider range, from 521 for students taking the Literature Achievement Test, to 652 for students taking the Level II Mathematics Achievement Test.

The SAT scores are used to adjust Achievement Test score scales, and the details of this adjustment are provided by Donlon and Livingston (1984). The effect of the scaling is higher average scale scores on Achievement Tests taken by students with higher average SAT scores than on Achievement Tests taken by students with lower average SAT scores.

No claim is made that the scaled scores on different Achievement Tests are equivalent, nor would such a claim be justified. This is evident from the following concluding comments by Donlon and Livingston (1984), regarding the Achievement Test scaling:

> Although the Achievement Test scaling procedure attempts to make scores comparable across subject areas, the comparability is not perfect. The main problem is that scores on the different Achievement Tests do not correlate equally with the SAT. When an Achievement Test is scaled, the mean score of students taking the test is assigned a scale value that depends on correlation of the students' Achievement Test scores with their SAT scores. The higher the correlation of the Achievement Test scores with the SAT verbal scores, the closer the scale value of the mean Achievement Test score will be to the students' mean SAT verbal score, and similarly for the SAT mathematical score. (p. 23)

Prediction

Prediction is the weakest of the five statistical forms that link results on one test or set of assessment tasks to another. Predictions can be made as long as there is some relationship between the performance on one assessment and the performance on another. The precision of the prediction will depend on the strength of that relationship; and just as important, the predictions are context and group dependent.

Mislevy and Stocking (1992) illustrated the group-dependent nature of predictions using the example of multiple-choice and essay sections of Advanced Placement (AP) Examinations. As they noted, there is an interaction between the relationship of the two sections and gender: the essay performance that would be predicted from scores on the multiple-choice section is different for boys than for girls. Ignoring gender, a boy and a girl with the same predicted score on the multiple-choice section would have the same predicted score on the essay section. If gender is considered in the prediction, however, a girl with a given score on the multiple-choice section would have a higher predicted score on the essay section than a boy with an identical multiple-choice score.

The fact that predictions are context and group dependent raises serious equity questions, particularly if scores from different assessments are to be used to make important decisions about individuals. If students in State A, for example, were administered only the multiple-choice section of an AP exam, while students in State B were administered only the essay section, the best prediction might require that the scores of boys from State A be adjusted downward relative to those of girls and that the reverse adjustment be made for scores from State B. Would boys from State A or girls from State B, however, consider it fair that they did not receive advanced placement credit for the same level of performance as a student from the opposite gender from their state who did receive credit? Ignoring the interaction with gender in making predictions, on the other hand, would give a handicap to girls in State A relative to their counterparts in State B, whereas the converse would be true for boys in the two states.

Another set of issues is introduced when one is describing group characteristics, rather than comparing the performance of individual students. The percentage of students who would perform above some specified level on, say, NAEP can be predicted from the performance of students on a state assessment, if the necessary data are collected. As Mislevy and Stocking (1992) noted, however, the techniques for making such predictions " . . . are complex, unfamiliar, and, perhaps most importantly, context-bound" (p. 6). That is, the predictions will depend on (a) the groups for which statistics are computed, (b) the specific demographic and educational variables taken into account in the prediction, and (c) the time at which the data are collected.

The potential importance of the time-dependent nature of predictions may be illustrated by considering the sixth example in the introduction, which described a state that wanted to link its assessment results to NAEP in 1992, and use that linkage in the interpretation of state assessment results in subsequent years. That type of use might be well justified if the state assessment and NAEP satisfied the requirements for an equating. However, if the state assessment emphasizes different content or poses tasks that require students to use different skill than those assessed by NAEP, then predictions that are justified in 1992 might not be justified in subsequent years. For example, increases in student performance in content areas that are well measured by the state assessment, but largely ignored by NAEP, could produce greatly inflated estimates of the percentage of students who exceed the NAEP achievement levels. These comments also apply to the eighth example in the introduction, which involves comparison of national and international assessment results.

Of course, it does not follow that because predictions might change with time that they necessarily will change. The fact that they might change, however, does suggest that procedures need to be implemented that allow for ongoing evaluation of the appropriateness of predictions over time or from one context to another. There are procedures for evaluating the continued appropriateness of predictions, but they require new data collection and therefore continued expense. Unfortunately, such efforts are necessary in order to adequately support inferences about student performance on an assessment such as NAEP, based on predictions from a state assessment that is designed to measure different skills or student achievement in somewhat different content areas.

JUDGMENTAL APPROACHES TO LINKING

The preceeding discussion focused on statistical approaches to linking one assessment with another. The following consideration of approaches relies primarily on judgment and only secondarily on statistical considerations.

Recently in this country judgmental scoring procedures have been used most widely in the area of writing. The introduction of performance-based assessments in other content areas has led to an increasing need for the use of judgmental scoring procedures in those areas as well. In a number of other countries, judgmental scoring and other open-ended exercises are the norm; and in some countries there are relatively well-developed systems for auditing and verifying scoring.

In principle, there is nothing to prevent the treatment of scores provided by expert judges as the data for any of the statistical approaches to the kind of linking discussed earlier. In practice, however, tasks that require judgmental scoring typically involve more extended answers and substantially more response time than do multiple-choice or short-answer, open-ended questions for which a single right answer is expected. Consequently, fewer extended-answer tasks can be administered, which in turn reduces the likelihood that one small set of tasks will be interchangeable with another in the sense required for a statistical equating. The unique features of each task, then, become relatively more important as the number of tasks is reduced.

The Question of Choice

Some assessment systems currently under development include, in addition to on-demand performances that might be completed in a single sitting or over the course of 2 or 3 days, projects that may require a week or more to complete, or portfolios of student work that may be collected over the period of a year or more. Another distinguishing feature of some of these assessment systems is that students may be allowed to choose among a number of tasks. Choice of task raises a number of questions about comparability that generally have not been the concern of people who have worked on the statistical equating and calibration issues encountered with traditional standardized tests. However, it is one of the issues that statistical moderation techniques have attempted to address.

Even if all students are required to respond to the same task (e.g., essay prompt or open-ended mathematics problem), the first question usually raised about judgmental scores is the comparability of scores assigned by different judges. Choice among tasks just exacerbates the problem of comparability of scores.

Social Moderation

Social moderation, also called *consensus moderation* (Bell, Burkhardt, & Swan, 1991), has been used most frequently for the review and coordination of teachers' ratings of student products. In one application, for example, teachers would rate the work of students in their own classes. Groups of teachers within the school would then meet to review the ratings assigned to a sample of papers by each teacher. After discussion, the ratings assigned by an individual teacher might be changed. The emphasis is on collegial support and movement toward consensus judgments.

Staff development is critical throughout this process. It is important that teachers develop a shared understanding of the criteria for rating before they actually do it for the first time. The criteria need to be illustrated by examples of student work. Example papers or other student products that exemplify the criteria of minimally acceptable, competent, outstanding, or other similar labels are often called *benchmarks* or *anchors*. Agreement that certain benchmarks or anchor products exemplify the criteria is a key part of the rating. Benchmark papers also may be interspersed with yet-to-be-rated papers to monitor the ratings assigned by individual raters during operational rating sessions.

In addition to training, social moderation might entail the independent rating of a sample of papers from an individual teacher's classroom by other teachers within the same school, or by teachers and expert raters from other schools. During such a meeting to assign independent ratings, differences in ratings would be discussed in an effort to achieve consensus.

A similar process could occur at the district level or for clusters of schools. A sample of papers from each cluster of schools would be brought to a central meeting place by team leaders representing each school. The panel of team leaders would then rate the sample of papers from all schools. Depending upon the size of the discrepancies of the centrally rated and locally rated papers, the original local ratings might be taken as assigned, or all the local ratings might be adjusted to account for the discrepancy. In either event, the team leaders would bring back the central scores to their schools so that they could be discussed and a broader consensus could be reached.

Verification, a process similar to the one just described, is used in Victoria, Australia (Victoria Curriculum & Assessment Board, 1991). Wilson (1992) provided a description of this process and some of the issues raised by its initial application in Victoria in 1991.

In the use of social moderation, the comparability of scores assigned substantially depends upon the development of a consensus among professionals. The process of verification of a sample of student papers or other products at successively higher levels in the system (e.g., school, district, state, and national) provides a means of broadening the consensus across the boundaries of individual classrooms or schools. It also serves as an audit that is likely to be an essential element in gaining public acceptance.

CONCLUSION

A variety of techniques are available for linking results of one assessment to those of another. A confusing array of terminology has come to be associated with those techniques and the terms are not always used consistently. In this chapter, we have tried to distinguish techniques in terms of their requirements for the assessments to be linked and the types of interpretations that can be made from them.

The degree to which students' scores on different assessments can be said to be comparable to one another or to a fixed standard depends fundamentally on (a) the similarity of the assessment tasks, (b) their cognitive demands, and (c) the conditions of administration. Strong inferences that assume the interchangeability of scores demand high degrees of similarity. Scores can be made comparable in a particular sense for assessments that are less similar. However, procedures that make scores comparable in one sense (e.g., the most likely score for a student on a second assessment) will not simultaneously make the scores comparable in another sense (e.g., the proportion of students that exceed a fixed standard). Weaker forms of linkage are likely to be context, group, and time dependent, which suggests the need for continued monitoring of the comparability of scores.

Although most of this chapter has been devoted to distinctions among statistical approaches to linking assessments, it should be noted that there is a growing interest in the use of social moderation. This interest has been stimulated by the increased reliance on performance-based problems that require extended student responses and that must be scored by professional judgment.

REFERENCES

American Educational Research Association, American Psychological Association, and the National Council of Measurement on Education. (1985). *Standards for educational and psychological testing*. Washington, DC: American Psychological Association.

Angoff, W. H. (1984). *Scales, norms, and equivalent scores*. Princeton, NJ: Educational Testing Service.

Beaton, A. E. (1992). *Considerations for national examinations*. A Policy Issue Perspective. Princeton, NJ: Educational Testing Service, Policy Information Center.

Bell, A., Burkhardt, H., & Swan, M. (1991). *Balanced assessment and the mathematics curriculum*. Nottingham, England: Shell Centre for Mathematical Education.

Donlon, T. F., & Livingston, S. A. (1984). Psychometric methods used in the Admissions Testing Program. In T. F. Donlon (Ed.), *The College Board Technical Handbook for the Scholastic Aptitude Test and Achievement Tests* (pp. 13–36). New York: College Entrance Examination Board.

Keeves, J. (1988). Scaling achievement test scores. In T. Husen & T. N. Postlethwaite (Eds.), *International Encyclopedia of Education*. Oxford: Pergamon Press.

Linn, R. L. (1993). Linking results of distinct assessments. *Applied Measurement in Education, 6*, 83–102.

Linn, R. L., & Hambleton, R. K. (1991). Customized tests and customized norms. *Applied Measurement in Education, 4*, 185–207.

Lord, F. M. (1980). *Application of item response theory to practical testing problems*. Hillsdale, NJ: Lawrence Erlbaum Associates.

McGaw, B. (1977). The use of rescaled teacher assessments in the admission of students to tertiary study. *Australian Journal of Education, 21*(3), 209–225.

Mislevy, R. M. (1992). *Linking educational assessments: Concepts, issues, methods, and prospects*. Princeton, NJ: Educational Testing Service, Policy Information Center.

Mislevy, R. M., & Stocking, M. S. (1992, March 11). Memorandum for the Record, Subject: Calibration. Internal ETS memorandum. Princeton, NJ: Educational Testing Service (cited with permission).

Petersen, N. S., Kolen, M. J., & Hoover, H. D. (1989). Scaling, norming, and equating. In R. L. Linn (Ed.), *Educational Measurement* (3rd ed., pp. 221–262). New York: Macmillan.

Skaggs, G. & Lissitz, R. W. (1990). Equating NAEP with state, local, commercial, or international assessments. Paper prepared for the National Assessment Governing Board (NAGB), Washington, DC.

Victorian Curriculum and Assessment Board. (1991). *VCE verification manual, 1991 mathematics.* Carlton, Australia: Author.

Wilson, M. (1992, February). *The integration of school-based assessments into a state-wide assessment system: Historical perspectives and contemporary issues.* Unpublished manuscript, University of California, Berkeley.

Yen, W. M., Green, D. R., & Burket, G. R. (1987). Valid normative information from customized achievement tests. *Educational Measurement: Issues and Practice, 6,* 7–13.

Chapter 6

Performance Assessment: Examining the Costs

Roy Hardy
Educational Testing Service

Do the costs for performance assessment really matter? Proponents of performance assessment have not argued that modes of assessment should be adopted primarily as a way to decrease costs. To the contrary, even the strongest advocates of performance assessment concede that the financial resources required to implement a program of this kind are likely to be significantly greater than the current expenditures for paper-and-pencil, multiple-choice (M-C) tests. Estimates of the increase in costs are, in fact, wide-ranging: Maryland estimates that the inclusion of performance tasks in their statewide assessment costs about four times as much as using paper-and-pencil tests, alone (Jordan, 1992); other estimates range from 5 to 10 times the cost of paper-and-pencil tests for performance-based assessments (Fremer, 1990; Carlson, 1991). If the value of performance testing does not reside in the likelihood of reduced costs, why then examine the costs at all?

The answer to that question is reflected in a 1991 survey of state directors of student assessment programs, which cites cost as the number one concern of the group surveyed (Aschbacher, 1991). Directors, like those within the group, must provide realistic estimates of costs for their divisions and for state legislators, who must in turn allocate funds for new testing programs.

The resources to develop and implement performance-based assessments may come from any number of sources: local school budgets, state testing program allocations, federal program funds, or private foundation grants. In every instance, however, the allocation of resources will have to compete with other worthy causes, such as reduced class sizes, programs compete with other worthy causes, such as reduced class sizes, programs for special populations, or additional computers for the classroom. Those who must make these allocation decisions will want to know not only the benefits to be gained from performance assessments, but the costs of such a program.

THE UNCERTAINTY OF COST ESTIMATES

Much of the cost of performance assessment is either unknown or disguised. To a certain extent, cost is unknown because of our limited experience with the development and implementation of the programs themselves. Cost may be hidden or disguised because proponents of the programs often work from within existing programs, without specific staff assigned and without specific budgets allocated (Pelavin Associates, Inc., 1991). This is especially true in the early stages of development. While the zeal of these pioneers is admirable, their mode of operation makes it difficult to obtain reasonable estimates of real cost. The evaluator of one state program reported that he was instructed not to track or analyze costs for a statewide portfolio project. In explanation, the program administrator told the evaluator, "I really don't want to know the costs at this point in the game" (p. 1–17).

This chapter examines the costs for large-scale performance assessment. At best, only estimates and rather broad ranges for the various costs can be provided. Nevertheless, in the belief that even limited information can improve decision making, the authors have (a) analyzed proposals for development, (b) reviewed experiences in tasks similar to those required by performance assessment, and (c) talked to those most directly involved in performance-assessment programs to obtain at least an educated guess as to the likely costs of development and implementation of performance assessment in the context of large-scale student testing programs.

ELEMENTS OF COSTS

The costs for performance assessment can be segmented into three categories: development, administration, and scoring costs. *Development costs* include those creative and quality control tasks that lead to an assessment exercise that is ready for large-scale use and interpretation. These tasks might include identification and specification of the learning and assessment objectives; exercise writing; editing, review, and other quality control procedures; pretesting, and then developing guidelines for scoring and interpretation. This phase might also include norming, but few proponents suggest that norming is appropriate.

Administration costs include the costs for any materials required to administer an assessment to students, as well as the costs for any special training for teachers, proctors, or others involved in the administration of assessment tasks. While in theory the cost of test administrator time should also be included here, with the exception of the National Assessment of Educational Progress (NAEP) virtually all performance assessments being planned for school-age students will use teachers or other school personnel without providing additional compensation. Therefore, no attempt has been made to place a dollar value on this staff cost.

Scoring costs include costs for training teachers or other professionals to assign numerical scores, narrative comments, or other forms of evaluation to student responses to assessment tasks. Costs in this area are significant because most forms of performance-assessment tasks require some form of scoring by people rather than by machine.

All three types of costs can be highly variable, depending on the nature of the assessment task, the work produced, and the amount of information and interpretation required from individual responses. For example, a 20-minute essay scored holistically will be much less costly to score than a writing portfolio of six to eight pieces scored to provide diagnostic feedback to the teacher and the writer. Therefore, in describing costs, we must also describe the unit for which the costs are estimated.

COSTS FOR DEVELOPMENT

If performance assessment were not so new, many users would not have to concern themselves with development cost, except as those costs are reflected in the price of commercial products. This is, for example, the case with norm-referenced tests (NRTs). Most user school districts do not worry about the development cost of NRTs, though they pay a portion of these costs in their purchase price. Because performance assessment is a relatively new concept, there are few commercial products for sale in this domain. Therefore, those who wish to implement performance assessment in the near future must consider their direct investment in the development of such assessments.

Development costs are easily hidden or disguised when an administrative unit uses current staff for this development. A better picture of expected costs for development is obtained in those instances when a state has contracted with an external agency for development. Even in such an instance, price may be a poor estimate of costs because contractors may choose to invest in these early programs to gain experience in performance assessment, or they may simply estimate costs poorly because they lack direct experience with this type of assessment.

One of the most highly publicized state movements toward performance assessment has been initiated in Kentucky. The Kentucky Request for

Proposal (RFP) called for the development of a totally performance-based assessment system to be developed for statewide use in selected grade levels and subject areas. A contract for this development was awarded to Advanced Systems, Inc. in July 1991 (Jennings, 1991). Separate analyses of the costs included in that chosen proposal and others received in response to the RFP were provided by Kentucky Department of Education (DOE) staff and by a committee of external consultants to Kentucky DOE (The Assessment Team Consultants, 1991; Kentucky Department of Education, 1991). Those analyses provide insight as to the estimated cost of development for performance tasks on a large scale.

Two tasks in the Kentucky RFP call for development of performance-assessment exercises. Task 3 is the development of scrimmage events that are less secure, pretested in state, and designed for use by schools in grade levels other than Grades 4, 8, and 12. Task 4 calls for the development of secure tasks, pretested outside the state, and designed for statewide administration at Grades 4, 8, and 12. The Advanced Systems proposal commits to the development of at least 35 exercises in the first year under Task 3 at a cost of $193,843 or about $5,500 per exercise. For Task 4, Advanced Systems promises the development of some 602 tasks over 5 years at a cost of $3,789,150, or about $6,294 per task. For a number of reasons, these are probably exaggerations of Advanced Systems' actual estimates. In each instance, some other activities are included in the description of work for each task. Also, the 5-year costs include some estimate of inflation.

These costs are projected across a variety of performance task formats, grade levels, and subject areas. Surely, some will be more complex and, therefore, more costly than others. The two sample exercises included with the proposal suggest activities designed for either individual or small-group administration in 30 to 60 minutes.

How do these costs compare to costs for multiple-choice (M-C) tests? One recent contract for a state testing program had costs ranging from $90 to $100 per item for writing, editing and preparation for field testing. If we assume about 50 M-C items per hour of testing, development costs amount to about $4,500–$5,000 per hour of testing time. Given that the cost estimates for both performance tasks and for M-C tests have considerable wobble, we can best conclude that development costs for performance tasks may be slightly greater, per student hour, than M-C tests, but the difference is not overwhelming.

Perhaps the more significant development cost is in terms of time. Development of performance-assessment tasks will typically require at least one school year and perhaps several years for field testing and refinement. This development time, along with development costs, represents a formidable impediment to implementation for many school administrative units.

Costs for Administration

Costs for test administration break out into two major categories: materials and staff training. If performance assessment is limited to paper-and-pencil activities, the cost of materials is minimized. However, cost constraints can severely limit the domain of content and skills measured in disciplines such as science, social studies, and even mathematics, whenever manipulatives are commonly used in instruction.

If programs permit the inclusion of performance tasks that use materials other than paper and pencil, the cost of materials must be considered. The expense of laboratory equipment, globes, calculators, and geometric solids can escalate quickly when an assessment is being planned for large-scale administration. In virtually all cases, program decision makers will have to limit both the number of tasks requiring such materials and the individual cost per exercise. What, then, are reasonable expectations for these costs?

In 1991, the Educational Testing Service (ETS) developed four prototype assessments in elementary science (*ETS Developments*, 1992; Hardy, 1992) for the state of Georgia. The most expensive prototype was an exercise requiring students to test and then identify six mineral samples. The assessment materials included the six samples (each labeled with a number), a small magnifier, a nail, a 2-inch square of glass, and a 2-inch square of ceramic tile. The materials were boxed together to form the assessment kit. A scientific supply house assembled the kits at a cost of $9 each.

Costs were considered in the selection of minerals (limestone is a lot cheaper than gold!), and at least one common test to identify minerals was excluded from the performance task due to expensive supplies.

The least expensive of the four prototypes developed by ETS for Georgia costs about 70 cents per assessment kit, and includes the design of a shipping carton to hold bars of soap. The materials consist of a block of wood the size of a bar of soap and a 6-inch plastic ruler. The two other exercises developed for this project cost between $1 and $4 per kit.

At $9 per student for materials alone, the cost for testing individually the 60,000 sixth-grade students in Georgia on a single 1-hour task measuring a limited area of content is clearly prohibitive. States faced with this dilemma have discussed a number of approaches to reducing the per-pupil costs, while at the same time including at least some materials-based performance tasks.

One such solution is to test only a sample of students. Although this approach can provide an accurate assessment of performance levels for a state at a fraction of the cost, it does preclude instructional feedback to individual teachers and students. Also, Aschbacher (1991) noted that policymakers at the state level often do not trust the results unless every student is tested. Aschbacher explained that, in at least one state, the sampling of students for performance assessment " . . . led teachers and administrators to think of performance-based activities as enrichment, not as mainstream assessment and instruction" (p. 8).

Another approach to controlling materials costs may be to test collaborative groups, rather than individual students. The Georgia prototypes were developed for administration to groups of two to four students at considerable savings in costs per classroom. However, collaborative group testing does limit the ability to assess the skills of individual students.

Some states have considered plans that call for a limited number of assessment kits that are then moved from classroom to classroom for the assessment. Although this approach reduces materials costs, it greatly increases staff time (i.e., cost) required to work out the logistics of this sharing.

Costs can also be prorated, if performance tasks are administered over multiple years. The science assessment in New York State used the same tasks for fourth graders for 3 consecutive years. This approach, however, can lead to teachers coaching students for the specific assessment tasks (Maeroff, 1991).

As performance assessment gains greater use in large-scale assessment, creative people will undoubtedly find ways of offering authentic tasks at lower costs. One such approach might be to define a set of equipment that should be available in every classroom at a particular grade level for instructional purposes, and then to design assessment tasks that utilize that instructional equipment. As an example, a skill-based assessment might call for students to weigh an object using a bucket balance. Although the cost of a bucket balance is probably not justified if it is used only once for an assessment, it may very well be justified as an instructional tool to be used in a variety of lessons throughout the school year.

Perhaps one note of caution should be added about materials costs from the Georgia experience. The mineral identification task required a piece of glass for a scratch test to determine the hardness of a mineral sample. The scientific supply house originally suggested glass one-sixteenth of an inch thick. Teachers quickly countered that glass that thin would easily break, presenting an opportunity for student injury. Safety being more important than cost, ETS opted for a thicker glass with rounded edges.

Costs for Staff Training

The cost for training staff to administer performance assessment tasks is perhaps the most difficult to estimate. Most states feel that some direct training is needed, particularly when performance assessment is introduced for the first time. Because of the large numbers of teachers and other school personnel involved in the administration of the typical state assessment program, any direct training is likely to be expensive. Of course, the expense will depend on the population and geographical size of the state and the particular logistics of the training. Because a day of training for administering performance tasks should cost about the same as a day of training for all teachers for any other purpose, it is assumed most states and individual school districts will have past experiences upon which to base a cost estimate.

The most significant cost in training teachers and others to administer performance assessments is an opportunity cost. Without additional dollars or training days, most agencies will have to substitute training for assessment for training on some other worthwhile topic, such as classroom management, collaborative learning, or accommodations for students with disabilities. Proponents of performance assessment have justified this opportunity cost by structuring training for assessment to include a broader context of instructional methods and approaches. These advocates argue that the training necessary for assessment also prepares teachers for improved classroom instruction. The costs are justified, therefore, on the grounds of improved instruction rather than only as a necessity for the administration of new modes of assessment.

Costs for Scoring

Scoring is a category in which performance assessment costs exceed, by far, the costs of current practice. For M-C tests, scoring is an almost negligible cost. Even with elaborate quality control procedures, answer sheets are scanned and scored for pennies per student.

Though performance assessment is not synonymous with hand scoring (the open-ended mathematics problems being planned for the new Scholastic Assessment Test [SAT] offer a counter example), most performance assessment tasks require some level of analysis and interpretation by human readers. This results in a significant expense added to the costs of performance assessment.

The magnitude of the cost for scoring performance assessments can depend on both the nature of the response and the nature of the type of scores or performance descriptions to be generated from the responses. Some proposed performance tasks require an observer to be present during the student performance to make ratings of student procedures. The Georgia Kindergarten Assessment Program is an example of such an assessment. With tasks scored by an observer, the primary cost is the staff time of the observer. Of course, there will also be costs for training these observers and for transportation if they observe beyond their own school. The Georgia Kindergarten Assessment Program requires about 1 hour per student to administer and score. In this instance, teachers judge the information available through this mode of assessment to be sufficiently superior to more time-efficient methods to justify the required teacher time (Tyson, 1990).

The recent experience with performance assessment in England, however, suggests there are limits to what teachers will accept as a reasonable time allocation for performance assessment. In that country, more M-C testing is now being considered in the wake of an early implementation of performance assessment that teachers complained took more than 30 hours per student (Chira, 1992).

To provide greater objectivity and reliability in scoring, most large-scale assessment programs will rely heavily on performance-assessment tasks that produce some permanent scoreable record of performance. This scoreable record may be an actual work product, such as an essay, or some indirect record of activities, such as a lab report. These scoreable records are likely to be collected, then scored in large groups by raters trained specifically for the task. Such a process provides greater efficiency and reliability, but negates the potential value of teachers examining the work of their own students. Many states arrange a compromise—papers are centrally scored, but the raters are selected from among classroom teachers.

The length of a typical student response as well as the number and complexity of the judgments raters are asked to make can have an impact on scoring costs. For example, a 500-word essay will be more costly to score than a 100-word essay; a paper scored on six dimensions will take longer (and therefore be more expensive) than one given only one holistic score; a work product requiring the rater to judge the logic of a geometry proof will require longer than one requiring only that the rater judge if a student has correctly drawn an equilateral triangle.

Diagnostic feedback on the quality of individual responses is seen by advocates of performance assessment as one of the method's most promising benefits. For large-scale assessments, however, the costs for providing this level of detail in scoring is likely to be prohibitive.

Because direct writing assessment has been widely implemented for several years, we have considerable experience upon which to estimate the costs for scoring narrative compositions. Table 6.1 gives some examples of typical costs for scoring essay-type responses as an assessment of writing skills.

There is some, though more limited, experience with assessments scored for subject-area content (rather than for writing skill) in programs such as Advanced Placement and NAEP. These experiences allow us to estimate the amount of scoring time per response for performance assessment tasks when the parameters and response format of those assessments are similar to existent programs.

A recent internal study at ETS catalogued all open-ended assessments scored by that organization along with calculations of the amount of rater time per average response for each of those programs (Educational Testing Service, 1992). The data in Table 6.2 are abstracted from that report.

Table 6.2 suggests that the scoring for performance tasks other than direct writing is considerably more expensive than essay scoring; and that conclusion is confounded by a number of factors including the complexity and the number of judgments required of the scorer and additional costs associated with the use of response formats other than paper and pencil, such as audio and videotapes. A recent study for the Georgia Assessment Program (Hardy, 1992) found both the reliability and the costs of scoring

TABLE 6.1
Scoring Costs for Writing Assessment

Program	Description of Scoring	Cost Reported	Reference
Connecticut Assessment of Educational Progress	25 minute essay, scored twice, holistically	$1.13 per student	Baron, 1984
Research study for SAT	45 minute essay, scored once, holistically	$.54-$1.47 per student	Breland, Camp, Jones, Morris, & Rock, 1987
California Assessment Program	45 minute essay, scored twice	$5.00 per student	Hymes, 1991
College Board English Composition	20 minute essay, scored twice	Approx. $5.88 per student	U.S. Congress, Office of Technology Assessment, 1992

TABLE 6.2
Performance Assessment Scoring Costs

Cost per Student	Number of Programs
Essay Scoring Costs	
under $2	3
$2–$4	8
$4–$10	3
over $10	4
Other Performance Tasks Scoring Costs	
under $10	2
$10 - $20	3
over $20	2

performance tasks in science to be similar to those aspects of scoring writing assessments.

JUSTIFYING COSTS

By most estimates, the costs for administering performance tasks will be from 3 to 10 times greater than the costs of assessment by multiple-choice tests alone (Office of Technology Assessment, 1992), although some estimates are as high as 60 times the cost of M-C testing (Jordan, 1992). Yet many believe that the additional costs are a good investment. California Assessment Director Dale Carlson noted that 60% of the costs of performance assessment goes directly to teachers for their participation in scoring. He considers that money a worthy investment in staff development: "Teacher involvement brings you support, new ideas, and most of all, rejuvenation" (Hymes, 1991, p. 45). There is some evidence that the implementation of direct writing assessment has led to increases in student writing (Office of Technology Assessment, 1992) and a similar change in curriculum and mode of instruction is the goal of advocates of performance assessment in other subject areas. The substantial additional costs are not considered as an assessment cost only, but as an investment in the improvement of instruction and consequent student learning. Some argue that the alternative of continuing the current dependence on multiple-choice tests will ultimately be far more costly in terms of the constraints of that mode of assessment on school restructuring and on improved instruction for higher order thinking (Schulz, 1992).

FUTURE PROSPECTS FOR ASSESSMENT COSTS

As activity in the area of performance assessment continues to increase, there is reason to believe that costs per assessment unit will decrease. Costs may decrease as more performance assessment tasks are developed and models can thereby be adapted for multiple use. Furthermore, as developers gain efficiency through experience and research with various formats, costs will more than likely decrease.

Administration costs are likely to increase in the short term as agencies acquire materials for assessment and absorb the significant costs of the initial training of teachers and test coordinators. Administration costs should, however, decrease as an administrative unit gains experience with performance assessment.

Scoring will remain a major cost factor in the near term, but may benefit considerably in the longer term from significant research in computer-assisted scoring. Researchers at ETS, for example, are experimenting with the uses of artificial intelligence in scoring natural language responses and have developed prototypes for computer-assisted scoring of architectural drawings (Educational Testing Service, 1990). Certainly, the widespread use of computer-based instruction and adaptive testing will open many new possibilities for performance-based assessment.

REFERENCES

Aschbacher, P. R. (1991). *Alternative assessment: State activity, interest, and concerns* (CSE Tech. Rep. 322). Los Angeles: UCLA Center for Research on Evaluation, Standards, and Student Testing.

The Assessment Team Consultants. (1991, June 27). *Recommendations on proposals to implement an interim and full-scale assessment program for the Commonwealth of Kentucky*. Frankfort, KY: Kentucky Department of Education.

Baron, J. B. (1984, Spring). Writing assessment in Connecticut: A holistic eye toward identification and an analytic eye toward instruction. *Educational Measurement: Issues and Practice, 3,* 27, 28, 38.

Breland, H. M., Camp, R., Jones, R. J., Morris, M. M., & Rock, D. A. (1987). *Assessing writing skill* (Research Monograph No. 11). New York: College Entrance Examination Board.

Carlson, D. (1991). Paraphrased from Donald L. Hymes. *The Changing Face of Testing and Assessment.* Arlington, VA: American Association of School Administrators.

Chira, S. (1992, January 8). A national curriculum: Seeking fairness for all. *The New York Times,* pp. A-1, B-7.

Educational Testing Service. (1992, Summer). Exploring the feasibility and educational potential of performance-based testing. *ETS Developments.* Princeton, NJ: Author.

Educational Testing Service. (1990). Helping America raise educational standards for the 21st century. *Annual Report.* Princeton, NJ: Author.

Educational Testing Service. (1992). *Performance scoring: Expanding ETS's capabilities* (Final report of the Performance Scoring Planning Project). Princeton, NJ: Author.

Fremer, J. (1990, June). *What is so real about authentic assessment?* Paper presented at the Boulder Conference of State Test Directors, Boulder, CO.

Hardy, R. A. (1992, April). *Options for scoring performance assessment tasks.* Paper presented at the 1992 Annual Meeting of the National Council on Measurement in Education, San Francisco, CA.

Hymes, D. L. (1991). *The changing face of testing and assessment* (Critical Issues Report). Arlington, VA: American Association of School Administrators.

Jennings, M. (1991, July 3). $29.5 million price tag for student assessment exceeds budgeted funds. *The Louisville Courier Journal,* pp. 1, 4.

Jordan, M. (1992, May 18). Subtracting multiple choice from tests. *The Washington Post,* p. A-1.

Kentucky Department of Education. (1991). *Kentucky Instructional Results Information System: Analysis of proposals.* Frankfort, KY: Thomas Boysen.

Maeroff, G.I. (1991). Assessing alternative assessment. *Phi Delta Kappan, 73,* pp. 273–281.

Office of Technology Assessment. (1992). *Testing in American schools: Asking the right questions* [OTA-SET-519]. Washington, DC: U.S. Government Printing Office.

Pelavin Associates, Inc. (1991). *Evaluating education reform: Assessment of student performance* (Tech. Proposal RFP 91–033). Washington, DC: Author.

Schulz, E. (1992, September). Enemy of innovation: Our obsession with standardized testing is impeding reform. *Teacher Magazine,* pp. 28–32.

Tyson, S. (1990, June). *Presentation on the development of the Georgia Kindergarten Assessment Program.* Paper presented at an Alternatives to Multiple-Choice Testing for Statewide Assessment Seminar, Atlanta, GA.

Chapter 7

Conceptualizing the Costs of Large-Scale Pupil Performance Assessment

David H. Monk
Cornell University

Cost analyses, particularly as they apply to evaluation in education, are of relatively recent origin and are not widespread (Catterall, 1988; Haller 1974; Levin 1991; Monk & King, 1993). Various reasons have been offered for the apparent neglect, including the absence of appropriate training (Levin, 1991) as well as the presence of deeply rooted conceptual and data problems that interfere with analysts' ability to draw the straightforward conclusions sought by policymakers (Monk & King, 1993; Thomas 1990). There is, nevertheless, no denying the salience of policymakers' interest in costs, and some impressive methodological progress has indeed been made. See, for examples, Barnett (1985, 1991); Jamison, Klees, and Wells (1978); and Levin, Glass, and Meister (1984).

This chapter is basically a conceptual investigation of cost analysis as it pertains to a particular educational reform: the advent of performance or authentic assessment on a large scale as a means of transforming entire educational systems. By organizing the inquiry around a specific instance of reform, I seek to make the analysis relatively concrete and useful to policymakers faced with decisions about whether and how to proceed with pupil performance assessment as a major component of school reform initiatives.

A further purpose of this chapter is to illuminate the sometimes contentious debate about pupil performance assessment costs. A number of reports on the costs of assessment in general and pupil performance assessment in particular have appeared recently, and it is important for the policymaking community to have the tools necessary to make intelligent use of the emerging estimates. (See, for examples, Bauer, 1992; Haney, Madaus, & Lyons, 1993; Koretz, Stecher, & Deibert, 1992; U.S. Congress Office of Technology Assessment, 1992; U.S. General Accounting Office, 1993.) I seek to provide those tools in this paper, and also have used the conceptualization developed here as the basis of my own set of cost estimates for large-scale pupil performance assessment reforms, which may be found in Monk (1993).

CONCEPTUAL ISSUES

The seemingly straightforward interest in estimating the costs of pupil performance assessment gives rise to a large number of significant conceptual problems. The chapter begins with a discussion of the important distinction that needs to be made and maintained between expenditures and costs. Much confusion stems from a lack of clarity here, and it is therefore a useful point of departure. Next comes an examination of issues that arise once an analyst has begun a bonafide cost analysis. These include the identification of relevant foregone opportunities and their measurement; the treatment of ambiguous costs; the allowance for the fact that costs can be very unevenly imposed across categories of actors within the system under study; the selection of the appropriate unit of analysis; and the appropriate adjustment for economic phenomena such as diminishing marginal rates of productivity.

Distinguishing Between Costs and Expenditures

Costs are measures of what must be foregone to realize some benefit. For that reason alone, costs cannot be divorced from benefits. *Expenditures,* in contrast, are measures of resource flows regardless of their consequence. A cost analysis requires a comparison of benefits; an expenditure analysis does not. The *cost* of pursuing one activity rather than another is the highest benefit foregone of devoting resources to the activity in question. An extensive literature has grown around the conceptualization of costs. For examples of quite thorough treatments, see Bowman (1966); Buchanan (1966); Thomas (1990). For a more accessible introduction, see Walsh (1970). For a good and nontechnical overview of cost analysis as it applies to evaluation, see Haller (1974).

Information about expenditures is generally more readily available than information about costs. While this is true in a relative sense, it is remarkable to observe how limited our actual ability is to keep track of expenditures for education. See Fowler (1992) for a discussion of the gaps in the federal government's school finance data collection. We hire armies of accountants to keep track of expenditures; there is no comparable corps of cost analysts. This is particularly true in education, where knowledge of costs is impeded by the multiplicity of possible benefits coupled with a rudimentary knowledge of how resources are translated into educational outcomes (Monk 1992). In short, there is no viable means of distinguishing between expenditures that are required given present technology from those that are due to inefficiency and waste.

The difficulties are only compounded when the goal is to estimate costs in an unexplored aspect of education such as the performance assessment of students. Ignorance about the production realities surrounding performance assessment is widespread if for no other reason than the fact that many of the initiatives are still being designed or are at very early stages of implementation (Pelavin, 1992). Moreover, the number of goals being pursued by performance assessment reforms is remarkably large. A review of the New Standards Project Proposal (1992) reveals no fewer than nine such goals, some of which have the potential to be contradictory. Here is a list of various objectives that the New Standard Project is seeking to achieve

- Fundamentally change what is taught and learned.
- Raise expectations that teachers have of students.
- Greatly increase student motivations and effort.
- Raise student performance across the board.
- Substantially close the gap between the best and worst performers.
- Reward student effort to master a thinking curriculum by providing access to college and jobs to those who do so.
- Reward school professionals who helped their students succeed against the new standard.
- Inform parents and the public of the standards to which students would be held and the material they were expected to master.
- Establish national standards but retain local initiative and creativity. (New Standards Project Proposal, 1992)

If the desire to raise student performance across the board translates into a desire to raise the mean level of achievement, there can arise a contradiction with the simultaneous desire to close gaps between the best and worst performers, assuming the resource base is finite. A serious commitment to estimating the costs of performance assessment must involve determining the resources necessary to accomplish these numerous goals. Anything short of this is an exercise in estimating expenditures.

Unfortunately, the more readily available expenditure data are of limited use for policymaking. They can be useful if a decision has been made to proceed with a project and the question is whether there are sufficient resources identified for implementation, or if there is curiosity about how much was spent on a particular activity. But expenditure data are quite useless if the more fundamental question is being asked about whether or not or how to proceed with a project. What makes matters worse is that expenditure data can masquerade as cost data and be misused in policy-making.

For example, if an analyst were to provide expenditure estimates associated with two approaches to pupil assessment, compare them head-to-head, and use the results to draw conclusions about how much more the one approach costs relative to the other, the analyst would be assuming implicitly that the two assessments are intended to accomplish the same goals and are each afflicted to the same degree with inefficiency. Only under these conditions would the comparisons be valid and have relevance to a decision about whether to do more or less of one or the other type of assessment. In cases where these demanding conditions do not hold, the comparisons are not valid and can be misleading.

This point can be illustrated further by examining an instance of expenditure data being cited in a cost context for the purpose of questioning the viability of relying more heavily on performance assessment for students in U.S. schools. Theodore Sizer, in a forum sponsored by *Education Week*, suggested that George Madaus' research indicated that the dollar costs of "truly authentic assessments" range between 6 and 20 times as much as current practice (*Education Week*, June 17, 1992, p. S4). Sizer used these figures to caution reformers about the potential high costs of authentic assessment. He went on to make the quite sensible point that costs need to be taken seriously since they represent a host of alternative reforms that might otherwise be pursued. I have no quarrel with Sizer's larger point about the importance of looking at costs. However, it would appear that the figures he cites are based on expenditure data and that he is overstating what we know about costs.

A closer look at what Madaus said about the costs of assessment is instructive. His observations occur in the context of a study he and a colleague, Thomas Kellaghan, conducted of student examinations systems in Europe. Among their findings is information about what Ireland and the United Kingdom spend on their external examination system (Madaus & Kellaghan, 1991). Specifically, they report a figure of $107 per examined student for Britain and Ireland, and estimate that if Massachusetts were to adopt one of these models to test its comparably aged students (16-year olds), the cost would be almost $7 million. These authors then compared this figure with the $1.2 million they claim Massachusetts currently spends to test the reading, writing, and arithmetic achievements of students at three grade levels (using machine scoring for the reading and mathematics tests), and concluded that were Massachusetts to adopt a European model of external exams, there would be "substantial financial implications" (Madaus & Kellaghan, 1991, p. 22).

What Madaus and Kellaghan report are differences in expenditures across quite different types of assessment efforts. They are correct to conclude that expenditures in Massachusetts would rise if the European model were adopted, but their figures cannot be used to conclude that the European model costs more, or that authentic assessment costs more than traditional assessment. The two approaches to assessment are fundamentally different and the respective expenditure levels are not strictly comparable. There have been a number of other attempts to make estimates of resource outlays for one or another type of assessment program. For example, Bauer (1992) surveyed Test Directors and estimated the average annual costs of testing per pupil to be $4.79. Haney, Madaus, and Lyons (1993) estimated a direct outlay of less than $.80 per student per test hour. The Office of Technology Assessment compiled a state-by-state listing of the costs of State Assessment Programs and reported that costs in 1988 dollars ranged from $1.12 to $39.42 per student (as cited in Haney, Madaus, & Lyons 1993, p.111). Finally, the General Accounting Office recently estimated that system-wide testing costs about $15 per student (USGAO 1993).

Discerning Costs

Having distinguished between expenditures and costs, we can take the next step and examine issues that need to be resolved before a cost analysis of performance assessment can proceed.

Costs cannot be defined in the absence of alternatives. Costs are incurred to the degree that some desirable alternative is foregone and the associated benefits are not realized. Thus, when a resource is devoted to one use, the benefits associated with all of the alternative possible uses of the resource are relevant to the task of determining the resource's cost.

Possible Restrictions on the Range of Alternative Uses. Which among all the possible uses is the relevant alternative use? Textbook definitions of opportunity costs identify the relevant alternative use as the *best* alternative use, but this is not always helpful since considerable ambiguity can surround what counts as best. The Office of Technology Assessment (U.S. OTA 1992, p. 27) speaks more generally about the "value of foregone alternative action," and risks generating confusion. It is not just any foregone alternative action that corresponds to the cost. It is, instead, the best or more highly valued alternative action. An example can make this point clear.

Suppose the task is to determine the cost of time a student might spend attending a Friday evening basketball game. By definition, the opportunity cost of the student's time is the best opportunity foregone by virtue of spending the Friday evening at the basketball game. The pertinent question concerns the broadness of the relevant range of alternative opportunities. Suppose the student in question is under close parental supervision so that the only alternative to going to the basketball game is spending a quiet evening at home, and let us suppose further that this is not a very attractive alternative use to the student. Indeed, the parents' supervision could be so close that the student is not even aware of a host of alternative uses. Under these conditions, the cost of the time spent at the basketball game (from the student's perspective) is quite low—not much is being foregone.

Now suppose that the conditions are different and the range of alternative choices is broadened to include going to a jolly party with really keen people. Assuming this is an attractive alternative use (again, from the perspective of the student), the cost of attending the basketball game has gone up, perhaps dramatically. We have reached two quite different conclusions about a cost, depending on how broadly we choose to define the relevant range of alternative uses.

This variability in the range of relevant alternatives can have bearing on our interest in establishing cost estimates for performance assessment. If we ask the question: "What is the cost of resources that are devoted to performance assessment activities?" the textbook answer will be: "The benefits of the best possible alternative uses to which these resources might have been put." This answer links the cost of performance assessment to the benefits of any conceivable alternative reform (within as well as outside of education). The more beneficial the alternative use, the more costly it becomes to devote resources to performance assessment.

However, there also may be a sense in which the range of alternative uses to which the resources required for performance assessment might be put is more severely constrained. Suppose, for example, that the only relevant alternative use for resources being devoted to performance assessment is conventional assessment. If this is the case, the costs of performance assessment will be measured in terms of the benefits of conventional assessment that are foregone. And to the degree that the benefits of conventional assessment are more modest than those associated with other possible uses, the costs of performance assessment will be lowered by virtue of the restriction on the range of relevant alternatives.

Why would it be appropriate to restrict the range of alternative uses? One justification could be based on behavioral expectations. If it is likely that performance assessment will substitute for conventional assessment, there is a sense in which the costs of devoting resources to performance assessment come at the expense of fewer resources going toward conventional assessment. Some data are beginning to appear that examine the degree to which new assessment approaches substitute for existing assessment efforts. For example, the U.S. General Accounting Office (1993) reports that 41% of the districts surveyed substituted a state provided test for local tests despite the fact that in the district's opinion the tests were quite dissimilar. In cases where the district thought the tests were similar, over 80% reported making the substitution.

However, assuming conventional assessment is not the best possible alternative use of the performance assessment dollars, it follows that foregone conventional assessment benefits are understating the true economic costs of performance assessment. The point is that a decision needs to be made about what counts as the relevant foregone use.

Sources of Variation in Benefit Levels. It is important to be more specific about the dimensions along which foregone benefits can vary. Essentially, they derive from two sources.

First, there is the direct contribution to the relevant decision maker's sense of well-being. It is a question of how well aligned the alternatives being foregone are to the relevant decision maker's preferences. Of course, this presumes clarity about who the relevant decision maker is. Suffice it to say that views about how valuable different foregone benefits are can vary substantially among those playing different roles. For more information about how it is reasonable for different actors within educational systems to disagree fundamentally over the value of a central resource such as student time, see Monk (1982).

The basketball example can help to illustrate this dimension of the valuation problem. Going to a party with a given set of characteristics contributes in a particular way to the student's sense of well-being. This may be high, low, or in-between, depending on how the student feels about parties. The more important party going is to the student, the more costly it becomes for the student to spend the time at the basketball game, assuming she or he is aware of the party option.

Second, there also is a productivity dimension to consider. Parties can be good or bad, jolly or not, and our student's sense of the cost of going to the basketball game will be affected by his or her perception of the level at which the party will operate. This concern over the level of production is conceptually distinct from a concern over how efficiently the party is produced. The student is less likely to be concerned about how efficiently resources are being transformed into party outcomes, largely because the resources are presumably coming from others. Even if we recognize that a party-going student will eventually be expected to host a party and thereby incur costs, it is not obvious that the student will be concerned about efficiency per se. Just because the student's associates run inefficient parties (and expend more resources than are necessary) does not mean that the student needs to follow suit. In other words, it may be the case that a party has the potential to be beneficial in the student's mind, but the reality may be quite different.

Again, there is a parallel with the problem of assigning costs to performance assessment. The foregone alternative used to assign value to the performance assessment resources may or may not be contributing benefits that are highly valued by the society. In other words, the benefits being produced may not align very well with what the society is seeking. If the relevant alternative is conventional assessment, it could be the case that conventional assessment places too much emphasis on rote learning and lower cognitive capabilities. It could be the case that conventional assessment (assuming this portrayal is accurate) is ill serving the interests of society as we move into the 21st century. Moreover, the alternative use may or may not be operating at a high level. Ergo, serious inefficiencies may be limiting production of the relevant benefits.

It follows that misalignment between the alternative use and the society's priorities as well as inefficiency in the production of the relevant alternative benefits have implications for the cost of performance assessment. This makes sense intuitively. It costs less to replace a poor practice than it does to replace a good practice. However, this kind of thinking begs the question about whether the poor practice could be improved. It also sidesteps the possibility that the restriction on the range of relevant alternatives is artificially drawn.

Lumpiness.   Costs can be conceived of at the margin (i.e., the cost of devoting additional resources to a given use) or in a cumulative sense (i.e., the sum of benefits foregone), given the allocation of some bundle of resources in a given direction. One reason why the two types of costs may differ stems from the potential for the alternative uses to be lumpy in their nature. In the basketball game example, the game may take more time than the alternative party. Thus, the cost of the time devoted to the game needs to be valued in terms of the benefits of the party plus the benefits of the best alternative use of time following the party. And in the case of performance assessment, the resources devoted to performance assessment may be greater than those devoted to the relevant alternative use, say conventional assessment. Under these circumstances, the cost of performance assessment consists of the foregone benefits of conventional assessment plus whatever benefits are foregone because of the additional resources devoted to performance assessment.

Implications for Measurement

Measurement questions quickly crowd discussions about foregone benefits or opportunities. Recall that the textbook definition of an opportunity cost makes reference to the best benefit foregone, not the most easily measured benefit foregone. And yet, cost analysts are under considerable pressure to develop metrics for the benefits they are assessing. A common strategy is to rely on market valuations of foregone benefits despite the fact that these dollar measures may not reflect the most highly valued foregone benefits.

The Friday night basketball game example can also help clarify this issue. Neither alternative use of the student's time that was just considered (spending the time at home or at the party) lends itself to a dollar metric. There is, however, a third alternative use that is relatively easy to cost in dollars—namely, the wage the student could command if he or she spent the evening working. Although this alternative use may be relatively easy to measure, it could be a very misleading cost estimate for the simple reason that it is hardly obvious that it represents the best alternative use in the student's mind.

The distinction between easy and hard to measure benefits has relevance for assigning costs to performance assessment. It would be desirable to have direct measures of the net benefits associated with the best alternative being foregone because of the proposed shift toward performance assessment. However, such measures are not readily available and would require a major effort with no guarantee of success. A second-best strategy involves accepting the claim that the net benefit of the alternative use can be measured by the dollar value of the resources devoted to it. If this strategy is pursued, an important part of analyzing the costs of performance assessment becomes the calculation of expenditures on the best alternative use to which the resources might be put. But, this is equivalent to calculating the dollar value of the resources devoted to the intended use, and the result is the use of either actual or anticipated expenditures on the intended use as the measure of the relevant costs. This approach to estimating costs is sometimes called the *ingredients approach* or *method.* It places a heavy emphasis on using expenditures to measure costs and can thereby contribute to the confusion surrounding the very important conceptual difference between the two. For a good overview of the ingredients method and its application to program evaluation, see Levin (1983).

The use of expenditures to measure costs has some merit. After all, dollars are broadly instrumental and their expenditure on a given ingredient does provide a measure of all the market based opportunities that are being sacrificed by virtue of the decision to spend. However, the underlying prices that give meaning to the dollar measures are generated by markets, and markets can vary widely in how well they function. Where markets do not function well, it is possible for the dollars spent on ingredients to be quite unrelated to actual benefits derived.

From a neoclassical economist's perspective, markets do not function well when they operate in noncompetitive environments. In the case of education, the deep involvement of the state is viewed by some as a serious limit on how well education markets can succeed at efficiently producing the correct mix of educational outcomes (see, for example, Chubb & Moe, 1990). If these critics are correct and if resources devoted to performance assessment will come at the expense of resources devoted to other educational uses, then the ingredients method for estimating the costs of performance assessment risks overstating relevant costs. In other words, under these assumptions, totaling the dollars that need to be spent on performance assessment would overstate the opportunities society would truly forego if performance assessment were implemented.

The point is not to debate the merits of public intervention in the functioning of education markets. Rather, the point is to recognize that the use of the ingredients method will overstate the costs of performance assessment to the degree that misalignment with social priorities and inefficiency in production characterize the relevant alternative use of resources that could otherwise be devoted to performance assessment.

These arguments pertain to questions about the costs associated with performance assessment. If we alter the question slightly and ask how much more it would cost to implement a system of performance assessment within an existing school system, there is an additional phenomenon to consider—namely, the possible absorption of performance assessment costs.

Costs will be absorbed to the degree that the performance assessment reform substitutes in practice for some aspect of the status quo. For example, to the degree that performance assessment can substitute for conventional assessment and existing staff development efforts, the marginal cost of implementing performance assessment will be diminished.

There is, however, an important difference between the degree to which one use of resources can substitute for another and the likelihood that the substitution will actually take place in practice. The complex decision making processes that give rise to actual practice in schools are difficult to assess and involve important political as well as economic phenomena. This mixing of political and economic phenomena gives rise to some ambiguity about the relevant costs. From a strict economic perspective, the cost is the best alternative foregone, regardless of what happens in practice. But, from a policymaking perspective, the potential for substitutions to take place is clearly relevant and has bearing on both the estimates of costs and their subsequent use in policy debates.

An important question that is much easier to ask than to answer concerns the degree to which misalignment with social goals or inefficient production of one resource use enhances the likelihood of substitution with an alternative. In the present context, the question is about the degree to which misalignment and inefficiency associated with conventional assessment is likely to enhance the prospects of substitution in practice with performance assessment. If this kind of link exists, it follows that misalignments and production inefficiencies have bearing on two aspects of cost: (a) the cost of the resources required for the reform; and (b) the cost of implementation. Figure 7.1 illustrates both of these cost components.

Illustration A in Fig. 7.1 represents a schooling system before the advent of performance assessment. The figure includes an admittedly artificial distinction between the costs of regular instruction and the costs of conventional assessment. Illustration B reflects the addition of the performance assessment reform where the costs are valued in terms of the full dollar value of the resources required for performance assessment and where performance assessment is considered a complete add-on to existing practices. In Illustration C, two things have happened: (a) there has been an adjustment to reflect the presumption that the dollar value of the resources required for performance assessment overstate the cost; and (b) an allowance has been made for the absorption of some portion of the costs of performance assessment into the costs of both the regular instructional program and the conventional assessment program. In other words, a substitution is presumed to have taken place between what was in place and the performance assessment reform. The figure is drawn to suggest that these two adjustments have a significant impact on the costs associated with performance assessment.

These arguments suggest that the conventional ingredients method can overstate the true economic costs of a reform such as pupil performance assessment, but they offer little guidance about the magnitude of the overstatement. A case can be made for making an offsetting adjustment, but for these offsets to be credible there needs to be reason to believe that the proposed new use (performance assessment in this case) will be less likely to suffer from both a misalignment with social welfare interests and an inefficiency in production.

It probably is easier to make the better alignment case for performance assessment than the productivity case. There appears to be consensus that the kinds of human performance dealt with by performance assessment are likely to become more and not less important to economic as well as social functioning as time passes (Marshall & Tucker 1992). However, it is hardly obvious that so-called conventional assessment has no role to play in assessing these kinds of capabilities.

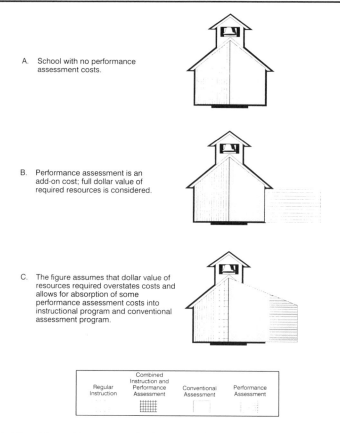

A. School with no performance assessment costs.

B. Performance assessment is an add-on cost; full dollar value of required resources is considered.

C. The figure assumes that dollar value of resources required overstates costs and allows for absorption of some performance assessment costs into instructional program and conventional assessment program.

Regular Instruction	Combined Instruction and Performance Assessment	Conventional Assessment	Performance Assessment

FIG. 7.1. Alternative conceptualizations of adding performance assessment to an existing educational system.

If the existing governance system gave rise to inefficiency within the conventional assessment program, what reason is there to expect performance assessment to suffer a different fate? Perhaps the sometimes parallel efforts to restructure school governance and to more directly involve teachers and parents will have salutary effects, but that is speculative. See O'Day and Smith (1993) for more on the kinds of governance changes that are part of systemic reform initiatives.

Handling Ambiguous Costs

Ambiguous costs involve real but in some sense unnecessary expenditures of resources. In a strict sense, they are not costs, since they are not necessary to accomplish some end. In another sense, they are quite real to the extent that those involved perceive the expenditures to be necessary.

The importance of these costs arose in conjunction with a cost analysis of the Texas Examination of Current Administrators and Teachers (TE-CAT). Shepard and Kreitzer (1987) drew attention to the issue when they showed that their cost estimates of the TECAT went up dramatically when they included a valuation of the time teachers devoted to preparing for the test. It is at least arguable that such preparation time was not intended by the state to be necessary. Nevertheless, teachers spent the time, and the time required them to forego opportunities. Resources were expended, and the question is whether or not to treat them as costs. It is possible for the new performance assessments to generate significant costs of this kind, particularly if the stakes associated with the test are high.

Defining the Locus of Costs

It also is important to be clear about whose perspective is being considered in a cost analysis, since the imposition of costs can vary widely across categories of actors within educational systems. An analyst might show that costs of a reform are relatively modest at the state level (or from a funding agency's perspective). Armed with these results, policymakers might go ahead and implement the reform only to discover subsequently that the neglect of costs borne by actors located at other levels of the system were sufficiently large to thwart the entire reform.

Shepard and Kreitzer (1987), for example, found that the contracted resource commitment for the teacher examination at the state level was on the order of 5 million dollars, but estimated that the total tax support for the program amounted to more than 35 million dollars when local costs were included. The Office of Technology Assessment (1992), hereafter OTA, also found a large discrepancy between the estimated outlays for a conventional standardized testing program (including contracted materials and services as well as district testing personnel) and a more comprehensive estimate of the outlays that took account of the time teachers spend preparing students for and administering the examination. The OTA estimates ranged between $6 per student per test administration and $110 per student per test administration, and illustrate how sensitive the results can be to decisions about what to include and what to exclude.

As further evidence of the importance of being attentive to the locus of costs, consider OTA's analysis of school districts' likely behavioral responses to alternative types of assessment programs. OTA distinguished between one hypothetical testing program that costs little in terms of direct dollar outlays but is quite costly in terms of the costs imposed on students, what OTA calls opportunity costs. By assumption, this testing program (Type I) has little or no instructional value. Whatever time a teacher spends preparing students for this type of test requires a like amount of time to be withdrawn from productive instructional use. The alternative (Type II) program has the opposite features. It is costly in terms of direct costs, but has minimal opportunity costs. This corresponds to a program where the development of assessment tasks and their subsequent scoring are quite costly, but where the assessment fits very nicely with instruction and even complements teachers' efforts to teach. Whatever time a teacher devotes to preparing students for this type of test has no adverse effect on learning.

According to OTA, the costs of the Type I test start low and increase as more time is devoted to assessment, whereas the costs of the second option are constant and do not vary with the amount of time devoted to the assessment. OTA identified a cross-over point where the initially lower costs of Type I meet and then go beyond the costs of Type II, and claimed that at the cross-over point the *district* (emphasis added) would be indifferent between the two testing programs.

This conclusion misses an important point about who bears what cost. To the degree that students bear the opportunity costs associated with the Type I assessment program, why would the district care about these costs? My conclusion is different from OTA's: At the crossover point, the district would still prefer to use the Type I assessments. The opportunity costs, which are assumed to be large and real, are imposed on students who are limited in their ability to organize and make their needs known. In sharp contrast, the additional direct expenditures associated with the Type II assessment program do occasion costs for district officials. They directly limit the ability of these officials to commit to programs such as investing in other reforms or providing a savings to taxpayers.

The key point is that the locus of costs has important implications for the accounting of costs as well as for the behavioral responses to innovation.

Discerning the Unit of Analysis

The results of cost comparisons of alternative approaches can be quite sensitive to the scale of the respective enterprises (Levin, 1983). It can matter whether the comparison is between traditional assessment and an alternative approach within a school district, region, state, or nation. Scale economies can be important, and an analyst might find a small scale application of a reform is considerably more costly on a per unit basis than is a much larger undertaking.

Care needs to be exercised when heavy emphasis is placed on relatively large units of analysis. One problem stems from the potential for aggregated data to gloss over sources of cost that are important on a small scale. For example, the amount of time needed to train teachers as scorers of performance assessments may vary substantially across Local Education Agencies (LEAs), depending upon factors such as the average amount of subject matter preparation present within a LEA's faculty. At the state level, the localities requiring more resources for staff development will, to some degree, be balanced by those requiring fewer resources, but costs could vary substantially across local sites. Moreover, to the degree that large units like states vary in the incidence of difficult as well as easy to train teachers, there could be variation in costs across states.

Finally, there is an important distinction to draw between the costs of developing a system and the costs of operating that same system. In the case of performance assessment innovations, there are substantial start-up costs that involve constructing the assessment tasks, testing their validity, achieving the initial interrater reliability, and so forth. There also are important operations costs. A good cost analysis needs to be attentive to both types of cost.

Discerning Instances of Diminishing Marginal Productivity

Economic research has generated a number of propositions about the behavior of production processes that have important implications for magnitudes of costs. For example, if the relevant production processes are beset with sharply diminishing marginal productivities of key educational inputs, unit costs may rise, perhaps substantially, as additional inputs are supplied. Alternatively, the production processes may be such that diminishing marginal productivities are neither widespread nor pronounced, in which case the upward pressures on unit costs will be minimal as more inputs are provided.

The central point here can be illustrated by sketching two alternative scenarios of performance assessment in education: one is a high cost scenario and includes an emphasis on diminishing marginal productivities, the other is a corresponding low cost scenario.

High-Cost Scenario. This is a world beset with diminishing marginal productivities. They affect teachers as well as students and occasion the following results:

- At any given moment there is wide variation in the ability of teachers to benefit from the in-service assessment training that is offered as part of the performance assessment reform. Some teachers benefit significantly and quickly; others not at all or minimally.
- The current cohort of teachers also varies widely in how able they are to implement the assessments that are developed.

- The teachers least able to benefit from the available training are the teachers performing at the lowest levels.
- For all the teachers who are able to benefit from the available training, the magnitude of the gain in performance drops as they reach higher levels of performance.
- A similar set of phenomena arises with respect to students. Namely, students vary in their ability to benefit from the feedback provided by performance assessment; they vary in their level of performance; the lowest performing students are the least able to benefit from the feedback; and the marginal effectiveness of the assessment information drops off sharply (for all students) as they reach higher levels of performance.

If this portrait comes close to describing the real world of performance assessment, the cost of the enterprise will be very high. Such high costs may still be worth bearing, but it is clear that their magnitudes will be substantial.

Low-Cost Scenario.   Here diminishing marginal productivities may be present, but their impact is much more modest; and education is viewed as a cumulative process such that useful assessment information provided today makes learning tomorrow less costly. Moreover, the assumption is that there are important scale economies that are possible such that assessment tasks developed by teachers in one locale are readily transferable to others. It can be further assumed that as teachers gain experience at both developing and utilizing assessment tasks, it becomes easier to make effective use of performance assessment within classrooms. Finally, the assumption is made that assessment becomes so closely aligned with instruction that it no longer makes sense to conceive of it as a separate entity.

This is clearly a low-cost scenario. Even if conservative estimates of the potential benefits associated with the reform are considered, the stage is set for finding a very favorable level of benefits in relation to costs.

Both the high- and the low-cost scenarios are plausible, but they both cannot be correct. Questions about which scenario is more accurate under what circumstances are ultimately empirical questions. However, the requisite empirical analyses will not be straightforward because proponents of performance assessment reform can easily claim that the high cost scenario, to the degree that it is played out as the reform is pursued, is more related to a failure to implement the reform properly than it is to more fundamental flaws in the more intrinsic merits of performance assessment as a reform.

CONCLUSION

This chapter has examined a series of conceptual issues that are central to any attempt to estimate the costs of an educational innovation such as large-scale pupil performance assessment. For many of the resulting problems there are no straightforward solutions, and my recommendation is to proceed by conducting cost analyses under a variety of explicit assumptions. In particular, alternative assumptions should be made about the following: (a) the degree to which costs are overstated by the ingredients method or absorbed at local levels; (b) the degree to which ambiguous costs are included in cost estimates; (c) the size or scale of the unit undertaking the reform; and, perhaps most important, (d) the degree to which diminishing marginal productivity is characteristic of the inputs being devoted to the reform.

Once the cost implications of these assumptions are worked out, consumers of the research will be in a position to choose a combination of assumptions with which they feel most comfortable. A major difficulty, of course, is the tendency for participants in the policy debate to choose assumption combinations for politically expedient reasons. The magnitude of this problem is compounded by the large amount of variation that can exist between the projected costs associated with best and worse case scenarios. For example, a cost analysis of the New Standards Project found differences on the order of 466% in my large state estimates between the best of the best case scenarios compared to the worst of the worst case scenarios (Monk 1993, p. 235). Other analysts also have wrestled with large discrepancies across their estimates. Haney, Madaus, & Lyons (1993, p. 118), for example, estimated that the total investment in state and district testing programs currently is between 311 million dollars and 22.7 billion dollars, annually.

It is nevertheless useful for policymakers to obtain upper and lower bound estimates on the costs associated with major reform efforts such as large scale pupil performance assessment systems. At minimum, having bounds begins to narrow the debate. Further, if the assumptions underlying the estimates are explicit, it becomes possible to interpret and place the numerical estimates in context.

It is heartening to know that these upper and lower bound cost estimates are becoming available with respect to a major reform effort such as the large-scale performance assessment of pupils. While these cost analyses are by no means straightforward and definitive, they will inform the debate and facilitate the development of sound public policy.

ACKNOWLEDGMENTS

This chapter is a condensed version of a monograph entitled: *The Costs of Systemic Education Reform: Conceptual Issues and Preliminary Estimates* by David H. Monk. Support for research was provided by the MacArthur Foundation and the Pew Charitable Trusts through grants supplied to the New Standards Project. Support also was provided by the Finance Center of the Consortium for Policy Research in Education (CPRE), a consortium of the University of Southern California, Rutgers University, Cornell University, Harvard University, Michigan State University, Stanford University, and the University of Wisconsin, Madison. The CPRE support was derived from grant #R1178G10039 from the U. S. Department of Education, Office of Educational Research and Improvement. The views expressed are those of the author and are not necessarily shared by the New Standards Project or its sponsors, CPRE or its partners, or the U.S. Department of Education.

REFERENCES

Barnett, W. S. (1985). Benefit-cost analysis of the Perry Preschool Program and its policy implications. *Educational Evaluation and Policy Analysis, 7,* 333–342.

Barnett, W. S. (1991). Benefits of compensatory preschool education. *Journal of Human Resources, 27*(2), 279–312.

Bauer, E. A. (1992). NATD survey of testing practices and issues. *Educational Measurement: Issues and Practice, 11*(1), 10–14.

Bowman, M. J. (1966). The costing of human resource development. In E.A.E. Robinson & J. Vaizey (Eds.), *The economics of education* (pp. 421–450). London: Macmillan.

Buchanan, J. M. (1966). *Cost and choice.* Chicago: Markham.

Catterall, J. S. (1988). *Estimating the costs and benefits of large-scale assessments: Lessons From recent research.* Paper presented at the annual conference of the American Educational Research Association, New Orleans, LA.

Chubb, J. E., & Moe, T. M. (1990). *Politics, markets, and America's schools.* Washington, DC: Brookings Institute.

Fowler, W. J., Jr. (1992). *What should we know about school finance.* Paper presented at the annual conference of the American Education Finance Association, New Orleans, LA.

Haller, E. J. (1974). Cost analysis for educational program evaluation. In W. J. Popham (Ed.), *Evaluation in education: Current applications* (pp. 401–450). Berkeley, CA: McCutchan Publishing.

Haney, W. M., Madaus, G. F., & Lyons, R. (1993). *The fractured marketplace for standardized testing.* Boston: Kluwer Academic Publishers.

Jamison, D. T., Klees, S. J., & Wells, S. J. (1978). *The costs of educational media.* Beverly Hills, CA: Sage.

Koretz, D., Stecher, B., & Deibert, E. (1992). *The Vermont Portfolio Assessment Program: Interim report on implementation and impact, 1991–1992 school year.* Santa Monica, CA: RAND.

Levin, H. M. (1983). *Cost-effectiveness: A primer.* Beverly Hills, CA: Sage.

Levin, H. M. (1991). Cost-effectiveness at quarter century. In McLaughlin & Phillips (Eds.), *Evaluation and Education: At Quarter Century* (pp. 189–209). Chicago: University of Chicago Press.

Levin, H. M., Glass, G. V., & Meister, G. R. (1984). *Cost-effectiveness of four educational interventions* [Project Rep. No. 84–A11]. Stanford, CA: Institute for Research on Educational Finance and Governance, School of Education, Stanford University.

Madaus, G. F., & Kellaghan, T. (1991). *Student examination systems in the European community: Lessons for the United States.* Unpublished manuscript.

Marshall, R., & Tucker, M. (1992). *Thinking for a living: Education and the wealth of nations.* New York: Basic Books.

Monk, D. H. (1982). Alternative perceptions of cost and the resource allocation behaviors of teachers. *Educational Administration Quarterly, 18*(2), 60–80.

Monk, D. H. (1990). *Educational finance: An economic approach.* New York: McGraw-Hill.

Monk, D. H. (1992). Education productivity research: An update and assessment of its role in education finance reform. *Educational Evaluation and Policy Analysis, 14*(4), 307–332.

Monk, D. H. (1993). *The costs of systemic education reform: Conceptual issues and preliminary estimates* [Final report to the New Standards Project]. Ithaca, NY: Department of Education, Cornell University. (ERIC Document Reproduction Service No. ED 376 210)

Monk, D. H., & King, J.A. (1993). Cost analysis as a tool for education reform. In S.L. Jacobson & R. Berne (Eds.), *The Reform of Education* (pp. 131–150). Newbury Park, CA: Corwin Press.

New Standards Project. (1992). *The New Standards Project, 1992–1995, A proposal.* Rochester, NY: National Center on Education and the Economy and Pittsburgh, PA: Learning Research and Development Center.

O'Day, J. A., & Smith, M. S. (1993). Systemic reform and educational opportunity. In S. H. Fuhrman (Ed.), *Designing Coherent Education Policy* (pp. 250–312). San Francisco: Jossey-Bass.

Pelavin Associates. (1992). *Evaluating education reform: Assessment of student performance.* Washington, DC: Author.

Shepard, L. A., & Kreitzer, A. E. (1987). The Texas teacher test. *Educational Researcher, 16*(6), 22–31.

Thomas, H. (1990). *Education costs and performance: A cost-effectiveness analysis.* London: Cassell.

U.S. Congress, Office of Technology Assessment. (1992, February). *Testing in American schools: Asking the right questions* (OTA-SET-519). Washington, DC: U.S. Government Printing Office.

U.S. General Accounting Office. (1993). *Student testing: Current extent and expenditures, with cost estimates for a national examination* (GAO/PEMD-93-8). Washington, DC: U.S. General Accounting Office, Program Evaluation and Methodology Division.

Walsh, V. C. (1970). *Introduction to contemporary microeconomics.* New York: McGraw-Hill.

Chapter 8

Change Has Changed: Implications for Implementation of Assessments From the Organizational Change Literature

Suzanne M. Stiegelbauer
University of Toronto

The 20-odd years of research on change in schools have provided a wealth of information on processes that work and do not work. For many, however, the successful implementation of new programs and processes, or innovations, remains a dilemma. The long-term commitment necessary for successful implementation and continuation is hard to keep in focus and even more difficult to keep funded, although the real goal of change remains always to have an impact on outcomes. Schools and teachers get involved in new things to make the educational process better and to improve themselves or their students' capacity to learn. Yet, reaching outcomes requires keeping up the pressure, getting past initiation to the real work of change—work that progressively has taken on new dimensions and new possibilities.

When we speak of change, we may be talking about a specific agenda, as in the use of assessments, but we also are talking about changing the way that people (including students) work together as they apply assessments, and we are talking about how those assessments relate to other aspects of school life. In short, our concern is with the school, not just the classroom.

This chapter deals with those elements important to the actual work of change: people, processes, practices, and policies (Loucks-Horsley, 1989). It is also about a new model for change, one which reflects a different way

139

of thinking about how change fits into today's educational systems (Fullan, 1991; Miles, 1992). To paraphrase Miles (1992), and at the risk of overstating the obvious, the secret of change still lies in the applied common sense of the people involved. People know more than they think they know; the problem is putting that knowledge into action, and that means reflecting on or processing what they think and developing a flexible sense of where they are going. This chapter takes some of the pieces of change as presented in the research of the last two decades and puts them together so that educators can use what they know to develop an environment wherein change succeeds.

CHANGE: OLD AND NEW

A Linear Approach

Back in the 1970s, when the research on change in schools began in earnest, change was viewed primarily as classroom change—one teacher, one classroom, one innovation. In fact, the central paradigm for planned educational change through the early 1980s provided an *innovation focused* perspective on the implementation of single changes in curriculum and instruction (Fullan, 1985). Thinking about change was linear in those days. One found or developed an innovation that would meet the needs and outcomes one had already defined. Not surprisingly, many desired results did not occur.

We now know a number of different reasons why—lack of match to the environment, lack of follow-through, lack of definition, lack of practice and training in the innovation. Change in these circumstances could be described as an *event*, because it was selected and announced; and it was assumed that change would then simply happen. Emphasis was on designing and adopting good programs, not on implementing them. Frustration with the lack of outcomes foreshadowed by such an approach was a major factor in the initiation of research on the change event, or on what happened between adopting a program and getting results.

An Overlapping Approach

Change is now approached a bit differently. The research on change has generated an emphasis on process and its context. Effective change no longer affects one teacher in one classroom, but the very culture of schools ((Fullan, 1991; Fullan & Miles, 1992; Horsley, 1990). As Cuban (1988) stated, many of the early efforts at change might be called "first order changes." They are addressed to more superficial elements of the classroom and the school system and do not stress the organization to any meaningful degree.

However, many of the changes required by current societal and educational demands go deeper than any surface treatment can address, and require what Cuban called "second order changes," changes that go deep into the structure of organizations and the ways in which people work together (Cuban, 1988). This kind of change is multifaceted, slower, and means changing attitudes, perceptions, behaviors, relationships, and the way people collaborate.

Many argue that making change operational and institutionalized within a system is only part of the challenge. Crandall, Eiseman, and Louis (1986) noted that the goal of institutionalization is often tantamount to routinization, which decreases the capacity of schools to integrate responses to new needs and issues. The assumption is that renewal (Hall & Loucks, 1977), rather than institutionalization, is a more appropriate focus for school improvement. Renewal implies an organizational culture geared toward continuous learning and improvement, rather than completing the implementation of individual changes (Stiegelbauer & Anderson, 1992).

In new models for change, organizational capacity for continuous renewal and growth points toward the direction of the future and "changing the culture of schools—what schools do and how they work—is the real agenda" (Fullan & Hargreaves, 1991). Planning for individual change is only part of changing the educational environment as a whole. This sounds imposing, and in many ways it is. However, the past 20 years have taught us something about strategies and processes that can be applied to good effect. (See Fig. 8.1 for visualizations of the old (linear) and the new (overlapping) processes of change.)

PEOPLE: THE MOST IMPORTANT ELEMENT IN CHANGE

The baseline for any change is working with people who will put plans into operation; people who will lead, support, and act as resources; and people who will act as catalysts and energizers. Early research recognized the necessity of people, but it took a long time to define what that recognition really meant to change itself.

One obvious meaning is that people are different and will respond to change in different ways—some will quickly become involved, some will resist, some will perhaps never engage themselves in the process. Another element that becomes obvious is that teachers, usually the objects of change, are historically *independent craftspersons* who often work in isolation and who place great value on the practical outcomes of their work (Crandall & Associates, 1982; Huberman, 1983). Finally, research shows that, given

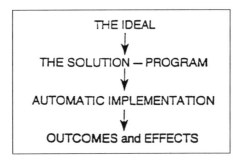

FIG. 8.1. A linear view of the change process.

these variables, the more contact that occurs, especially one-to-one supportive contact (Hall & Hord, 1987) and group problem solving or *process analysis* discussions (Miles, 1992), the more likely it becomes that these independent individuals will take on the change.

Fullan (1991) asserted that an individual's involvement with and commitment to change is motivated largely by his or her subjective understanding of the meaning of change. Within this *subjective reality*, individuals have to decide "what's in it for them" and how they will deal with this new opportunity. Some see it as a "loss" of what they know well (Marris, 1975); others see change as an opportunity. It is the "transformation of subjective realities," or the establishment of a new meaning or relationship to the change, that is the essence of any substantive change process (Fullan, 1991).

Sometimes subjective meaning can be mediated by dealing with the objective reality of the change (i.e., what the change really is, how it relates to current practice, and what its effects will be). This is Fullan's second factor related to meaning. On the one hand, there is the individual and his or her personal being; on the other hand is his or her professional life and responsibilities. Somewhere within this framework, change lives or dies.

Teachers are very concerned about what might be called a *practicality ethic* (Doyle & Ponder, 1977; Huberman, 1983). Objectively, a change has to have practical outcomes for them and for their students. A change also has to be sound, not superficial; be clear in its goals and procedures; have a role within the organizational status quo that will lend it long-term support and ongoing clarification; and finally, change has to be valued by the organization and by the teachers within that organization. Many teachers feel burned by putting effort into changes that were short-lived, not valued, not clear when implemented in the classroom, and not practical for students. Such negative experiences reinforce the subjective reality that change is not worthwhile.

Learning-Related Actions

In this context, it makes sense that schools use assessment as an area around which to focus a number of learning-related actions, which can in turn contribute to future innovations. What can teachers learn about talking to each other about assessments? What kinds of assessments work best for them? What do students think about assessment? How can commitment to experimentation be encouraged? Group dynamics focused on problem solving and implementing solutions can help clarify how teachers will approach change; and the dynamics of the group also go a long way toward developing consensus around the value of change within the organization.

The Need for Information. In the early stages of response to change, there is a need for information about how the innovation will affect individuals personally (*self*); later, individuals need both time to practice the change even as they manage it (*task*); and finally, individuals will be interested in refining what they are doing to better meet the needs of their students (*impact*). These change-related concerns describe the process that teachers go through as they take on something new (Hall & Hord, 1987). Individuals will go through these stages at different rates, but facilitators can use certain guidelines for the kind of information and support individuals or groups will need at different points in time.

The Need for Leadership. First of all, change requires leaders—those who keep up the pressure and provide visible sanction for what is happening; and change also requires support in terms of policy and funding. The research makes it clear that district, board, and school administrators are the main determinants of whether or not change gets implemented (Hord, Stiegelbauer, & Hall, 1984). Without their continued and highly visible support, change has little chance to succeed. Leaders may or may not be facilitators; however, they must be communicators who are committed to the goals of the change and demonstrate the sincerity of their intentions to all members of the system. Their experience can guide those who are more conservative in their response to change and who want to see more concretely what the change is all about (Fullan, 1988; Crandall & Associates, 1982).

If school leaders are not facilitators themselves, they must find someone to provide that secondary leadership and support. Facilitators are those whose role it is initiate, problem solve, and maintain action related to the change. They may be principals, resource people, vice-principals (Hord et al., 1984), teachers, or consultants to the process. Facilitators seem to have a number of qualities in common: They understand the technical require-ments of the change effort, they possess a conceptual and technical understanding of the dynamics of change as it relates to the specific environment, they have and make use of interpersonal skills, and they demonstrate that the change is a worthwhile effort to be engaged with (Horsley, 1990). Given that schools and systems are frequently working with more than one change simultaneously, it is the role of a facilitator to provide implementing teachers with the ongoing training, classroom problem solving, materials, and other resources necessary to clarify and refine innovation use.

These leadership and support functions of change illustrate Fullan's (1985) idea of *pressure and support* as necessary ingredients to a change process. Without a certain amount of pressure nothing happens, nor will anything happen without support to tailor change to the needs of individu-als and individual contexts.

PRACTICES: NEED, COMPLEXITY, CLARITY, QUALITY, PRACTICALITY

The qualities of an innovation make a difference to successful change. The best practices are classroom friendly, well-defined, practical, and relevant to teachers' needs and interests. Portfolios have been adopted widely because they have most of these qualities. Teachers like to feel that any new practice has clear benefits for them and for their students. Practices that are too similar to or too different from conventional approaches present problems of implementation because teachers either do not clearly distinguish what is new or feel a sense of loss or resentment in being asked to change from what they perceive as successful current practice (Fullan, 1991; Marris, 1975).

Need and Complexity

The one-teacher/one-classroom innovations of the 1970s and 1980s were frequently developed from the perspective of *technical rationality* (Miles, 1992). Innovations were developed because they were in some way tech-nically better than current practice and would presumably lead to better results. This decision about better results was seldom the decision of the implementing teacher. Some teachers did develop and market innovations that worked for them, such as the "Programs that Work" of the National Diffusion Network. Initially, the movement toward technical rationality led to an insistence on "innovation quality, fidelity of implementation, and to a search for 'teacher-proofness'" (Miles, 1992, p. 9). In other words, a technically good innovation should be able to be introduced anywhere with the same results. This turned out not to be so, and that circumstance launched much of the research on the implementation and diffusions of innovations as we know it currently (Sashkin & Egermeier, 1991).

On the contrary, it turned out that many innovations are high on cost, low on fit, and involve *false clarity* (i.e., they appear easy to implement, but actually involve more effort or change than people anticipate (Fullan, 1991, p. 70) or are superficially interpreted). Practical changes are those that address salient needs, fit well into real teacher situations, are focused, and include concrete how-to-do-it possibilities (Mortimore, Sammons, Stoll, Lewis, & Ecob, 1988). Huberman (1983) described a number of factors that affect innovation implementability and attractiveness to teachers, including:

- *Craft legitimization.* Was the product field tested?
- *Compatibility.* Is the social context of prospective users, particularly with regard to opportunities and incentives for action, incorporated into the innovation?
- *Accessibility.* Is the innovation designed to relate to the conceptual framework of a person who does not already share the assumptions of change?
- *Observability.* Is there opportunity for the prospective user to assess the knowledge in light of his or her own reality—such as vivid descriptions of the ideas at work?
- *Adaptability.* Do the innovations encourage local adaptation?
- *Inspiration.* Does the innovation have a strong inspirational thrust? Are idealistic-altruistic values an important component of its message?

Given the "classroom press" of teachers for immediacy and concreteness, innovations have to be accessible and beneficial for teachers and students in both an immediate and long-term way (Crandall & Associates, 1982). Change does not always equal progress, especially if it is not practical for teachers or systems.

Clarity, Quality, and Practicality

Two elements of practices that affect clarity and quality of implementation are size and the complexity issue described above. According to several large studies of implementation, the larger the scope of change and the more personally demanding it is, the greater the chance for success (Crandall, Eiseman, & Louis, 1986; Fullan, 1991). Although size and complexity may initially deter a potential adopter, in the longer term the greater the teacher effort and energy expended in implementing a new practice, the greater the potential outcome. Small innovations often do not succeed in the long run because they are not perceived to be worth the effort or because teachers cannot distinguish the innovation clearly enough from other practices. On the other hand, innovations that are too large require too much of the organization as a whole and frequently result in distortion or partial implementation to make them manageable (Crandall et al., 1986): In essence, "the greatest success is likely to occur when the size of the change is large enough to require noticeable, sustained effort, but not so massive that typical users find it necessary to adopt a coping strategy that seriously distorts the change" (Crandall et al., 1986, p. 26). In short, innovations must be practical.

A method to improve clarity in innovation use and to reduce the potential of distortion employs the concept of *innovation configurations* (Heck, Stiegelbauer, Hall, & Loucks, 1981) or *practice profiles* (Loucks & Crandall, 1981). This method outlines (a) core components of the change developers believe is required if desired results are to be obtained, and (b) related components which enhance the operation of core components or increase the likelihood of achieving desired goals. It also lays out implementation requirements and the necessary resources, such as user knowledge and skills, or materials and equipment, which may be required to implement the change. A profile checklist also can be used to explain the innovation to users and to design strategies addressed to support specific components. Profiles also may help evaluate the fit between the innovation and the teacher and the school more accurately, allowing the school to adapt components, as necessary, or determine what adaptations are likely to affect goal outcomes. Assessing implementation requirements is critical to ensuring that the resources necessary to implementation are in place and whether the system is ready to give the support demanded by the innovation (Crandall, et al., 1986).

PROCESSES: WHAT MAKES CHANGE WORK

Strategies

Strategies to support the understanding of innovations are as important as support for individuals working with the innovations. Such strategies need to be directed at a number of factors at once. Successful change, however, requires a long-term process of action, refinement, and support to clarify

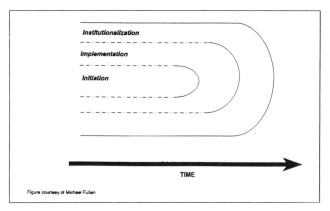

FIG. 8.2. Overlapping phases of the change process.

and to integrate innovation use. When we talk about process, we mean those factors that go into the three phases of change (see Fig. 8.2). They are (a) *initiation*: deciding on an agenda and beginning work; (b) *implementation*: putting the innovation into action, in context; and (c) *institutionalization or continuation*: seeing the innovation in place and integrated into the daily life of the school. Going through these phases can take three to five years for stable implementation and predictable outcomes.

At any point in this sequence, the direction of the process may be altered, resulting in adaptations to the innovation or even in dropping it. The more lock-step, technical rationality approach to change would see this as undesirable, though occasionally inevitable. In fact, a *hyperrational approach*, which views change in terms of "what should be changed" (Wise, 1977; Fullan, 1991) often acts as a barrier to setting up an effective process of change, given the nonrational quality of social systems (Patterson, Purkey, & Parker, 1986). New views on change look at this process and the events within it as opportunities to improve goals and outcomes for the health of the organization—systems, teachers, and students alike.

Both the change process and the people involved in it go through something like developmental stages. Different kinds of activities are needed to address each stage. At its simplest, an image of this process can be configured around Hall and Hord's (1987) Stages of Concern model: Early in the process, activities need to be addressed to personal issues, then to management tasks, and, later, to refinement issues. Implementation and organizational requirements for resources and support also must be considered early in the process. Involving teachers early on in problem identification and task-related strategies, such as peer coaching for skills, helps develop commitment. True commitment, however, is usually the effect of seeing outcomes occur, not the cause. "The commitment of teachers increases as they simultaneously see themselves master the practice and perceive that their students are doing better" (Crandall, et al., 1986, p. 34). Finally, the organization has to provide resources, ongoing training and coaching, and monitoring to nurture the immediate process of implementation (Hall & Hord, 1987). Strategic conceptualizations like these provide facilitators with a starting point.

Another way to begin is through the use of *temporary systems*—project groups, task forces, consultative relationships that " . . . at some more or less clearly defined point in time will cease to be" (Miles, 1992, p. 9), but which support the change through the process of implementation. These temporary groups have the advantage of being able to define themselves and are often more egalitarian and experimental than the organizational environment around them. These kinds of bounded groups become a model for the management of change, such that " . . . creative attention given to the invention and use of new types of temporary systems could show very high payoff" Miles stated in 1964 (1992, p. 10). As they form new norms within the team, they are often able to influence the norms around them to good effect. When the team disbands, members have new skills they can contribute to other projects.

Research and Organizational Themes

Research on temporary systems has influenced thinking on the management of change, including what the organizational environment should look like. With that as a given, enter the reality of larger, multilevel efforts for change. Here other factors come into play, including nonrationality, or nonlinear effects in the process. Research suggests that activities directed to some broader but consistent *organizational themes* also have a positive effect on a change process (Fullan, 1991; Louis & Miles, 1990). Organizational themes include:

- *Vision Building*, or the capacity of the school to develop a shared vision of what the school and its change should look like. When this shared purpose is present, schools are better able to build consensus and credibility through the use of symbols, public dialogue, and the example of those for whom the change makes sense.
- *Evolutionary Planning*, closely related to the first theme, embodies the capacity of organizations to "take advantage of unexpected developments in the service of vision" (Miles, 1987, p. 13). "Have a plan, but learn by doing" (Fullan, 1991, p. 83).
- *Initiative-taking and Empowerment* allow leadership to come from a variety of sources, including cross-hierarchical steering groups in contact with other groups with similar interests. Collaborative work cultures that reduce the professional isolation of teachers increase

the potential of social progress to support implementation. As one gains the recognition of one's peers, incentives to succeed increase.

- *Staff Development and Resource Assistance* are often seen as start-up training for innovation use, not as a continuing process. One of the least developed yet most important elements of staff development is follow-up. New conceptions, skills, and behaviors require continuous, interactive, cumulative learning to be fully taken advantage of. This means in-service training must happen all the way through the process of implementation, not just at the beginning. Fullan (1991) describes it this way:

Implementation, whether it is voluntary or imposed, is nothing other than a process of learning something new. One foundation of learning is interaction. Learning by doing, concrete role models, meetings with resource consultants and fellow implementors, practice of the behavior, and the fits and starts of cumulative, ambivalent, gradual self-confidence all constitute a process of coming to see the change more clearly. (p. 85)

- *Monitoring, Problem-coping, and Restructuring* the change process are just as important as measuring its outcomes. This is in part an information issue: information about what is working can be shared, while information about what is not working can serve as a stimulus to *problem-coping*—arriving at solutions that make sense. This is another form of Miles' (1992) *process analysis*—shared, self-analytic behavior, "a sort of sustained mindfulness that leads to further diagnosis and action taking" (Miles, 1987, p. 6).

Needless to say, perhaps, evaluation is always a delicate point. Getting monitoring right requires sophistication and trust. In this context, restructuring refers to how the school as a workplace is or is not organized to support change, which includes policies, organizational arrangements, roles, funding, availability of time to hold meetings, and demands on teachers and other staff. Working with innovation may require that the organization change to make the change work.

Interactive Change

The change process being described in these themes is interactive and complex. While these themes may be a part of all three of the phases of process—initiation, implementation, and institutionalization—they are especially in demand during the implementation phase, when most of the learning about change occurs. It also is the phase requiring the most person support, in group and one-on-one consultation and coaching, in order to problem-cope as matters progress. This is the time to hang fast and wait for group consensus, cumulative learning, and critical mass to have an effect.

Institutionalization

The last phase of the change process, *institutionalization*, has its own requirements. Institutionalization depends upon change becoming embedded in the context and structure through policy, budgets, and timetables; and through generating a critical mass of administrators and teachers skilled in and committed to change (Huberman & Miles, 1984). Although institutionalization may seem to connote a final phase, it actually is difficult to complete. In fact, evidence suggests that, rather than support institutionalization, organizations tend to enter a process of renewal, which may result in either tailoring the innovation to more current needs or to replacing it as emphasis is given to yet another change. Institutionalization succeeds best when all phases of the change process are considered at the beginning (e.g., how will funding be maintained for ongoing in-service activities and needed materials?).

The Bottom Line

Rather than implementing single innovations, schools are beginning to develop their capacity for continuous improvement as a generic skill, based on changing needs and new programs. This is not to say that successful innovations should not be continued, only that they should be viewed in terms of their relevance to renewal and to the improvement of practice, not just in terms of mastery. The single innovation approach often has benefits in mediating the chaos of change, especially early in the process. The bottom line to any change, however, is how it fits within the organization, since it is organizational health that will make the longer-term difference. Educational reform is largely a local process wherein central support is vital; effective linkage systems among leaders, facilitators, and users within a system are essential; and wherein emphasis is on continuous evolution, with a focus on classroom practices and outcomes (IMTEC, 1992).

POLICIES: SUPPORTING CHANGE

How change is supported through policy can make the work of those implementing the change more or less difficult. Good policies can make people more flexible, and they can clarify directions and priorities, help focus people, and validate whatever is going on.

Focus on Policies

The focus of policies should be on the people and activities that put the change into action. Questions that must be asked include: If policies are not in place to support those kinds of things, what policies need to be in place? What kinds of linkages are there and what linkages need to be developed? How will finances be found to actually make the necessary changes? The goal of policies should be directed toward whatever it takes to develop the desired outcomes, given the social reality of various systems.

Generally, when we are discussing policy issues, we are talking about administration and organizational linkages. What has been said about change as it affects people, practices, and processes now takes another turn as we consider what it takes to support and maintain strategies related to all of the above. This can be discussed at a number of levels—the school, the district, the state, and the nation. The conditions for success remain the same at all levels: Administrative support is vital to change, and policy decisions make and break change efforts.

Learning to Support Local Schools

The issue for upper administration (district, board, ministry, state, national) is learning to support local schools in their efforts: " . . . in other words, how to make demands on, support, encourage, empower, enable, and build a strong local school" (IMTEC, 1992). Supports within the system must be built around the real needs of the schools in development. One of those supports is assessing necessary linkages beyond the school that contribute to the school's work. Another support is developing easy relationships across the system.

Learning to Support System-Wide Initiatives

Policy can support system-wide initiatives and learning as well as local projects. Fullan and Hargreaves (1991) made a number of recommendations for school systems: (a) develop more trust and ability to take risks as a system, especially in the selection, promotion, and development process; (b) foster increased interaction and empowerment in the system; (c) give the curriculum content back to schools; and (d) restructure administration to meet current needs. Such recommendations emphasize the need of systems to develop connectedness and real empowerment—the sharing of power with students, with teachers, and with principals. Rosenholtz (1989), in studying what makes a difference in the capacity of schools to deal with change, found that moving schools to action placed a great deal of emphasis on the selection of good personnel and on learning opportunities for all. Moving districts to action might mean considering the same criteria. Collaborative cultures may emerge in such schools, but they still require support at the district level, in the spirit of interactive professionalism laced with cross-school and cross-district contact.

Teachers, parents, and students are more likely to develop commitment and collaboration around issues of local interest. Whether the solution to local concerns comes from the inside or from the outside, the process and the potential power of interaction across levels remains the same. The task of local districts is to " . . . set goals and standards to provide funds, research and resource materials and the means to achieve those goals" (Fullan & Hargreaves, quoting Landsberg, 1991, p. 103). The specific goals, once the framework is established, become an agenda for the school.

THE USE OF ASSESSMENT IN CHANGE

Besides clarifying and supporting changes after they are implemented, assessment can be a major contributor to the change process itself. At the people and practices level, once individuals are comfortable with assessment or monitoring materials as problem-solving or problem-coping devices, assessment can play a role in making the change more practical and workable. At the process level, various forms of assessments and monitoring tools (e.g., those of the concerns model) can help facilitators learn how to work with individuals or help temporary systems teams understand the effects of their efforts. At the policy level, assessments have the potential to determine where linkages and support are most needed and to validate ongoing efforts as a part of continuous improvement.

The Dual Purpose of Assessment

Assessment serves a dual purpose in the process of change, and may be considered part and parcel of a specific innovation—for example, finding the best way to use portfolios, reflective strategies, or student monitoring worksheets effectively and training people to use them. Assessments may at the same time be part and parcel of the innovation process, helping to check on progress. In a reflection of the restructuring movement of the last few years, schools are more and more engaged with changes that involve both process and content assessment. This duality acknowledges that however good a change is, it is still a change, and people will need time to learn about it and learn how to use it to clarify their work.

An Example of Change

The restructuring of a high school in northern Ontario (Stiegelbauer & Anderson, 1992) offers one example of the use of assessment strategies embedded in the innovation and implementation of change. Like many other schools in the United States and Canada, this one faced budget cutbacks that potentially meant the loss of a number of programs the school staff and board saw as important. They decided to find another way to organize their school so that they could keep these programs.

The result of their efforts is a student-centered high school called Project Excellence, which puts teachers in the role of student advisors, subject monitors, and coaches for student learning. Students, on the other hand, completed course units, were tested for mastery at the end of each unit, were coached by teachers if they had problems, and participated along with teachers in the design and implementation of the program as it evolved (Anderson, Stiegelbauer, Gerin-Lajoie, Partlow, & Cummins, 1989). Monitoring and assessment were essential in determining how to implement the innovation and also were part of the implementation process. During the first three years of implementing and clarifying the innovation, teachers, administrators, and occasionally parents and students met biweekly to assess, adjust, and maintain consensus about what they were all doing. The result is a restructured school that works, proving that monitoring and ongoing assessment are an important part of how and why it works.

Project Excellence is only one example of people working together to apply assessments and relate those assessments to other aspects of school life. Whether the use of assessment is narrow or broad, related to a specific curriculum or part of a larger change process, some kind of reflection and monitoring can only facilitate change. A cautionary note, however—many people have had negative experiences with assessments in the past or see assessment strategies as compromising their own independence as teachers. Working on this issue will probably be part of the change process, and an important one at that. Unless people see assessments as beneficial to them and understand how to use and apply them well, assessments will not have their greatest possible effect on change. People, in effect, must want change to work.

CONCLUSION: CHANGE HAS CHANGED

Key research on the do's and don'ts of change suggest that, rather than developing a new strategy for each change, systems must engage in continuous improvement. Instead of seeing change as distinct from other events within a system, systems must learn to view change as a part of everyday reality.

The emphasis of change used to be on the management and implementation of single innovations—one teacher, one classroom. The new emphasis, based on the research of the past 20 years, is on developing systemic capacity for change. In this framework, change is part of a continuous learning process for educational professionals. Strategies for working with change can benefit from the work done on managing single innovations. At the same time, however, specific change efforts offer opportunities for different kinds of interactions that contribute to a kind of organizational learning that develops the whole system, not the teacher-implementor alone.

As part of the new paradigm of change, we look at change differently. To borrow here from Fullan and Miles' 1992 article "Getting Reform Right," and paraphrasing a bit:

Change Is a Journey, Not a Blueprint. Rational, planned change is certainly helpful in the beginning, but in work with people in schools on implementation projects, there inevitably comes a moment when something happens. Perhaps it is the *implementation dip,* perhaps it is a change in personnel, but whatever it was is, it means diverting from the plan and changing what is being done. If we think about the process of change as a blueprint directing us from Point A to Point B to Point C as in Fig. 8.2, it is a little harder to see a diversion as an opportunity. When we believe from the beginning that the process of change is a journey where detours, interesting villages, or waterfalls are potential opportunities, then change is not so intimidating. Miles, in his AERA presentation (1992), reminded us that when you have groups of people working on things together, you have the capacity for a journey. Collaborative work not only provides a problem-coping focus, but also the support to make the risk taking more rewarding.

Change Is Systemic. Change projects are often initiated to solve one problem without looking at the relationship of that problem to other issues in the school or the overlap of personnel and resources that will be a part of all that the school does. Having a larger vision for the school or system puts change in perspective regarding where the school or system is going and how resources can be shared to get it there. Any major reforms in complex systems such as schools, school districts, or boards need to build structures and capabilities at all levels. "Ad hoc solutions will not work in the long run; only institution-building based on sustained commitment works." (IMTEC, 1992)

Change Is Learning; Reform Is Risky; Resolution Is Uncertain; Problems Are Our Friends. On a journey through change, you may get where you are going, but sometimes you get somewhere else. You may get waylaid for a couple of years. All of that opens up opportunities for different kinds of learning and different ways of accomplishing a desired effect. It is always a little risky to be open to opportunity, yet from the perspective of learning, it has advantages. Thinking about change as a learning process opens the door to opportunities to reframe, look at results differently. Taking on unexpected problems and finding solutions to them creates the capacity to continue to do so. "Deep coping," as Fullan and Miles stated, appears more likely when schools are working on a "clear, shared vision of where they are heading" and when they create an active coping structure (such as a temporary group) to tackle problems and focus energy (1992, p. 750). Know ahead of time that no journey is without problems.

Change Programs Do Not Run Themselves; Change Is Resource Hungry. Change will eat up as many resources as you want to give it. You need people, you need money, you need supplies, you need special facilities, you need time. Ongoing resources are an important part of making change work. Looking at innovation in terms of discrete changes makes this kind of resource management all the more imposing. On the other hand, looking at the bigger picture, developing capacity for management, and seeking overlap help to manage this resource problem. The more linkages, relationships, and networks that you can develop between parts of the system, the more likely it is that you will have effective problem-coping management. Linkages develop commitment, help with resources and support, empower and train people, and provide personnel for facilitation and leadership. They provide support for the substantial effort which needs to be devoted to such tasks as checking on progress, keeping everyone informed of what's happening, linking with other change projects, and solving problems. In schools where change succeeds, these kinds of activities occurred more frequently than in other schools (Fullan & Miles, 1992). You cannot assume that change will come into being, other than in name only, without this kind of work.

All Large Scale Change Is Ultimately Local Implementation. If it does not work at the school or classroom level, it is not going to work at the system level, no matter how good the idea or the innovation. When individuals are able to work with the change, no matter what its source—mandated or locally developed—schools and systems will work with the change. Evidence says that the school is the center of change and focus on classroom practice makes change meaningful to teachers. It is the school's vision and collaborative work that put the change in action; the qualities of the change which demonstrably address real classroom issues give momentum to that action. Schools do need the support and commitment of other levels for a top–down, bottom–up balance, but change has to happen in one place, the place where the most work must occur.

Changing the Culture of Institutions Is the Real Agenda. Finally, the new perspectives on change have a different agenda from the earlier, technologically-based frameworks. When we are talking about change, we are talking about new ways to deal with education and its institutions which better allow us to address problems and find solutions on a continuing basis. New ideas on change see this as an issue of constant learning for all, not a one-shot implementation effort. These ideas on change also emphasize the value of collaborative work in the process of change, work that institutionalizes the interaction between different levels and participants in the system, that is addressed to both global and specific concerns, and that respects all elements of the system for what they can contribute, not for what they conventionally are.

For change to be effective, we have to find new ways of interacting as human beings in organizational settings. Any innovation, such as performance assessment, can serve as a starting point. These new ideas on change are even more complicated than the old ones and making them work requires a new mind set and a different style. In tandem with that complexity are two givens: Change is a constant, and "wishful thinking and legislation have a poor track record for social betterment" (Fullan & Miles, 1992, p. 752). Understanding the factors that influence the success and failure of change opens the door to a fresh approach and " . . . is the best defense and the best offense" (Fullan & Miles, 1992, p. 752) for improving schools.

The following guide to change implementation incorporates the central ideas contained within this chapter. Its intention is to provide the reader with an easy-to-use reference to the most important elements in the process of innovation.

SUMMARY

CHANGE HAS CHANGED: GUIDELINES

People: The Most Important Element in Change

- Change is a process, not an event. While mandates have a role, it is the long-term process of engaging and supporting people working with change that will make the most difference.
- A variety of roles play a part in any change process. These roles can add up to consultative and interactive processes that support not only a specific change, but strategies for any change.
- Change is a highly personal experience; people respond to change differently.
- People go through developmental stages related to the self, to management or task, and to the refinement of change in relation to student results. Understanding these stages will help facilitators address individual needs and interests, as people work with a specific change.

- Change involves adaptations in behaviors, practices, skills, and often beliefs about what is important and valuable. People often experience initial work with change as a loss of what they do well. Finding ways to combine their areas of strength with what is new will promote comfort with change.
- Teachers are guided by a *practicality ethic*. They want to know that a change has practical outcomes for themselves and for their students.
- Success in facilitating change requires pressure and support from leaders and one-on-one interactions with teachers to solve problems and to support innovation.

Practices: Need, Complexity, Clarity, Quality, Practicality

- Practices must fit into teachers' situations, be clear, and include concrete how-to-do-it information.
- Practices must demonstrate clear benefits for students.
- Change is not always progress; practices must be relevant to local needs, concerns, and adaptation.
- Too small or too large an innovation may result in no change at all. The greatest success occurs when change requires noticeable, but manageable and sustained effort.
- Change affects not only teachers, but schools and school systems. Practices need to be viewed in relation to other practices and to system goals.
- Change in practice requires change in behavior, skills, attitudes, beliefs, and frequently, ways that people work with one another. Each one of these is a kind of innovation in itself.
- Examining new practices in terms of core components, related components, and implementation requirements can help in determining fit and in designing implementation strategies.

Process: What Makes Change Work

- The process of change involves three phases: initiation, implementation, and continuation. From the beginning, all should be considered in planning.
- Organizational themes contributing to successful change include developing a shared vision, evolutionary planning, providing for initiatives, empowerment, ongoing training, developing strategies for problem coping, analysis, and restructuring organizational norms to support implementation and ongoing learning. These themes are interactive and interwoven throughout the process of change.

- The social reality of systems undergoing change creates a nonrational and nonlinear setting wherein unexpected events should be viewed as opportunities for growth and for a redefinition of goals.
- The change process goes through developmental stages related to the concerns of individuals working with change: personal, management, and the refinement of work. Strategies need to be addressed to these concerns as part of the innovation process.

Policies: Supporting the Change

- The focus of policy should be the development of organizational supports and linkages that enable schools to improve.
- Districts and schools can improve system capacity for change through selecting good people and providing them with opportunities to learn.
- Change requires the interaction, connectedness, and the sharing of power across different components of the system. Empowerment means giving people responsibility and support to actualize that responsibility.
- The presence or absence of supportive policies can make or break a change effort.
- People will be more committed to changes that are of local interest to them, whether those changes come from the outside or from the inside. Change as a local initiative should fit within system goals and priorities, but still address local needs.

REFERENCES

Anderson, S., Stiegelbauer, S., Gerin-Lajoie, D., Partlow, H., & Cummins, A. (1989). *Project Excellence: A case study of a student-centered secondary school.* Toronto: Ministry of Education, Province of Ontario.

Crandall, D., & Associates (1982). *People, policies and practice: Examining the chain of school improvement* (Vols. 1–10). Andover, MA: The Network, Inc.

Crandall, D. P., Eiseman, J. W., & Lewis, S. K. (1986). Strategic planning issues that bear on the success of school improvement efforts. *Educational Administration Quarterly, 22*(3), 21–53.

Cuban, L. (1988). A fundamental puzzle of school reform. *Phi Delta Kappan, 70*(5), 341–44.

Doyle, W., & Ponder, G. (1977–78). The practicality ethic in teacher decision making. *Interchange, 8*(3), 1–12.

Fullan, M. (1985). Change processes and strategies at the local level. *Elementary School Journal, 84*(3), 391–420.

Fullan, M. (1988). *What's worth fighting for in the principalship? Strategies for taking charge.* Toronto: Ontario Public School Teachers' Federation.

Fullan, M. (1991). *Overcoming barriers to educational change.* Paper commissioned by the Office of the Under Secretary of the U.S. Department of Education for the New American Schools Development Corporation initiative.

Fullan, M. G., & Hargreaves, A. (1991). *What's worth fighting for: Working together for your school*. Toronto: Ontario Public School Teachers' Federation.

Fullan, M. G., & Miles, M. B. (1992). Getting reform right: What works and what doesn't. *Phi Delta Kappan, 73*(10), 744–752.

Fullan, M. G. with S. Stiegelbauer (1991). *The new meaning of educational change*. New York: Teachers College Press.

Hall, G. E., & Hord, S. M. (1987). *Change in schools: Facilitating the process*. Albany: State University of New York Press.

Hall, G. E., & Loucks, S. F. (1977). A developmental model for determining whether the treatment is actually implemented. *American Educational Research Journal, 14*(3), 263–76.

Heck, S., Stiegelbauer, S., Hall, G., & Loucks, S. (1981). *Measuring innovation configurations: Procedures and applications*. Austin: Research and Development Center in Teacher Education, University of Texas and Southwest Educational Development Laboratory.

Hord, S. M., Stiegelbauer, S., & Hall, G. (1984). How principals work with other change facilitators. *Education and Urban Society, 17*(1), 89–109.

Horsley, D. (1990). *Many roads to fundamental reform: Getting started*. Andover: The Regional Laboratory for Educational Improvement of the Northeast and Islands.

Huberman, M. (1983). Recipes for busy kitchens. *Knowledge: Creation, Diffusion, Utilization, 4*, 478–510.

Huberman, M., & Miles, M. (1984). *Innovation up close*. New York: Plenum.

IMTEC International Newsletter (1992, June). *School improvement and evaluation: How schools improve*. Oslo, Norway.

Loucks, S., & Crandall, D. (1981). *The practice profile*. Andover, MA: The Network, Inc.

Loucks-Horsley, S. (1989). Workshop format based on Crandall, D., & Loucks, S. (1983). *A roadmap for school improvement, executive summary of the study of Dissemination Efforts Supporting School Improvement* (DESSI). Andover, MA: The Network, Inc.

Louis, K. S., & Miles, M. B. (1990). *Improving the urban high school: What works and why*. New York: Teachers College Press.

Marris, P. (1975). *Loss and change*. New York: Anchor Press/Doubleday.

Miles, M. B. (1987). *Practical guidelines for school administrators: How to get there*. Paper presented at the American Educational Research Association Meetings.

Miles, M. B. (1992, April). *40 years of change in schools: Some personal reflections*. Address to Division A (Administration), American Educational Research Association Meeting, San Francisco.

Mortimore, P., Sammons, P., Stoll, L., Lewis, D., & Ecob, R. (1988). *School matters: The junior years*. Somerset, UK: Open Books.

Patterson, J., Purkey, S., & Parker, J. (1986). *Productive school systems for a nonrational world*. Alexandria, VA: Association for Supervision and Curriculum Development.

Rosenholtz, S. (1989). *Teachers' workplace: the social organization of schools*. New York: Longman.

Sashkin, M., & Egermeier, J. (1991, April). *School change models and processes: A review of research and practice*. Symposium conducted at the 1992 Annual Meeting of the American Educational Research Association, San Francisco.

Stiegelbauer, S. M., & Anderson, S. (1992). *Seven years later: Revisiting a restructured school in northern Ontario*. Paper presented at the American Educational Research Association Meetings, San Francisco.

Wise, A. (1977). Why educational policies often fail: The hyperrationalization hypothesis. *Curriculum Studies, 9*(1), 43–57.

Chapter **9**

Arizona's Educational Reform: Creating and Capitalizing on the Conditions for Policy Development and Implementation

Lois Brown Easton
Eagle Rock School and Professional Development Center

Paul H. Koehler
Peoria Unified School District, Arizona

A state reform effort based on radical changes to an 11-year old testing program has been quietly occurring in Arizona. This reform effort is unlike many others because it has focused on systemic (rather than piecemeal) reform through changes in assessment. Although not making the headlines that Connecticut, California, or Vermont have made, the Arizona reform deserves national attention, for Arizona has succeeded in taking advantage of (and sometimes generating) policy conditions so powerful that the Arizona Student Assessment Program (ASAP; see Fig. 9.1) was written as legislation in November, 1989, and signed into law 6 months later.

According to Stout (1987), the testing situation in Arizona before the ASAP was confusing and unfocused. In 1971, the legislature passed a law requiring that districts have a Continuous Uniform Evaluation System (CUES); despite state curriculum documents, the law was not specific about what curriculum CUES should test, nor did the law require monitoring districts to make sure they implemented CUES. Furthermore, districts were not required to report CUES scores.

Without data and concerned about the strength of Arizona's educational system, legislators in 1979 mandated norm-referenced standardized testing for all students (except those exempted by law) from Grade 1 through Grade 12, every year, in the spring. With that mandate, Arizona implemented what might be described as the epitome of high stakes testing (Madaus, 1988). In 1988, the legislature was convinced by a lobby group associated with a whole language network and other educators to allow 1st- and 12th-grade testing to be optional except for a sample at each grade. Testing other students—every grade, every year, in the spring—continued until the spring of 1991.

Before the ASAP, Arizona had two testing mechanisms: (a) CUES, which required district testing that referenced no particular curriculum and was neither monitored for effectiveness nor a source of data to the state; and (b) extensive norm-referenced standardized testing, which served as the sole source of state information about achievement. Educational reform initiated at all levels died hard against these barriers.

What got Arizona interested in an alternative to such a testing program? What conditions made the state consider integrated performance assessments matching broad curriculum framework documents, reduction of norm-referenced testing, and a broad, contextual reporting system with local goal-setting?

THE ASAP

- Reduced norm-referenced standardized testing and moved it to the fall;
- Provided performance-based, integrated assessments that measure broad products or outcomes and processes and are based on the state's curriculum framework documents. The assessments are transparent to the curriculum and also transparent to each other with district forms (A, B, and C) matching the state form (D);
- Requires districts to make curriculum decisions about the state curriculum framework documents and to implement some way of measuring student competence on district implementation of the state curriculum standards. Assessment strategies may include
    -use of the district forms (A, B, or C) of the state assessments,
    -use of a portfolio system,
    -use of district-developed or selected assessments that match the district curriculum developed on the basis of the state curriculum framework documents, and
    -a combination of these assessment strategies;
                                                                (cont.)

(cont.)
- Requires assessment of third, eighth, and twelfth graders with one of the state forms (D) of the performance assessments in each subject, randomly chosen for each student so that all students need to be prepared for all assessments (and, therefore, competent on all of the curriculum standards);
- Provides for scoring of the state form (D) of the assessments by Arizona educators at regional scoring sites.
- Provides for collection of data on factors that affect and reflect achievement through surveys of teachers, principals, and superintendents and use of other data collected by the Department of Education;
- Requires the publication of school, district,and state profiles that present achievement information as well as information on factors that affect and reflect achievement and points of interpretation for both.

FIG. 9.1. The ASAP.

CONDITIONS FACILITATING THE DEVELOPMENT OF THE ASAP AS POLICY

Several conditions coalesced to make Arizona ripe for a far-reaching reform effort, one that has gone beyond its effect on testing to affect the entire system of education in the state.

The Spirit of Reform

For example, the spirit of reform that was mobilizing change across the country was also having an effect in Arizona. The national urgency to restructure schools led Arizona educators to implement site-based management practices. At a grass roots level, teachers embraced a whole language philosophy, despite strong pressure to "teach to the test," that led to a reconceptualization of elementary school education based on a commitment to literacy through meaningful texts. This was matched at the upper grades by movement to middle school philosophy and structures.

The national reform agenda had an effect at the state level, too. Like many states, Arizona initiated reform legislation in response to national reports, such as *A Nation at Risk*. In 1987, the Arizona legislature initiated a reform bill called Goals for Educational Excellence (GEE). The GEE called for setting high standards for students in terms of K-12 achievement, graduation rate, and postsecondary success; and the GEE empowered a joint legislative committee that included representatives from education, business, and community sectors. This committee, in turn, convened task forces for each of the three components (K-12 achievement, graduation rate, and post-secondary success) of the bill.

A Collaborative Opportunity

In addition, the GEE legislation required collaboration between the legislature and educators in the state, particularly the State Board of Education and the Department of Education. This condition, which had far-reaching effects on the development of the ASAP, was rather unusual in a state in which the legislature usually passed laws that the State Board of Education and the Department of Education translated into rules and regulations and implemented with districts. The result of the work of Jacque Steiner, then Chair of the Senate Education Committee, working with Bev Hermon, Chair of the House Education Committee, and C. Diane Bishop, State Superintendent of Schools, made it possible for educators to respond to the work of the task forces, particularly the task force on K-12 achievement.

The Department responded to the specific learning objectives set by the task force on K-12 achievement during its brief summer work with the following statement:

- The state already has excellent curriculum framework documents that could do the work of the specific objectives set by the task force. Furthermore, adoption of the task force's objectives would create a condition of curriculum chaos; districts already had too many curriculum masters. The state's curriculum frameworks should be adopted in lieu of the task force's objectives;
- Testing as established by the state in 1980 would not be able to measure achievement of the goals as articulated by either the task force's objectives or the state's curriculum framework documents; and
- If those objectives were to be measured so the legislature would know how close the state was to meeting its K-12 achievement goals, assessments closely aligned to the curriculum had to be developed, current standardized testing had to be substantially reduced to allow for the new assessments, and district testing (CUES) had to be reconsidered.

Once the Joint Legislative Committee became convinced of the worth of the state's curriculum framework documents (and appreciative of the process by which these documents were written), all else followed. The Committee abandoned its own objectives, required development of assessments to match the state curriculum frameworks, and agreed to reconsider state and district testing.

Thus, the GEE inadvertently opened a pathway to reform of assessment, and educators in the state took advantage of it. Although initially not intended to address the testing situation in the state, the GEE required the setting of higher achievement goals and caused legislators to wonder how these goals might be measured. Educators, seeing the opportunity to change a situation that had grown intolerable, were able to convince legislators that they could not achieve higher educational goals for students if they continued current testing practices.

Capitalizing on Dissatisfaction

Educators had long been saying that current testing practices were not working for Arizona students. At last, legislators began to say the same thing, although for somewhat different reasons. Dissatisfaction, therefore, was another condition that enabled the GEE legislation and the resulting ASAP to be successful. Through the GEE, legislators expressed their concern about higher order thinking skills and their beliefs that higher order goals for student achievement needed to be defined and legislated. They acted on their belief that educators would not orient themselves toward teaching for higher achievement without a legislative mandate. Underlying these beliefs and resulting actions was a fundamental perception that they did not know enough about student achievement, particularly in higher order thinking skills. Lacking data and suspicious about what they perceived as a void in stating goals for higher achievement, legislators sought some way of mandating excellence.

Their dissatisfaction with the current system was shared by educators who may not have agreed on precisely what was wrong with education in Arizona nor how to fix it, but did agree that something had to change. Educators were clearly troubled by the limits of the current testing situation. Although intended to spur student achievement in Arizona, the norm-referenced standardized tests had, in educators' minds, depressed achievement. Haladyna, Haas and Nolen (1990) and Smith (1990) attested to the effects of the high-stakes norm-referenced testing system in Arizona. Tests, initially not meant to have much of an effect on curriculum, began to serve as curriculum as the 1980s progressed. "Teaching to the test" became the norm, especially in the months preceding April testing. Educators, particularly those seeking to implement a whole language or middle school philosophy, became frustrated with the influence of norm-referenced testing over curriculum and instruction. This difference was made more poignant when educators noticed the discrepancy between the state curriculum frameworks that supported their educational philosophies and the state's testing structure. Even Department of Education specialists became frustrated when, in the middle of exciting work on writing process, for example, teachers would query, "But is this on the ITBS?"

Exacerbating the testing problem in Arizona was the reporting system. Lacking any knowledge about district testing (CUES), the state could only publish scores from the norm-referenced tests as evidence of educational achievement. Every July, these were published district by district (sometimes school by school) as front page stories. The scores lacked context since the publishing of other educational indicators along with test scores was not mandated. Any casual newspaper reader could jump to conclusions about a school—warranted or not—based on its test scores. Already hot in the summer, Arizona grew hotter every July when the test scores were published.

Progress in Curriculum Reform

Another condition that contributed to the success of the ASAP as policy was the progress that had already been made in curriculum reform. The Arizona Board of Education and the Department of Education had, as early as 1985, turned their attention toward curriculum reform. Embarrassed by state curriculum documents that were lists of discrete and isolated skills representing a hodgepodge of curriculum theory, the State Board put into effect a regular curriculum revision process preceding textbook adoption in each subject area according to a seven-year cycle.

The first curriculum list to be revised was in language arts. The broad-based, State Board-appointed committee revising this document set the standard for all subsequent revisions by first creating a foundation statement for language arts that defined and described the language arts according to the best current thinking of researchers and practitioners in the field. The beliefs in the foundation statement led to curriculum guidelines that required:

- Processes and whole products or outcomes, rather than isolated skills;
- An integrated language arts approach;
- Language across the curriculum; and
- Holistic evaluation of language use.

Like the California frameworks, this document was a framework for language arts curriculum in Arizona districts; it set expectations for third, eighth, and twelfth grades rather than curriculum for all grades. Arizona's language arts document was recognized as an outstanding curriculum document by the National Council of Teachers of English.

Subsequent subject area frameworks largely followed the format of the language arts document and emerged with solid foundation statements and related processes, content, and products or outcomes instead of isolated skills. District committees throughout the state reviewed and responded to all framework documents, and statewide hearings were held in order to revise the documents before final drafts were presented to the State Board of Education for adoption.

If the Department of Education, following the mandate of the State Board of Education, had not required curriculum development of this sort, the Joint Legislative Committee might have clung to the specific objectives written by their task forces, and testing in Arizona might not have changed much. The effect of high stakes testing on all aspects of education in Arizona would have continued. Instead, since the ASAP was based on curriculum frameworks already respected throughout the state, the ASAP had credibility even before its particulars were aired for the first time.

State Research Efforts

State research efforts also aided Arizona in moving from its dependency upon norm-referenced tests to measure student achievement. In 1987, the State Board of Education by law had to determine which norm-referenced standardized tests to use for the next few years. The committee it appointed to make the determination decided that it wanted a correlation between the language arts and mathematics tests and the state curriculum framework documents. A research effort directed by Noggle of Arizona State University (1988) demonstrated that on average, across three tests submitted for adoption, three grade levels and three subjects (reading, language arts, and mathematics), only about 26% of the skills in the curriculum framework documents were measured by any of the tests. Legislators, dependent upon these instruments for information about student achievement, were appalled; they wanted to know what the tests did test and were disturbed to find that the tests largely measured lower level skills rather than the higher level skills they valued. They also were disturbed to think that teachers might devote considerable teaching time to the fraction of outcomes in the curriculum frameworks that actually were tested.

As part of the Department of Education's response to the GEE, researchers at Arizona State University, West Campus, were asked to determine the effect of norm-referenced standardized testing in Arizona. Haladyna, Haas, and Nolen (1989) prepared three technical papers for the Department. The first looked at the literature related to test pollution; the second reported on questionnaires distributed to principals, teachers, and superintendents about curriculum, instructional, and testing practices as well as climate factors that were influenced by norm-referenced testing in Arizona. The third presented anecdotal data as a result of follow-up interviews with teachers, principals, and administrators. The researchers suggested that the effects of test pollution made data from the norm-referenced testing less than trustworthy; they also documented instances of curriculum change, instructional time devoted to test preparation, and practice tests; and finally, they illustrated through teacher, principal, and superintendent anecdotes that norm-referenced testing was taking a professional (and sometimes personal) toll in Arizona.

Smith (1990) of Arizona State University focused on the last of these effects in a study that was independent of the Department of Education. In this study, she compared the effects of testing in a traditional school and a whole-language school. Although she found that the effects on students and teachers were debilitating and demoralizing in both schools, she found more profound effects in the school working to transform itself from a basal workbook curriculum to a literature-based curriculum.

All five of these studies appeared at the appropriate time, the first four commissioned by the Department of Education, the fourth an independent study. The 26% found by Noggle (1988) became a number much cited by legislators to explain their interest in performance assessment correlated to the curriculum frameworks they valued. *Test pollution* became a familiar phrase to describe the doubts legislators had about what they were learning from test scores. Stories of first graders crying on test day and twelfth graders "blowing off" the test were heard in legislative halls. All five studies had a profoundly positive effect on the move from reliance on norm-referenced testing to the ASAP.

Technical Support

Readiness to offer technical support for the ASAP is another condition that advanced the reform effort. Before 1985, the Department of Education had been largely a monitoring and regulatory agency. In 1985 a unit known as the School Improvement Unit (SIU) was formed. This unit was dedicated to service, curriculum innovation and support, and technical assistance. Specialists in writing, reading, mathematics, social studies, science, and general pedagogy who were hired during 1986 and 1987 made their first priority working with schools and districts on a variety of staff development needs. This unit was operative and had gained a good reputation by the time the ASAP needed technical assistance, particularly in curriculum and assessment innovation. The state writing specialist, for example, found herself on call to assist with writing assessment and its impact on teaching writing in the English classroom and across the curriculum.

National innovation in assessment also paved the way for the ASAP. What writing assessment experts had discovered was being translated into other subject areas, and states across the country were beginning to develop and use performance assessments based on the model of the writing assessment. If English language arts teachers had not been, as Wiener (1986) put it, wrestling " . . . with the issue of testing student writers and [devising] an assessment system whose history is a notable model for the profession at large," performance-based assessment in other fields would have been less likely, or slower, to develop (p. 13). Indeed, according to Wiener, other subject area teachers were encouraged by the success of English teachers in direct assessment of writing to " . . . shape valid assessment programs that reflect the important tenets of their disciplines" (p. 13).

Innovations in assessment allowed test makers to measure students' ability to demonstrate knowledge and skills, particularly in writing but also, gradually, in other subjects. These innovations were being refined and developed in other areas when a performance-based assessment system was proposed for the ASAP. The innovations made it possible for the Department of Education to answer the query, "But how can you test that?" with a description of direct assessment of writing, an evaluation of a variety of responses to reading, and a measurement of student application of mathematics. The Joint Legislative Committee became convinced that the higher-order requirements they appreciated in the state curriculum framework documents could be measured.

The development work that states such as Connecticut, California, New York, Illinois, Michigan, Vermont, and Maryland had accomplished by the time the ASAP was proposed allowed the Department of Education to answer the question important to all legislators, "But, who else is doing that?" with a list of respected leaders in education.

Thus, curriculum frameworks that mandate more than selection of a correct answer could be assessed. The language arts curriculum framework and assessments require students to write in a variety of genres following a writing process, and read and respond thoughtfully to intact pieces of real literature or worthy nonfiction. The mathematics curriculum framework and assessments require use of mathematics to solve real problems and communicate about mathematical thinking. The social studies and science frameworks and assessments require sophisticated and integrated problem-solving. Multiple-choice, norm-referenced standardized tests could never have done the job for Arizona. The work of Wiggins, Mitchell, Linn, Shepherd, Madaus, the Resnicks, and others, and application of their work in other states, eased Arizona's move toward alternative assessment.

Open-Minded Professionalism

Two other conditions facilitated the ASAP as policy. Leaders in state government, districts, and the professional associations were thoughtful, open-minded, and influential. Furthermore, they collaborated with one another to bring about the ASAP; informal meetings and phone calls were frequent, and formal meetings of a GEE Advisory (and, later, an ASAP Advisory Committee) united these people. The chair of the Senate Education Committee at the time of the GEE and the ASAP, Jacque Steiner, had worked for several years prior to the GEE to bring about just such legislation. Steiner was a former teacher, and she had worked with another former teacher, Jim Green, chair of the House Education Committee, who was later replaced by yet another former teacher, Bev Hermon. All three would solve many educational problems; the logical extension of the GEE with the ASAP appealed to them. The chief state school officer, C. Diane Bishop, a former high school mathematics teacher, also had a vision of education that translated into the eventual Arizona Student Assessment Program.

State leaders were backed by thoughtful and effective assistants. Legislative education staff Judy Richardson (who later directed School Finance at the Department of Education), Louann Bierlein (who later worked at the Morrison Institute for Public Policy at ASU), Michelle Blaine, and Martha Dorsey assisted the Joint Committee on the GEE, facilitated collaboration among the legislature, the State Board, and the Department of Education, drafted and revised the legislation, and facilitated the formal hearings and less formal conversations legislators had about the ASAP. The State Board and Department of Education were served by Paul Koehler, Associate Superintendent, and Lois Easton, Director of Curriculum and Assessment Planning.

The professional associations, including the NEA affiliate, the Arizona Education Association (particularly Donna Campbell), and the Arizona School Boards Association (particularly Joanne Mortensen), similarly swung their agendas and lobbying efforts toward the ASAP once they recognized its potential for advancing their own educational agendas. Lest their support sound too self-serving, let it be stated that all also recognized the inherent good within the ASAP. For example, the AEA saw empowerment of teachers within the ASAP; the ASBA saw more possibility for site-based management and local control. Both entities favored diminished norm-referenced testing, more educationally healthy performance testing tied to agreed-upon curriculum standards, and better data about student achievement.

One legislator who voted for the ASAP in the form of Senate Bill 1442 declared, "I don't know when I've seen all the alphabets behind an educational initiative like this. If they're all behind it, it must be good, so I'll vote for it."

Superintendents from several districts followed the legislation carefully and worked for the ASAP once they realized the support it would lend to their own district reform efforts. According to one superintendent, "Authenticity is a nice incentive, doing something that is real, that is important" (Easton, 1991, p. 338). He also stated, "The ASAP is seen as a breath of fresh air . . . teachers with a strong support base and pedagogy embrace the ASAP because it validates what they believe about teaching and learning" (Easton, 1991, p. 286).

More than once, teachers testified at hearings on the ASAP, often taking personal days in order to do so. According to one teacher, the ASAP helps teachers to be "mindful" about their teaching (Easton, 1991, p. 310).

AN ANALYSIS OF THE ASAP'S SUCCESS AS POLICY

How well did these conditions work to advance policy? Succinctly put, they enabled the passage of the ASAP during a single legislative session.

Senate Bill 1442 was drafted in November 1989 and heard by the Senate Education Committee in January 1990. It was approved by an 8 to 1 vote and presented to the House Education Committee, which approved it after slight amendment 12 to 2, with one member abstaining. The bill in its revised form was reapproved by the same margin in the Senate Education Committee and sent to the full Senate, where it was approved 21 to 9. The bill was heard in the full House and passed by a 45 to 7 vote. The Governor signed the bill into law in May 1990.

Application of Policy Analysis Criteria

Other criteria for effective educational policy may help explain the successful passage of the ASAP. Pipho (1990) described several criteria for successful policy in a "Forum" section of *Education Week*. Among these criteria, his suggestion that going fast is better than going slowly is most pertinent: "Speed is the name of the game" (Pipho, 1990, p. 24). The rapid passage of the ASAP (6 months from the writing of the legislation to the Governor's signature) may have served the state well. As one state cynic pointed out, "The more time there is for people to fuss, the more they'll find wrong with a perfectly good bill." Two years of work on the GEE before the ASAP, however, provided a solid basis for the legislation. The several years over which the ASAP has been implemented has also provided needed time for districts to make the global changes they needed because of the ASAP.

Pipho also suggested that "once you start, keep the momentum" (1990, p. 24). From August 1989 through May 1990, over 200 forums and public meetings were held regarding the ASAP. Almost daily, somewhere in the state, someone was talking about the ASAP. An elaborate and frequently revised task analysis for the process of getting the ASAP from first draft to the Governor's signature helped the ASAP "get there" in 6 months.

The public forums and meetings helped address another reason the ASAP was successful: The planners of the ASAP did not "sell the public short" (Pipho, 1990, p. 24). Many vehicles for communication about the ASAP helped deliver a consistent message. The Department invited even its most outspoken opponents to discuss the ASAP. Similarly, the ASAP planners did not "hide the product or process" (Pipho, 1990, p. 24). The assessments, in the spirit of openness, were there to be viewed by everyone. Influential business groups who reviewed the ASAP assessments responded enthusiastically to the question, "Wouldn't you like to see students able to do this when they come to work for you?". On the other hand, because the ASAP happened so fast, opponents did not have much chance to marshal resources; it is likely that some who would have been outspoken against the ASAP had not heard of it by the time it had been signed into law.

Of all his political rules for educational change, Pipho's last is most striking: "Stand firm—don't flinch" (Pipho, 1990, p. 24). Legislators, State Board of Education members, educators at the Department of Education, and educators from throughout the state who supported the ASAP had moments of genuine discomfort, even agony. The authors, expecting a quiet chat with two Arizona senators, were subjected to a 2-hour assault by about 30 members of a far-right fundamentalist group, for example. Still, the leadership persisted in believing the change was right, and the bill was passed into law.

Pipho's admonition to "get the basics right—use the right mix of incentives, rewards and sanctions" (Pipho, 1990, p. 24) relates to Mitchell's (1986) criteria for evaluating educational policy. Current incentives may not be sufficient as districts struggle to implement the ASAP. Relief incentives may be more effective than either sanctions or rewards.

The six criteria Mitchell (1986) identified for evaluating educational policy provide another way of looking at the ASAP. Mitchell suggested that educational policy may be examined according to:

1. How well it meets the needs of the stakeholders (ranging from students to employers of students) and how well it balances the needs of the individual stakeholders with the overall needs of the general public;
2. How well it supports the organizational integrity of schools;
3. Whether or not it has a realistic means-end linkage;
4. How integrated it is to other state policy;
5. Whether or not it has a positive cost-benefit ratio; and
6. Whether or not it is politically feasible or even palatable. (p. 14)

Extensive interviews by Easton (1991) with seven Arizona educators from all areas of education suggest that the ASAP:

1. Is democratic; that is, it does consider the needs of all stakeholders but does not overbalance itself in favor of any one stakeholder nor lose sight of the general good;

2. Supports the organizational integrity of schools if schools are moving towards improvement based on current learning theory and doing so according to a site based plan through collaboration;
3. Does have a realistic means–end linkage, at least for the present;
4. Is the keystone for refocusing current state policy and shaping future policy;
5. Has a positive cost-benefit ratio; and
6. Is politically feasible or palatable for schools already independently moving toward improvement. (p. 377)

Elaboration on several of these findings illuminates some important aspects of the ASAP as policy, particularly its likelihood of faithful implementation.

Attitudes Toward Reform. The second and sixth findings indicate a critical split in the state between those alert to and adapting current research to present practice and those ignoring current research and seeking to preserve the status quo. As in most states, some districts (even some schools within districts) have differing attitudes toward reform and are at various places along a continuum of readiness for reform. Those already moving toward reform on their own embraced the ASAP; it validated what they were trying to do on their own. Others, particularly districts that performed well according to the way Arizona used to test students, were resistant to the ASAP. Thus, for some, the ASAP supported their learning paradigm and organizational structure and was palatable and feasible; for others, the opposite held true.

The Challenge of Incentives. The ASAP contained no incentives for implementation such as rewards or sanctions (Number 3). In fact, no threat stronger than the reporting function was embedded into the ASAP. Legislators felt that public reporting of various achievement and achievement-related indicators would serve as sufficient incentive for implementation. However, districts asked, sometimes in roundabout ways, "What happens if we don't do this?". Some legislators since the passage of the ASAP have speculated on the power of rewards and sanctions tied to the profiles. The ASAP may need stronger incentives; educators hope they'll come in the form of relief from legislative and State Board rule constraints.

Fit with Existing Policy. Although the ASAP does not fit into coherent state policy (Number 4), this is through no fault of the policy itself; there was no coherent state policy until the ASAP. For example, recent and current laws, other than the ASAP, established pilot studies of various techniques to improve education, such as career ladders. The ASAP required substantial housecleaning of old legislation, particularly legislation regarding curriculum and testing. The ASAP also forged a stronger link between State Board rules and statutes on these issues.

Funding Reform.   Finally, the ASAP did not require an appropriation (Number 5); it was implemented on a financial platform of reallocated testing money. While most saw the immediate and long-range benefits worth almost any cost, both the state and districts have struggled to implement the ASAP without financial assistance. A policy analyst stated, "I've never seen teachers talking the way they are talking about what happens in the classroom. They're studying, thinking. We're ultimately going to be getting more, far more, close to a 100% return on our investment rather than the 10% we've been getting with our old testing" (Easton, 1991, p. 355). Still, most reforms require financial support, and requests for financial support occurred in the years after the ASAP was legislated even as the state faced severe budget shortfalls. Policy implementation at both the state and district levels was jeopardized without financial assistance from the state, although as the ASAP moved from its pilot status to full implementation, additional state funding was secured.

CONDITIONS THAT HAVE FACILITATED
POLICY IMPLEMENTATION

Conditions that facilitated the passage of the legislation also may have smoothed the way for ASAP implementation.

Department Actions

The Department of Education, already geared up to implement curriculum reforms such as writing as process and the use of manipulatives in mathematics recommended in the state curriculum framework documents, switched course slightly so as to help educators understand the assessment implications of these curriculum reforms. Department specialists became ASAP liaisons for districts, so that every district had a personal contact person within the department to call on for help with the ASAP. The Department concentrated on getting out a consistent message by utilizing a variety of techniques:

- A fall 1990 statewide ASAP conference involving 800 people from nearly all 220 districts;
- Spring regional follow-up conferences serving all districts closer to home;
- A videotape;
- A videotape library of conference presentations;
- A User's Guide periodically updated with new information; and
- A newsletter.

Basha's, a statewide grocery chain, donated bags that were sent home from the 1990 conference with materials that participants could use to begin their work on the ASAP by informing and helping their communities to perceive the value of the ASAP. Many of these activities, or variations on them, continued in order to assist districts throughout Arizona.

Flexibility

More importantly, the Department, with legislative support, recognized the need for flexibility in implementing the ASAP. Pushing through the reform according to a legislative rather than an educational timeline would have doomed the ASAP to failure. Once it became enthusiastic about the ASAP, the Legislature wanted it implemented immediately. It finally conceded that the ASAP should be implemented in a single year. The Department of Education persuaded the Legislature to allow implementation over a three-year period and then presented the case for another pilot year. Extending the time to implement the ASAP in general as well as with regard to several of its particular aspects alerted the districts to the sincerity of the effort.

Other examples of flexibility include efforts to obtain and utilize feedback before making decisions. The Form D assessments are an extreme example of this effort to be flexible and involve districts, schools, and teachers. The Department of Education sent masters of all the Form A assessments to all school districts and strongly encouraged districts to use these during the 1990-91 school year. Teachers used them as teaching units and as assessments; they scored them by themselves or involved others in the scoring processes. District administrators used the assessments for staff development. Regardless of the use, educators were asked to evaluate the assessments. Feedback forms from educators and meetings enabled the Department of Education fully to evaluate the Form A assessments on which all other assessments are based (see Fig. 9.1).

Feedback

Significant revisions on Form A as a result of feedback meant an unexpected delay in issuing Forms B and C and building the official state form, Form D. For example, because the mathematics assessments were described as "doing too much thinking for students," and as making inappropriate use of manipulatives, they were extensively revised and a "hold" put on Forms B and C until the more appropriate Prototype A could be fashioned. While some educators were upset that the Department did not meet its own deadline for issuing Forms B and C and delayed administration of D, most were delighted that the call for feedback was sincere, and that feedback was utilized to create a more credible product.

Involvement

The involvement of Arizona educators in the review process and in other aspects of the ASAP is another factor that has facilitated implementation of the reform. The fact that educators score assessments at regional scoring sites also increases the credibility of the ASAP and has helped districts more willingly implement the program. As piloted with a few districts in 1990, and statewide in 1992, the scoring process is a time- and money-intensive but worthwhile process. In 1992, 577 teachers received a small stipend or reimbursement for substitute expenses for 4 days of scoring at 15 regional sites. They were trained and certified (they had to pass a performance test with real papers), and calibrated against prescored papers as they evaluated performances by third, eighth, and twelfth graders in mathematics, reading, and writing. The staff development benefits of their work have been described as worth the cost of paying these teachers for scoring the more than 115,000 papers.

Openness

Another aspect of the ASAP that has enhanced the implementation process is correlated to a virtue of the ASAP: The ASAP promotes transparency of what is usually secret and secure (see Schwartz, 1990). The assessments are closely correlated to known and valued curriculum guidelines. District forms (A, B, and C) of the assessments were revised until satisfactory, and only then was the state form (D) developed. Nothing is secret in the form of the D assessments, although specific assessments are secure until students take D. This aspect of the ASAP has brought about sufficient good will to ensure implementation in districts otherwise used to mysterious mandates from state government.

CONDITIONS WITH NEGATIVE IMPACT

Despite conditions that have facilitated both the development and implementation of the ASAP as policy, there have been problems. Communication problems have plagued the process.

Information

Partial information and misinformation have created a variety of realities in Arizona districts and communities. At one point in the development process, parent groups thought the state had adopted the NAEP (National Assessment of Education Progress, which was conducting its state-by-state trial in Arizona and other states at the time) which they then confused with the MEAP (the Michigan Educational Assessment Program). Because the MEAP was under attack by special interest groups, the ASAP was condemned by local versions of these groups as part of a national conspiracy to control curriculum. Some conservative parent groups also worried about asking students to write about themselves and a scoring process they perceived as arbitrary. One group denounced the ASAP because "the atheists who score the papers would give lower scores to students who write about Christian values." Parents and educators who dote on strategic applied phonics and other methods of teaching not consistent with current learning theory also were troubled by the ASAP.

Access

Policy implementation problems with small and rural districts abound; substitutes are rare, and many such districts cannot send (or afford to send) representatives to meetings, even when they are close-by. Implementing the ASAP in a one-room school brought with it special challenges, although most small and rural districts welcomed the grouping flexibility implied by curriculum that respects individual progress.

Decisions about the ASAP and special populations were controversial: Should the assessments be required for special education students? How can the assessments be used with these students? Although special education students were not required to take the tests, their teachers were allowed to use whatever form (A, B, or C) was appropriate in whatever way it was appropriate (as an instructional unit or assessment).

What about students who have just entered from Mexico and are barely literate in either Spanish or English? Should they be exempt, as they were from the old testing program? Does this exclude them from the curriculum? Spanish versions (not just translations) were developed and mediated administration of English versions were tried to respond to this access need. Discrimination in education through testing remains a problem, even though the state has not yet mandated use of the results of ASAP testing for decision making about student progress. According to a spokesperson from the Arizona Education Association, "We cannot be fooled that we're getting around discrimination in education with the new assessments and the ASAP. We must be vigilant about discrimination. We cannot assume fair treatment" (Easton, 1991, p. 293).

Time and Role Changes

Time, though extended considerably, could always have been further extended for better implementation. Staffs at Department, district, and school levels were reorganized to implement the ASAP; more people than expected were needed to do the jobs that needed to be done in this reform effort. Often, job refocusing was the answer, though usually not without some pain. For example, district test coordinators usually concerned with the mechanics of test administration had to consider new problems such as how far teachers, who are interactive with students during administration of the assessments, can go in helping students understand the context of a problem; how to obtain manipulatives; how to score district versions of the assessments; and how to provide staff development on new assessment practices.

Administrators, in particular, had a hard time. According to a spokesperson from the Arizona NEA affiliate, administrators "into control" were going to have a difficult time; "they will not be able to adjust to coordination of effort" (Easton, 1991, p. 294). Also, those "tied to the need for simple numbers . . . will find that easily scored bubble sheets for students and teachers" are not compatible with the implications of the ASAP (Easton, 1991, p. 294). A policy analyst suggested, however, that administrators can view the ASAP as a "tool to use as leverage with their local boards to make changes in their schools. They can blame the ASAP for anything" (Easton, 1991, p. 286).

Staff reorganization, particularly toward a more collaborative model, was seen as a potential problem, particularly for administrators who "rule with a heavy hand," according to an Arizona Education Association spokesperson (Easton, 1991, p. 327). Teachers, too, were expected to have trouble with distributed authority. The AEA spokesperson described the situation in many Arizona districts when the state asked educators to review Form A assessments: "When they received the assessments and were told they could suggest changes to them, these teachers were aghast. They'd never been asked to participate in an educational innovation" (Easton, 1991, p. 327). In a somewhat similar vein, while the ASAP cleaned up some confusing and contradictory legislation, some statutes and State Board rules remained on the books to contravene the intent and actuality of the ASAP. Among the statutes seen as potentially contradictory was the career ladders legislation because career ladders programs promote competition rather than collaboration, a feature of the ASAP. Among the State Board rules seen as not advancing the ASAP were the certification rules and state teacher testing. The former did not ensure meaningful preservice experiences in assessment and the latter more closely mirrored norm-referenced standardized testing than the ASAP performance-based assessments.

The relationships of local districts with the Department of Education, though improved by the shift in focus in the Department (in 1985) from regulation to service and a further shift to service oriented toward implementing the ASAP, continued to be a problem for some districts. Those not wanting to participate in the decision-making process with the Department simply said, "Just tell me what to do, and I'll do it." The ASAP requires district adaptation of state curriculum and assessment techniques, but according to one district superintendent, adaptive activities may be foreign to districts used to " . . . one right answer. Just as students may be baffled by assessments that ask them to think, schools and districts may be baffled by a policy that has some room for them to maneuver" (Easton, 1991, p. 328).

Districts accustomed to waves of reform confidently predicted, "This too shall pass," and geared themselves up to do nothing. Districts that wanted the state out of local decision making expressed their point of view with vigor: "We will decide what we are going to teach and how we are going to test what we are going to teach." Many used local control as an excuse for preserving the status quo; few used it to reform what they were doing. A state policy analyst took a different point of view: The ASAP as policy does not imply a single right way of doing things. Districts, she said, will discover that they can implement the ASAP in a variety of ways, whatever is right for them (Easton, 1991, p. 324). A district superintendent maintained that "the ASAP actually frees them from much that has bound them, namely the high stakes testing we've done. We won't need escape clauses from the ASAP" (Easton, 1991, pp. 328–329). The Department of Education consciously tried to follow the model Honig (1987) espoused in explaining California's reforms. Referring to the work of Peters and Waterman, he called for a "simultaneously loose and tightened management system. You define what you want in general so that people have the same definition and a carbon copy of the same general accomplishments, but you are loose enough so that you have flexibility in implementation" (p. 7).

High-performing districts that did well under the previous system of testing in Arizona were especially anxious about performance under the new system. Obviously successful districts, according to an Arizona policy analyst, were likely to see the ASAP as more of a threat to their satisfying status quo. Districts doing poorly had nothing to lose and didn't feel threatened by the ASAP (Easton, 1991, p. 288). Since the status quo most often was the old paradigm of teaching and learning, the ASAP was important for all Arizona districts, even those appearing to educate students well according to norm-referenced, standardized test scores.

A former legislator took a slightly different point of view about this tension. "Only in places where we've really failed to educate our children will there be radical upheaval and immense changes to accommodate the ASAP. And those places are where the upheaval is worth it," she stated (Easton, 1991, p. 360).

Funding

Without any special appropriation in its first and second years (and only small hope for an appropriation its third year), funding remained a problem at state, district, and school levels. Among the new costs for the state and for districts were the costs of copying and distributing the district forms of the assessments for review during school year 1990-91. "No one thought about how much it would cost to print those pilot assessments," stated an Arizona Education Association representative, "but that's one area of resistance. Some districts never did get them out to teachers because they claimed it cost too much" (Easton, 1991, p. 352).

Uses of Better Data

The fact that the ASAP results in better data for legislators to use, data centered around their Goals for Educational Excellence and based on a mix of norm-referenced test scores, performance assessment scores, and non-test indicators, has a downside according to an Arizona policy analyst. She said of legislators, "They'll be forced to do something. With an absence of data, they can ignore problems" (Easton, 1991, p. 287). They will also "have the facts and not just be hoping they're getting a straight story on needs from schools and districts" (Easton, 1991, p. 287). A former legislator realized the significance of good data: "If all 220 districts aren't doing well, we plow the field and replant with new systems, but we have to have some measure of how they're doing before we make such radical changes. We must have a framework for doing something" (Easton, 1991, pp. 336–337). Data were expected to change the relationship of educators and legislators, a change that can be both good and bad for education, good because the processes and results of the ASAP would yield authentic data, bad because those hiding from the data—either educators or legislators—would have to emerge and take action.

Equity

The question of equity frightened some educators and policy makers used to a sorting system for students, schools, and districts. Those accepting the world as haves and have nots expressed discomfort about the ASAP. A principal reinforced this point:

The kind of education being promoted in the ASAP is the kind of education usually possible only in private, even exclusive, schools. We're doing an upper class thing here with all students. We're making it possible for all students to assume leadership roles. We're helping them think, giving them problem-solving experiences, teaching students how to access resources so they'll have some equity when they leave our system. (Easton, 1991, p. 307)

According to an Arizona school superintendent, the ASAP offers all students entry into a life equal to or better than that achieved by their parents. It advances the higher skills needed for higher level jobs. Families, therefore, get an economic boost out of the ASAP, and they can take comfort from the knowledge that their children are being prepared for jobs that will be available in the 21st century (Easton, 1991, p. 299).

CONCLUSION

Despite the problems in development and implementation of the ASAP, it will make a significant difference in Arizona, greatly affecting what matters most in education: the teacher working with the individual student (McLaughlin, 1987). The ASAP, established and implemented because conditions were right for its time and place in Arizona educational history, is in turn establishing and nourishing favorable conditions for that work.

REFERENCES

Easton, L. (1991). *The Arizona Student Assessment Program as educational policy.* Unpublished doctoral dissertation, University of Arizona.

Haas, N., Haladyna, T., & Nolen, S. B. (1989). *Standardized testing in Arizona: Interviews and written comments from teachers and administrators* (Tech. Rep. 89–3). Phoenix: Arizona State University, West Campus.

Haladyna, T., Haas, N., & Nolen, S. B. (1989). *Test score pollution* (Tech. Rep. 89–1). Phoenix: Arizona State University, West Campus.

Honig, B. (1987). How assessment can best serve teaching and learning. *Assessment in the Service of Learning: Proceedings of the 1987 ETS Invitational Conference.* Princeton, NJ: Educational Testing Service.

Madaus, G. F. (1988). The influence of testing on the curriculum. In L. N. Tanner (Ed.), *Critical Issues in Curriculum: Eighty-seventh Yearbook of the National Society for the Study of Education: Part I* (pp. xx–xx). Chicago: University of Chicago Press.

McLaughlin, M. W. (1987). Learning from experience: Lessons from policy implementation. *Educational Evaluation and Policy Analysis, 9*(2) 171–178.

Mitchell, D. E. (1986, September). Six criteria for evaluating state-level education policies. *Educational Leadership, 44,* 14–16.

Noggle, N. L. (1988). *Testing of achievement.* Tempe, Arizona: College of Education, Arizona State University.

Nolen, S. B., Haladyna, T., & Haas, N. (1989). *A survey of Arizona teachers and school administrators on the uses and effects of standardized achievement testing* (Tech. Rep. 89–2). Phoenix: Arizona State University, West Campus.

Pipho, C. (1990, May 30). Political rules for educational change. *Education Week*, p. 24.

Schwartz, J. L., & Viator, K. A. (Eds.) (1990). *The prices of secrecy: The social, intellectual, and psychological costs of current assessment practice*. Cambridge, MA: Harvard Graduate School of Education, Educational Technology Center.

Smith, M. L. (1990). *The role of testing in elementary schools*. Los Angeles: UCLA Center for Research on Evaluation, Standards, and Student Testing.

Stout, R. (1987, Spring). Testing policy in Arizona. *Arizona Briefs* [pamphlets]. San Francisco: Far West Regional Laboratory for Educational Research and Development.

Wiener, H. S. (1986, Fall/Winter). Writing assessment: An evaluation paradigm. *WPA: Writing Program Administration, 10*(1–2), 13–16.

Chapter 10

Performance Assessment and Equity[1]

Eva L. Baker
University of California at Los Angeles

Harold F. O'Neil, Jr.
University of Southern California

National educational reform in its most responsible incarnation requires us to take seriously the aspirations and competencies of all citizens. It challenges us in unprecedented ways to integrate our moral policies with our most trustworthy scientific and practical knowledge. The National Education Goals demand competitiveness for all students, "leaving none behind" (National Council on Education Standards and Testing, 1992). In part, the goals will be realized through proposed national education standards and assessments.

The beliefs underlying the value of national education standards owe much to our national observation of the successes of foreign educational systems, particularly those of the economically developed world. Because Americans wish to emulate the high performance of students in those countries, we are examining and considering adopting some of the attributes of their educational systems. One such attribute shared by many countries is a well-established national examination system, through which individual students obtain credit for their accomplishments and admission tickets for higher education or job opportunities.

---

[1]Portions of the text were previously printed in the article, "Performance Assessment and Equity: A View From the USA," by E. L. Baker and H. F. O'Neil, Jr., *Assessment in Education*, 1(1), 11–26. Reprinted with permission.

Yet, the United States differs drastically from most of the countries we believe to have exemplary educational systems. First, the United States is much more diverse—in economics, in culture, and in first languages spoken—than any of our competitors. We are both a larger and more culturally expansive nation whose population may be close to 50 times the size of many of the countries we would copy. Our schools reflect our society, and our problems are complicated, as perhaps only American society can be complicated.

Even under the best circumstances, where an enthusiastic public awaits results of our new assessment products, serious technical questions about the design, analysis, and interpretation of performance assessment remain to be answered before we can legitimately have confidence in the use of measures we might apply. A primary purpose of this chapter is to identify and report on the status of the technical side of performance assessment, diversity, and equity.

ASSESSMENT AND EQUITY: FIRST QUESTIONS

From the perspective of equity, let us briefly confront three assumptions underlying the use of assessment in educational reform—three unpleasant, even dark views of assessment-led reform. First is the tacit understanding that, without accountability-based assessment, teachers cannot or will not of their own volition undertake the preparation and actions necessary to teach all children. The threat of exposure and ensuing sanctions of high-stakes assessment is thought to be essential to rid the profession of the slothful and incompetent. Second is the assumption that, despite contrary evidence (Mickelson, 1990; Steinberg, Dornbusch, & Brown, 1992), poor children from families with no history of achievement will perceive their self-interest to be connected to performance on assessments and will mobilize for the promise of explicit rewards. Third is the assumption that the minority community will embrace as its own the procedural details of reform, particularly performance assessment.

It is this third point, the minority community's perception of the self-evident merit of performance assessment, that deserves additional exploration. An anecdotal experience is enlightening here. One of us had the occasion to speak before an audience principally composed of minority educators and community members, a group unusually committed to, and active in the educational reform agenda. After a sunny exposition of the benefits of performance assessment—its emphasis on integrated learning, long-term engagement, a set of sensible and concrete accomplishments—the reaction from at least some members of the large audience was astonishing.

Performance assessment was attacked by minority group members on a number of fronts and for a number of reasons. The major assertion was that performance-based assessment reform is a creation of the majority community intended to hold back the progress of disadvantaged children. This attack was both unexpected and vehement. It was supported by stated beliefs that performance assessment was a strategy to "change the game" from the known attributes of standardized achievement tests to a set of requirements that would keep minority children in a second-class position. The argument was bolstered by the assertion that the achievement gap was being closed, particularly by approaches that emphasized an "effective schools" strategy (Edmonds, 1979) involving pre- and posttesting, test-taking preparation, and other clearly instrumental approaches to improving test scores.

Performance-based assessment is obviously grounded in a different instructional model, one for which the majority of teachers of disadvantaged children may be unprepared. Even the terminology of new forms of assessment led the audience to suspect assessment reformers' intentions. The use of the term "alternative," the reform code for anything not multiple-choice, raised concerns in this group. "Alternative" assessment was construed to mean nonstandard—in fact, substandard. Their referent was an outgrowth of "alternative schools," a term used to describe either remnants from the counterculture excesses of the 1970s or present-day "continuation" schools for students who cannot make the grade in regular schools. Alternative also suggested to some the idea of nonstandard assessment criteria (and sliding scales have not resulted in the application of high standards for these minority children). While alternative or performance-based assessments are intended to generate nonstandard reports of performance—models, and examples sensitive to the contexts and interests of the schools and students—this attribute was perceived to be a mechanism to avoid the collection of hard data and to permit the erosion of educational opportunity.

There also was a perception by the minority group members that much of performance-based assessment required strong language skills by students to explain or document their accomplishments. This set of requirements seemed ominous to some, and was predicted to result in either a structural disadvantage in performance requirements for nonstandard English speakers or promotion of policies to exclude, on the basis of limited English proficiency, large numbers of minority students from reported assessments. Colleagues both of and apart from minority communities have subsequently shared similar, though perhaps less volatile, experiences. Paradoxical beliefs are held: either new gates—higher barriers—will block access, or performance assessments will drop the standards expected of minority children.

Although this experience was a strong reminder of the role of context in interpretation, these perceptions must be directly addressed by those who promote a transition between assessment systems. If we are to embrace more complex, more intensive, and more relevant assessment systems, we must be sure that all communities understand and cogenerate assessment solutions.

CHARACTERISTICS OF PERFORMANCE TASKS

Almost any description of performance assessment includes a set of key attributes (Linn, Baker, & Dunbar, 1991). These are, for example, complex learning, higher order thinking, stimulation of a wide variety of active responses of students, tasks requiring multiple steps, and significant commitments of student time and effort. Performance-based assessment also may emphasize authenticity, that is, the task is intended to be inherently valuable to students, either immediately or because they can see its longer-term connection to an important goal. It also is argued that performance-based assessment generates an opportunity for the integration of high quality subject matter learning into implicitly useful tasks. Although there is no necessary reason why performance assessment and good subject matter must be linked, the connection between the design of new subject matter or content standards and performance assessment has been forged. In practice, most efforts at performance assessment also require the student to communicate his or her understanding of content, of process and strategy, and of the results obtained. This communication component reinforces the real world aspects of tasks.

As observed by members of the minority community, performance task characteristics may present special challenges for low performing minority students. Some of these challenges inhere in the transitional period, during which performance assessment tasks become more regular parts of educational expectations. Other difficulties may be more persistent because of their fundamental relationship to the education of diverse students.

One example of the more ephemeral problem involves a key attribute of performance-based assessment: its open-ended, challenging quality. While complex learning and higher order thinking are in the repertoire of virtually every child entering school, their formal imposition in performance-based assessment tasks is a different matter. Their use presupposes that children will have relevant instructional experiences as preparation. Students report in studies of performance assessment that they have rarely if ever experienced similar tasks in instruction—in one set of studies (Baker, Linn, Abedi, & Niemi, in press), they claimed they were never asked to read new material, integrate it with prior knowledge, or explain a complex historical idea to someone else. This research was conducted mainly in classrooms of middle-class students, those most likely to have been exposed to newer instructional approaches. As is well and unfortunately known, studies of the instructional experiences of many disadvantaged students report that higher order thinking tasks are represented in teaching less often than in classrooms of middle-class children. In a period of transition, then, minority children and their teachers will likely have less experience than children of other groups. Even apart from differing entry experiences, the starting point of these children is often behind that of others and they will have much farther to go.

Now consider the intrinsic and extrinsic motivational properties thought to be associated with authentic performance-based assessment. Although it may be possible to identify common purposes and tasks that will be equally effective in providing meaningful experiences for students, studies of context sensitivity and cultural specificity suggest otherwise (Miller-Jones, 1991; Ogbu, 1978). It is more likely that individuals and members of diverse groups will need to be given tasks that uniquely stimulate their interest, relate to their particular world and prior knowledge, and otherwise adapt to their special backgrounds (Laboratory of Comparative Human Cognition, 1982; Rogoff, 1982; Rueda & Moll, 1994; Sharp, Cole, & Lave, 1979). Tasks likely to appeal to the majority culture are the more likely to be represented on assessments with comparative or accountability purposes. The impact on disadvantaged students is likely to be negative. One palliative to this situation has been suggested by Gordon (1991), who advocated providing choices for minority students in the content of assessment tasks. This solution would be useful under a certain set of conditions—where tasks are used to monitor the effects of classroom learning and goals are not necessarily uniform, or where students are likely to be skilled estimators of needed prior knowledge or other resources critical to their ultimate success in the task. Recommendations to use multiple measures and to use tasks that sample the domain "in question" for the "culture in question" (Laboratory of Comparative Human Cognition, 1982, p. 654) make intellectual sense, but run up against current conceptions of comparability. Functional equivalence of different tasks has yet to be demonstrated.

On the matter of extrinsic motivation, it is often assumed that consequences of performance assessments—school recognition, opportunity for more challenging educational experiences, or improved career potential—will appeal to all students. However, if the incentives were not equally attractive to all, the group for whom the incentives were less compelling could be expected to perform less well. Studies of motivation have shown that social class and ethnicity modify the impact of various motivational events (Ogbu, 1978; Steinberg et al., 1992). Fordham and Ogbu (1986) documented that African-American adolescents are strongly pulled between desires to perform well in school and to win peer approval, a commodity not typically rewarded for academic prowess. Further, they are reported as less able to defer rewards. Thus, delayed incentives for success on performance assessments are less likely to be useful for children whose families have not experienced benefits of reward for hard work.

Is the problem of incentive transitional or more enduring for disadvantaged learners? There is some evidence on this question. In the case of intrinsic motivation, there is every reason to believe that cultural specificity of task knowledge and interest will continue as motivators (Rogoff, 1982). The impact of extrinsic motivation will be in part a function of the extent to which severe socioeconomic disadvantage persists. Until members of disadvantaged communities perceive their group as profiting from success in school, it is likely that an emphasis on delayed extrinsic motivation (such as college admission) will disadvantage minority students. Only when cousins and older siblings make progress will models of consequences be likely to change. Simply stated, if assessments motivate disadvantaged students less than others, and the importance and frequency of measures increase (leading others to try harder and providing more practice), then gaps in performance will increase.

Emphasis on communication is a third characteristic of performance-based assessments that may present problems to minority group members. For nonstandard English speakers, the dependence of performance tasks on explaining, writing, and extended communication creates added difficulty. A case in point comes from the standards of the National Council of Teachers of Mathematics (1991). Many of the mathematics tasks require students to discuss and explain their processes or inferences. While not disputing that English language proficiency is an important educational goal, equity concerns arise in assessment of a population with large numbers of nonnative speakers of English and an increasing number of immigrants. Students who know information and can perform desired tasks must have a way to obtain credit for their expertise, and language emphasis should not continue to obscure their ability to demonstrate competence, except, of course, in language competence itself.

ADMINISTRATION OF PERFORMANCE ASSESSMENTS

In addition to important design issues in performance assessment, we also must attend to the potential inequities caused by differences in task administration. As has been frequently demonstrated, in the National Assessment of Educational Progress (NAEP) anomaly and elsewhere, small variations in assessment administration context may translate into regular, persistent differences in results. Considering the fact that performance-based assessments can involve extended administration periods and the use of a wide range of materials, it is a considerable challenge to assure comparability in administrative conditions. One would need to assure that three facets of administration are controlled: setting, time, and support for the assessment.

Setting

Elements of the setting that must be addressed to promote equity in administration involve climate, context, and environment. Equity of climate implies that all students, within the same and among different classrooms, have an equivalent picture of the purpose of the task, the seriousness of the implications of the results, and the overall affect conveyed by the teacher or other administrator. Included in this analysis is the potential impact of having the same ethnicity or race of the administrator as the students, and the language(s) of task administration, for example. Research findings suggest that there is a long way to go before such assurances are met on the practical level.

A second aspect of setting is the specific context in which any task is embedded. Is the task a part of regular instruction or demonstrably a special event? Are students permitted to work within typical social or spatial arrangements or does the task change requirements? Is the task familiar or will students need extended preparation to begin? These questions are difficult because they are likely to be setting-specific and a function of individual teachers' approaches to classroom management. Also, they are affected by students' strategy repertoires, especially their likelihood to use less usual representations (Franklin, 1978).

Third, seemingly straightforward elements of task administration may affect the performance of different groups. Are settings arranged so that distractions are minimal? Are they functionally equivalent for different groups? Are materials accessible for all students in an easily replicable way? Are rules for the participation of observers or other adults explicit?

Time

A second major element in administration is the time allowed for tasks. The amount of time allocated for directions, data collection, and completion of various tasks will have an impact on performance. While this constraint may seem obvious—for example, everyone has 2 hours—in operation, it is a problem of great complexity. For instance, how tightly should time of tasks be monitored? If it takes longer to understand directions for groups less familiar with performance-based tasks, is the additional required time subtracted from the total allocation? Is it added? If comparability of understanding is desired, time would vary. If comparability of administration conditions are to be optimized, time would be controlled for all students. If students do not finish an initial task in the allocated time, must they go on to the next even if their likelihood of success is undermined by their partial completion of the prerequisite? How are students made aware of time constraints?

As tasks increase in their authenticity, it also is likely that estimates of time needed for various components will differ from reality. Data collection may be more difficult or findings may need corroboration, and such events will affect total available time. Although a correction for time can be statistically manipulated, the implications of such an adjustment are not at all clear. Allowing time to vary and focusing on task completion may be a reasonable approach to time differences. However, extended time may add factors of fatigue or anxiety to the assessment situation. Cole and Scribner (1973) found that time and tasks needed to be adjusted so that children could perform competently.

Support

The third element of task administration is support, the need to have appropriate materials, trained teachers or administrators, and reasonable procedures for recording results. Early efforts in large scale performance assessment in England failed because of inadequate support (Nuttall, 1992), as teachers using performance-based assessments were unable to collect detailed information about students and maintain a reasonable learning environment for children.

In the United States, support will have different shading as class size differs. In classrooms which include students of differing cultural and language experiences, support needs also will vary. While it is unlikely that all variables can be anticipated, it is essential that convenient procedures to document these aspects of administration be a regular part of the assessment administration process.

THE RATING PROCESS

Assuming that the tasks designed are appropriate for all children, that scoring rubrics are not inappropriately reactive to ethnic differences, and that variations in administrative conditions can be held to a minimum, a central technical concern in performance-based measures is the process through which student performance is judged and assigned to different levels of accomplishment. A key issue is whether ethnic group membership of raters predicts the score given to children of like or different ethnic groups and what might account for such interactions.

Part of the answer depends upon whether raters are (a) rating live or recorded versions of student performance, such as speeches, or (b) judging products prepared by students which give no information about group membership, such as reports. Clearly, opportunities for bias are stronger in the first case. Raters' expectations for different group members or their reactions to cultural differences, such as speech patterns, eye contact, and movement, would be issues where student performance-in-process is observed and judged. When student products are being judged, linguistic patterns could easily trigger responses that might inadvertently influence one's judgment of the content quality of student performance.

Equity of rating also derives from the characteristics of raters. If there are significant differences among rater groups, then those differences might be expected to have an impact on the scores raters assign. A simple model of the potential for interaction is presented in Fig. 10.1.

To understand potential interactions, a more refined set of characteristics

	Raters' Ethnicity		
Students' Ethnicity	1	2	3
1			
2			
3			

FIG. 10.1. Interactions among raters' and students' ethnicity.

of raters can be analyzed. A partial list of rater characteristics which could be expected to influence their performance as scorers of performance assessments appears in Fig. 10.2. Raters' knowledge, including specific content knowledge, relevant prior knowledge, and world knowledge, would be expected to have strong influence on judgments. In research reported by Baker, Linn, Abedi, and Niemi (in press), it was found that raters differed in their knowledge of immigration topics and that those differences affected the extent to which they were able to distinguish

```
┌─────────────────────────────────────────────┐
│                                               │
│               Knowledge                       │
│                                               │
│               Training                        │
│                                               │
│            Linguistic Facility                │
│                                               │
│              Expectations                     │
│                                               │
│            Instructional Model                │
│                                               │
└─────────────────────────────────────────────┘
```

FIG. 10.2. Characteristics of raters as potential sources of both equitable and inequitable rating.

students' use of prior knowledge in written explanations. If such differences were consistent by rater group, then the likelihood of equitable rating among groups of raters would be greatly reduced.

Raters can also differ in terms of training. This can mean both in their experience with the rating process and the level of training competence attained in a fixed period of training.

Third, the raters' own level of linguistic competency will undoubtedly affect their tendency to distinguish among and value alternative levels of communication competence.

Fourth, raters may differ in the overall expectations they hold for students, and believe, for instance, that fourth-grade children should demonstrate a particular set of accomplishments. In cases where scoring rubrics are ill-defined or there is considerable latitude in interpreting the rubric, it is possible that raters or teachers will apply their contextually derived expectations, and that these may result in main effects irrespective of student group membership.

More likely, however, interactions will be found. For example, African-American children demonstrate higher levels of activity and need for stimulation (Boykin, 1982). This propensity might affect a rater's judgment of task-specific performance, particularly if the rater overvalues subdued or controlled performance.

A last factor is the type of instructional model held by the teacher/rater in the content or performance area under assessment. Persistent instructional beliefs—for instance, about the use of appropriate steps or strategies—may exert subtle influences in the rating process. For example, inferring from earlier research (Cohen, 1971), preference for analytic rather than relational concepts by raters may negatively impact their judgment of performance of African-American children. Because rater training rarely attempts to discern these instructional beliefs and preferences, their impact in the rating process will less likely be detected, but nonetheless could explain systematic differences based upon group membership of raters.

Research Findings

Few research findings exist about the performance of ethnically different groups of students on performance-based assessment in its present form. However, as noted earlier, considerable research has been conducted from the theory of cultural practice (Scribner & Cole, 1981). Main effects have been found recently in performance assessments in history, with clear advantages for Asian-American students over White and Latino students at the secondary school level (Baker, Niemi, & Sato, 1992). The authors have not been able to find studies of the interaction of raters and student ethnicities in educational settings. However, reviews of the literature conducted in the industrial and military sectors provided some evidence with regard to the impact of ethnicity in the scoring process. The summary will focus on job performance ratings in these two settings.

Research on Industrial Performance Ratings: A Summary

In general, the literature on performance ratings in the industrial sector indicated that ratees receive higher ratings from raters of the same ethnicity (Kraiger & Ford, 1985). The effect is small but consistent. White raters rated the average White ratee higher than they did 64% of African-American ratees. African-American raters rated the average African-American ratee higher than 67% of White ratees.

Four classes of variables were hypothesized by Kraiger and Ford in their meta-analysis to moderate this effect. The first was the setting of the rating, whether in the laboratory (or under training conditions) or in the field. It was expected that the effect of ethnicity would be stronger in laboratory experiments, where a limited amount of information is available to the rater, than it would be in relevant field settings, where a rater (usually the supervisor) would have more extensive and integrated information. A second class of variables was rater training in its grossest form, specifically whether it was offered or not. It was expected that training should reduce the ethnicity effect. Third, it was hypothesized that the composition of the workgroup would have an impact on rating. Assuming a majority group rater, it would be expected that increasing the proportion of minority to majority group members would diminish the ethnicity effect by reducing the salience of minority members. A fourth variable was the degree to which the scoring rubric called for low or high inference judgments by raters. It would be expected that low inference ratings, where attributes are counted, would be less susceptible to ethnic effects than rubrics calling for categorical judgments.

Let us consider these potential moderator variables in turn, drawing from studies limited to comparisons between Whites and African-Americans.

The research evidence on setting (Kraiger & Ford, 1985) indicated that, whether training was laboratory- or field-based, it did not mitigate the ethnic rating effects. Rater training, contrary to expectation, did not reduce the ethnicity effect. Further, neither level of inference of rating nor rating purpose (high stakes or research) moderated the ethnicity-rating interaction. Only composition of the workgroup was found to have the predicted impact. The effect of ethnicity was higher (favoring Whites) when African-American ratees constituted a smaller percentage of the workgroup. However, in one study (Sackett, DuBois, & Noe, 1991), no effect of this variable was found.

In summary, the research literature conducted in industrial settings supports the generalization that persons receive higher performance ratings from raters of the same ethnic group. Given the proportion of White teachers to minority students, the implications of this finding are somewhat troubling.

There also has been research on industry performance measures other than ratings. Cognitive criteria such as training tests and job knowledge tests have been used, as well as behavioral indicators such as absenteeism and tardiness. Finally, direct performance indices, such as units produced, and indirect performance, such as accidents or customer complaints, also have been measured. The results of a meta-analysis (Ford, Kraiger, & Schechtman, 1986) indicated a significant ethnicity effect on these variables. In this meta-analysis, Whites performed better than African-Americans on performance indices such as accidents and complaints, although it is possible that a reporting bias was in operation. There may be moderator variables such as unknown organizational practices (e.g., minorities given less desirable work territories, or lack of mentors). More pronounced differences linked to ethnicity of personnel were found for training and job knowledge measures than for absenteeism and performance data.

Military Studies of Ethnicity and Performance: A Summary

In contrast to the industrial studies, military studies on ethnicity and performance ratings shared particular characteristics. First, all research was conducted in field settings, and rater training was always provided. Moreover, African-Americans constitute a higher percentage of the workforce (approximately 30 to 40%). The samples also included Latinos. Low inference measures were used on a range of job performance areas, and all studies reported performance for entry level jobs.

According to Pulakos, White, Oppler, and Borman (1989), ratees received slightly higher ratings from raters (either peers or supervisors) of the same ethnicity (the effect found was very small [1% of variance] but consistent). Among attributes rated were technical skill and job effort (cognitive), and personal discipline and military bearing (noncognitive). Results did not vary by job. These findings lend some support for the four classes of moderator variables identified by Kraiger and Ford (1985). Reduced impact of ethnicity occurred where consistent rater training focusing on ratee job performance was provided. In addition, workforce composition and an institutionalized view of equity in the military would predict lower impact of ethnicity.

The remaining sources of information on ethnicity can be found in the body of literature labeled "test fairness" in industrial and military settings. In industrial studies, Whites typically score about one standard deviation above African-Americans on pretraining aptitude tests, with an obtained point biserial correlation of .50. Ethnic impact is less on job knowledge tests ($r = .34$) and further is reduced when actual on-the-job performance is studied ($r = .16$) (Ford et al., 1986, p. 334). In military studies, the average White job incumbent scored above the average African-American job incumbent in the following manner: on an aptitude test, .85 standard deviation; on job knowledge tests, .78 standard deviation; and on hands-on tests, .36 standard deviation (Wigdor & Green, 1991, p. 179). These findings suggest that ethnic differences when measured by performance assessment will be reduced, compared to more traditional measures of aptitude or job knowledge.

Within the military environment, similar ethnic findings were attained with respect to the diminishing effects of ethnicity on performance ratings (Wigdor & Green, 1991). The military uses the Armed Services Vocational Aptitude Test Battery (ASVAB) as a predictor to assign job classifications to incoming personnel. Studies (Wigdor & Green, 1991) have documented the relationship of this test and subsequent job performance ratings. On cognitive criteria, such as on a job knowledge written test, the ASVAB predicted better for Whites than African-American service personnel (Whites = .43; African-Americans = .26). In contrast, on hands-on tests (more objective performance measures), there is less differential predictability of aptitude (ASVAB) due to ethnicity (Whites = .29; African-Americans = .22). In general, aptitude measures are more accurate for Whites than for minorities. The lack of accuracy for African-American soldiers results in overprediction of their job performance. Similar overpredictions were reported by Maier and Fuchs (1978) for the Army Classification Battery on performance and by McLaughlin, Rossmeissl, Wise, Brandt, and Wang (1984) for the ASVAB and the Skill Qualification Test. Overprediction means that minority students do less well on performance measures as predicted by their aptitude scores.

Another form of pre-employment performance measure is the employment interview. An extensive study on interview ratings was provided by Lin, Dobbins, and Farh (1992). The ratings were provided by same-, mixed-, or different-ethnicity panels for same- or different-ethnicity potential employees for a janitorial position. The data indicate that the same-ethnicity effect could be avoided by using mixed-ethnicity interview panels. Further, the use of a more structured interview reduced the same-ethnicity effect. Certainly, the low status of the job in this research has effects on the findings, and replications for higher status jobs are essential before conclusions can be inferred.

IMPLICATIONS

The systematic differences in effects for ethnicity and the interactions of rater and ratee ethnicity present a complex agenda for the designers and would-be users of performance assessments. At issue is whether or not there exist demonstrably lower performances in ethnic groups that cannot be explained by assessment attributes, administrative conditions, or rater characteristics and behavior. If such differences do exist, attention must be turned to the learning conditions to which students are exposed. It is likely that these conditions or delivery standards (National Council on Education Standards and Testing, 1992) will be observed to vary systematically and will provide explanations for performance differentials.

If, however, one returns to the prospect that aspects of both performance assessment and instruction systematically differ for ethnically different students, and if raters systematically rate students of other ethnic groups lower (and, as we all know, the vast proportion of teachers are White), we must conduct validity studies to assure that such ratings are not the product of inappropriate application of knowledge. If ethnically different raters vary in terms of key characteristics for valid ratings—for instance, internalized instructional models or relevant prior knowledge—then rater qualification procedures and training to assure their representation will need to be undertaken.

THE ROLE OF VALIDITY

In any case, the role of validity in performance assessment will need to be strengthened. Research must be conducted to demonstrate that performance-based assessment results have validity for the particular assessment purpose served, whether it be diagnosis, accountability, or certification. Moreover, validity studies must demonstrate consistent results for the particular ethnic groups of students and of raters in the performance-based research. Studies must also demonstrate that children of different ethnicities and language backgrounds can profit from instruction designed to lead to performance-based outcomes. To make sense, these studies will undoubtedly require measures of instructional and school delivery. These measures should include the extent to which students have had exposure to similar tasks, the degree of content sampling, the training of teachers, and availability of relevant materials.

Because it is unlikely that inequities in education will be mitigated by research results, however terrific, in the short term we must develop interpretative models that will support the honest reporting of differences as they may exist, and that will not perpetuate or gloss over real performance differences. For example, such interpretative models may report the relative position of a child or a school compared to students or schools with similar characteristics, say, language proficiency, but performance also must be reported in terms of the standard intended for all to achieve.

Finally, specifications for the design of performance assessments, rubrics for their rating, and models or benchmark examples of performance all must be available for parent, teacher, and student participants. Rules for the inclusion or exclusion of special population students must be made public. Furthermore, safeguards against misuse of assessment results must be developed and implemented. Audits by experts or community groups may be required to assure the fairness of the system.

CONCLUSION

Although it is tempting to believe that the new assessments also will result in dramatic improvements along all dimensions, performance assessment is in for a rough time on the equity issue, even if only for the short term. The reason the United States developed such a love affair with objective tests is that they promised fairness. Despite documented evidence of the past bias of many of these measures, in design they still have some appeal. Everyone gets the same test; and scoring is standardized and not subject to particular prejudices. The scorer's ethnicity, for instance, is a matter of great indifference for traditional tests.

If performance-based assessment, while not the single solution, is to be at least a critical component of integrative educational reform, we must attempt to remedy its obvious potential for inequity. These remedies include improving the design of measures and scoring procedures so that differences in students' world knowledge, specific prior knowledge, perception of meaningfulness, and language facility are considered explicitly; and administration conditions, including climate, setting, and logistical support must be comparable. Furthermore, qualifications of raters, including training to avoid ethnic interactions, models of student performance, and comparable standards of judgment must be made public and subject to independent review. The real key is that students receive comparable and equitable teaching offered in safe environments from qualified teachers with high expectations. As researchers, we must support the continued documentation of process and search for validity and equity of new performance measures.

ACKNOWLEDGMENTS

The work reported herein was partially supported under the Educational Research and Development Center Program cooperative agreement R117G10027 and CFDA catalog number 84.117G as administered by the Office of Educational Research and Improvement, U.S. Department of Education.

The findings and opinions expressed in this report do not reflect the position or policies of the Office of Educational Research and Improvement, the U.S. Department of Education.

REFERENCES

Baker, E. L., Linn, R. L., Abedi, J., & Niemi, D. (in press). The dimensionality and generalizability of domain-independent performance assessments. *Journal of Educational Research*.

Baker, E. L., Niemi, D., & Sato, E. (1992). *The impact of ethnicity and instruction on performance-based assessment* (CRESST Deliverable to OERI). Los Angeles: University of California, National Center for Research on Education, Standards, and Student Testing.

Boykin, A. W. (1982). Population differences in the effect of format variability on task performance. *Journal of Black Studies, 12,* 469–485.

Cohen, R. (1971). The influence of conceptual rule-sets on measures of learning ability. In C. L. Brace, G. R. Gamble, & J. T. Bond (Eds.), *Race and intelligence* (pp. 41–57). Washington, DC: American Anthropological Association.

Cole, M., & Scribner, S. (1973). Cognitive consequences of formal and informal education. *Science, 182,* 553–559.

Edmonds, R. (1979). *What do we know about teaching and learning in urban schools? Vol. 6. A discussion of the literature and issues related to effective schooling.* St. Louis: CEMREL, Inc., Urban Education Program.

Ford, J. K., Kraiger, K., & Schechtman, S. L. (1986). Study of race effects in objective indices and subjective evaluations of performance: A meta-analysis of performance criteria. *Psychological Bulletin, 99*(3), 330–337.

Fordham, S., & Ogbu, J. U. (1986). Black students' school success: Coping with the burden of "acting White." *Urban Review, 18,* 176–206.

Franklin, A. J. (1978). Sociolinguistic structure of word lists and ethnic-group differences in categorical recall. *Institute for Comparative Human Development Newsletter, 2,* 30–34.

Gordon, E. (Speaker). (1991). Alternatives for measuring performance (Video Conference No. 4). *Schools That Work.* Chicago: North Central Regional Educational Laboratory.

Kraiger, K., & Ford, J. K. (1985). A meta-analysis of ratee race effects in performance ratings. *Journal of Applied Psychology, 70*(1), 56–65.

Laboratory of Comparative Human Cognition. (1982). Culture and intelligence. In R. Sternberg (Ed.), *Handbook of human intelligence* (pp. 642–722). New York: Cambridge University Press.

Lin, T-R., Dobbins, H. G., & Farh, J-L. (1992). A field study of race and age similarity effects on interview ratings in conventional and situational interviews. *Journal of Applied Psychology, 77*(3), 363–371.

Linn, R. L., Baker, E. L., & Dunbar, S. B. (1991). Complex, performance-based assessment: Expectations and validation criteria. *Educational Researcher, 20*(8), 15–21. (ERIC Document Reproduction Service No. EJ 436 999)

Maier, M. H., & Fuchs, E. F. (1978, September). *Differential validity of the Army aptitude areas for predicting Army job training performance of Blacks and Whites* (ARI Technical Paper 312). Alexandria, VA: U.S. Army Research Institute for the Behavioral and Social Sciences.

McLaughlin, D. H., Rossmeissl, P. G., Wise, L. L., Brandt, D. A., & Wang, M-M. (1984, October). *Validation of current and alternative Armed Services Vocational Aptitude Battery (ASVAB) area composites* (ARI Tech. Rep. 651). Alexandria, VA: U.S. Army Research Institute for the Behavioral and Social Sciences.

Mickelson, R. (1990). The attitude achievement paradox among Black adolescents. *Sociology of Education, 63*, 44–61.

Miller-Jones, D. (1991). Informal reasoning in inner-city children. In J. Voss, D. Perkins, & J. Segal (Eds.), *Informal reasoning in education* (pp. 107–130). Hillsdale, NJ: Lawrence Erlbaum Associates.

National Council of Teachers of Mathematics. (1991). *Professional standards for teaching mathematics*. Reston, VA: Author.

National Council on Education Standards and Testing (1992). *Raising standards for American education*. Washington, DC: U.S. Government Printing Office.

Nuttall, D. (1992, September). *Moderation: Lessons from performance assessments in the United Kingdom*. Presentation at the UCLA/CRESST conference "What Works in Performance Assessment," Los Angeles.

Ogbu, J. (1978). *Minority education and caste*. San Diego: Academic Press.

Pulakos, E. D., White, L. A., Oppler, S. H., & Borman, W. C. (1989). Examination of race and sex effects on performance ratings. *Journal of Applied Psychology, 74*(5), 770–780.

Rogoff, B. (1982). Integrating context and cognitive development. In M. E. Lamb & A. L. Brown (Eds.), *Advances in developmental psychology* (Vol. 2, pp. 125–170). Hillsdale, NJ: Lawrence Erlbaum Associates.

Rueda, R., & Moll, L. C. (1994). A sociocultural perspective on motivation. In H. F. O'Neil, Jr. & M. Drillings (Eds.), *Motivation: Theory and research* (pp. 117–137). Hillsdale, NJ: Lawrence Erlbaum Associates.

Sackett, P. R., DuBois, C. L. Z., & Noe, A. W. (1991). Tokenism in performance evaluation. The effects of work group representation on male/female and White/Black differences in performance ratings. *Journal of Applied Psychology, 76*(2), 263–267.

Scribner, S., & Cole, M. (1981). *The psychology of literacy*. Cambridge, MA: Harvard University Press.

Sharp, D., Cole, M., & Lave, C. (1979). Education and cognitive development. The evidence from experimental research. *Monographs of the Society for Research in Child Development, 44*(1–2), 1–112.

Steinberg, L., Dornbusch, S. M., & Brown, B. B. (1992). Ethnic differences in adolescent achievement: An ecological perspective. *American Psychologist, 47*(6), 723–729.

Wigdor, A. K., & Green, B. F., Jr. (Eds.). (1991). *Performance assessment for the workplace* (Vol. 1). Washington, DC: National Academy Press.

Author Index

Subject Index